Secrets of

Home Theater

Secrets of Home Theater

Mike Wood

TechTV Press is published in association with Peachpit, a division of Pearson Technology Group.

Peachpit
1249 Eighth Street
Berkeley, CA 94710
510/524-2178
800/283-9444
510/524-2221 (fax)
Find us on the World Wide Web at: www.peachpit.com and www.g4techtv.com

Editor: Carol Person
Production Coordinator: Myrna Vladic, Simmy Cover
Copyeditor: Peggy Gannon
Compositors: Rick Gordon, Emerald Valley Graphics; Deborah Roberti, Espresso Graphics
Indexer: FireCrystal Communications
Cover Design: Aren Howell
Cover Illustration: Alan Clements
Interior Design: Kim Scott
Illustrations: Kelly Person

Notice of Rights

Notice of Liability

Trademarks

ISBN 0-321-27836-4

9 8 7 6 5 4 3 2 1

Printed and bound in the United States of America.

This book is dedicated to my wife, Cristina
and my daughter, Alana
for giving me the encouragement and inspiration
to follow my passion and write about it.

Acknowledgments

To Russ Herschelmann, Joe Kane, Anthony Grimani, Mark Peterson, Norman Varney, Tomlinson Holman, Floyd Toole, Brent Butterworth, Kevin Voecks, and numerous other audio/video writers, manufacturers, and Industry "gurus" for teaching me what I know about home theater.

To Anthony Grimani (Performance Media Industries, LTD), Larry Houser (AVT), Brent Butterworth (Curtco Robb Media), John Taylor (LG Electronics), Marc Finer (Communications Research for Sony Electronics), John Dahl (THX), Craig Eggars (Dolby Laboratories), Jim Noyd (Jefferson Acker for Ultralink), Hank Finke (ReQuest), Marty Zanfino (Mitsubishi Electronics), David Butler (XM Satellite Radio), and Ron Rodriguez (Sirius Satellite Radio) for their help in fact checking various portions of the book. And the dozens of people that were willing to send me the product images you see throughout its pages.

To Carol Person for editing and Kelly Person for the illlustrations, and all the production people at Peachpit for putting up with my constant revisions and helping make this happen and to Wendy Sharp for giving me the opportunity.

None of the above should be held responsible for the opinions contained and expressed herein. My apologies to anyone I left out.

Table of Contents

Chapter 11 Electrical Power   225

Chapter 12 Sound and Room Acoustics   235

Introduction

Watching a movie or television show on a large, high-definition video screen with a full-range, multichannel audio system is a kick in the pants. To realize what home theater can truly deliver, you have to experience it first-hand. I've been enthralled with home theater since its inception. Maybe you have or maybe you would like to and that's why you're reading this book. Do you get confused at the apparent complexity of a typical home system or did you feel lost as you checked the options available? If so, don't worry; you're not alone. In this book, I'll answer all of your questions about home theater (and some you may not know you should be asking), including such mystifying topics as:

- Do you really need five, six, or even seven speakers?

- What exactly is a ".1" channel?

- Should you buy an all-in-one receiver or separate preamp-processor and power amplifier components?

- Do you have HDTV? Should you get it? Is it available through satellite or cable?

- Why is a 65-inch big screen TV called a "microdisplay?"

This book is written for novices and enthusiasts alike, or anyone who wants to assemble a top-notch home theater system for as little or as much money as you want to spend. I'll talk about what features you need and what you don't. I'll give you an idea of how much you might spend, and where you can save money. And I'll explain how you can put the whole thing together yourself, or what to consider when hiring someone else.

How to Use This Book

I've been writing about home theater for nearly ten years and one thing I've found is that organizing information about the topic so it makes sense and is interesting is probably more difficult than research-ing and writing the information itself. Various topics are interrelated. Understanding one topic often requires an understanding of another. I could start with the physics of sound and vision, explain the mathe-matics of sound waves and frequencies and eventually, several chapters later, get to buying and installation tips that you actually want to know about. At that point, though, I might as well call the book *Secrets of Home Theater While Curing Insomnia*. There are many important aspects of audio and video systems, and I will discuss most of them eventually, but they are not all vital to your immediate enjoyment of movies, music, and television programs.

This book is primarily written as a collection of independent chapters. You can certainly read it from beginning to end, if you are so inclined, but I expect you might be interested in one or more particular topics. You can therefore read a specific chapter or subchapter to find the information you need for that particular subject without missing (or needing) much information from previous chapters. If you're planning to buy a TV, for example, you might only want to read Chapter 7, "TV and Video Monitors."

Each chapter starts with a description of the product, what it does, and why you might be interested in it (assuming you aren't already). There might be certain aspects of a product that are better explained elsewhere in the book, and where appropriate, I'll tell you where to turn to so you can find more information. Similarly, while I've tried to keep the terminology simple, there might be particularly confusing words or phrases that are used throughout the book. For brevity's sake, these words are explained only once, in the chapter where it is most appropriate. There is a glossary in the back, however, where you'll find a working definition for most home theater-related words or phrases.

Each product chapter contains three sections titled: "What to Look For," "Getting Started," and "Secrets." The first section, "What to Look For" outlines the important features and topics that you should understand or things you need to know before buying that product. "Getting Started" discusses how to connect and configure the component into your system. In the "Secrets" section, you'll find additional information that you don't necessarily need to know before you buy or install a product but that will help you get better performance or enjoyment from whatever product you do buy. In most cases, this information can even be applied to products you already own.

Tips and Notes are scattered throughout the book as well. These are various bits of information that you might find interesting or useful, or both.

The only exception to this format is in Chapter 10, "Audio and Video Wire," which discusses the various types of cables and connectors used in a home theater system. There are a few secrets for various cable types scattered throughout the chapter.

If, however, you're starting from scratch, or don't know where to begin, read Chapter 1, "Anatomy of a Home Theater (Where to Start)." This chapter offers an overview of the various components used in a home theater system and how they interrelate with each other. From there, you can skip around as you see fit.

History of Home Theater

Film

Watching videos at home may seem like second nature now, but there was a time when even the idea of seeing projected images move was considered magic. Movies, or at least projected still images, date back to the 1600s, when the magic lantern was popular. But the real inspiration came in the early 1800s when Peter Mark Roget recognized and wrote about the physiological effect called persistence of vision. The eye retains images briefly after they've gone. A series of still images can therefore be shown sequentially and perceived as a single image. If objects in the image move from one still to the next, the object will appear to be in motion. Aristotle discussed these "after images" much earlier.

Around the same time as Roget's discovery, Joseph Niepce took the next significant step in the birth of the film industry with what he called a heliograph (a "sun drawing"), which imprinted the image of his hometown onto chemically sensitive material. Hannibal Goodwin invented light-sensitive emulsion on celluloid, though it was a similar invention by George Eastman for his Kodak camera that became more popular. Eadweard Muybridge and Thomas Edison and others combined photography with their understanding of persistence of vision to create motion pictures.

The early film pioneers recorded moving images on film at 24 frames per second (fps) to fool the eye into thinking it was seeing a moving image. While the image did appear to have motion, since it was ultimately projected onto a large screen, the image also had flicker, or an unsteady or wavering light. The human eye is more sensitive to flicker than flashing images, particularly as the light source gets brighter. To reduce the perception of flicker in movie theaters, each image is flashed twice when it's projected, creating a 48 fps frame rate.

One other interesting development in the history of film is the shape of the screen. Originally, movies had the same shape, or aspect ratio as a frame of a 35mm filmstrip. Television adopted this same aspect ratio. When it became obvious that television was going to be a huge draw, and to attract people back to the theaters, studios came up with wider aspect ratios, or wide-screen movies.

The next step for film is, ironically enough, video. *Star Wars: Episode I-The Phantom Menace* was the first movie released in what's called digital or electronic cinema. Various parts of the film were recorded or transferred to the high-definition video format (see Chapter 3, "Choosing Source Components: TV Programming"), then played back in the theater through a massive digital video projector. There are numerous advantages to digital cinema over regular film. The next film in the Star Wars series was shot entirely in high-definition video. Digital cinema is already available at home.

Film Sound

Before I talk about what's available at home, though, I have to discuss the incredible impact sound has had on motion pictures. Until the 1920s, the first films were "silent." At the time, there was no real way to record sound for the film and play it back in synchronization with the picture. Combining sound and pictures (beyond that of a pianist playing in the theater along with the movie) was an obvious next step.

The big break came in 1926, when Warner Brothers, in collaboration with Western Electric and Bell Labs, created the Vitaphone Corp. The first commercial movie to use the Vitaphone system—a phonograph synchronized with the filmstrip—was Warner's *Don Juan* (starring John Barrymore). It wasn't until the success of Al Jolson's *The Jazz Singer* in 1927, which included recorded dialogue, that film sound was truly accepted. Film sound would later be standardized as a mono, or single channel recorded optically directly onto the filmstrip.

Multichannel sound would be a few years away. Disney introduced *Fantasia* in 1940, along with its groundbreaking soundtrack, dubbed "Fantasound." Leopold Stokowski had recorded an orchestra with nine separate optical tracks. These were mixed down to four master surround sound tracks and played back on special equipment synchronized to the film.

A handful of other studios used their own techniques with various films to create multichannel sound, but the next big advance came with *This is Cinerama* (1952) presentations, which used magnetic sound. Cinerama used seven channels, five directed to speakers behind the ultrawide screen and two surround channels played through an array of surround speakers. *The Robe* (1953) used CinemaScope's four-track system (left, center, right, and mono surround), with a magnetic recording applied to the film. Todd-AO introduced a 6-channel magnetic system that was played in sync with the movie *Oklahoma!* (1955); however, after only a few films, this system would be replaced with 70mm presentations, which used a 6-channel magnetic soundtrack (initially five screen channels and a single surround channel), recorded onto the filmstrip itself.

Surround sound didn't become the norm it is today until 1974 when Ray Dolby introduced Dolby Stereo. Adopting many of the principles that came before it, but accepting the economic and compatibility issues that prevented other technologies from becoming universally accepted, Dolby Stereo made multichannel surround sound successful to a wide audience. The system standardized two optical tracks that could be recorded onto the filmstrip. Within these left and right channel tracks, a center and mono surround channel track could be encoded. If a theater had the appropriate equipment, it could decode the four tracks and play them back through appropriate speakers. Three front speakers placed behind the screen reproduced the left, center, and right channel information, while an array of speakers along the side and back walls played the surround channel. If the theater lacked this equipment, it could just play one or two of the optical tracks, with no loss of any audio information.

Theaters used, and in some cases still do, Dolby's decoding equipment to play back all four channels, plus a subwoofer signal through their surround speaker systems. *Star Wars* was one of the first movies to use Dolby Stereo to great effect, followed quickly by *Close Encounters of the Third Kind*. Hearing space ships "fly" overhead and around the audience added tremendous impact to the groundbreaking films.

Rumor has it, though, that George Lucas, creator of the *Star Wars* and *Indiana Jones* films was disappointed with the inconsistent quality of the audio presentation he heard at various commercial theaters. Lucas hired audio maven Tomlinson Holman to develop a certification program, called THX, which outlined numerous parameters that were important for good sound quality in a theater. (The program either gets its name from Lucas's first film, *THX-1138*, or is an acronym for Tomlinson Holman's eXperiment or both, depending on whom you ask.) One of the advantages of the THX program is that the film soundtrack can be recorded in any format and, when played back in a THX theater, will sound good.

As digital audio came into play, several companies worked to bring it to the theatrical arena. In 1990 Eastman Kodak and the Optical Radiation Corp. released the first digitally recorded soundtrack for the movie *Dick Tracy* in CDS or Cinema Digital Sound. The digital soundtrack replaced the optical soundtrack with compressed digital information and provided 6-channels of dynamic, crystal-clear digital audio. Five discrete, full-range main channels, plus a "low frequency effects" (LFE) or boom track could be used in a layout now referred to as 5.1 (five point one). The CDS format was used for a handful of titles including *Dick Tracy, Days of Thunder,* and *Terminator 2: Judgment Day.*

Batman Returns, released in 1992, utilized Dolby's digital format, which proved to be a better solution to bringing digital audio to the movies. Recording the digital audio signal in the space between the sprocket holes, Dolby Stereo Digital (then called SR-D or AC3, though now just referred to as Dolby Digital) compresses 5.1 channels onto the film without displacing the Dolby Stereo optical tracks. The format sounds great, but the playback equipment was initially expensive.

In 1993 Steven Spielberg released *Jurassic Park* with a competing digital surround format named after the company that created it, Digital Theater Systems (DTS). The system uses a digital time code on the filmstrip, which synchronizes to an external CD-ROM player that reproduces the soundtrack but leaves the optical track unaffected. DTS uses the same 5.1 speaker configuration as Dolby Digital.

As if two competing theatrical formats weren't enough, Sony Corp. developed a compression system format called Sony Dynamic Digital Sound (SDDS) that offers up to eight audio channels. It is similar in configuration to the old Cinerama speaker layout and stores the digital information in the space on the filmstrip outside the sprocket holes. Sony has not made any attempt to use SDDS as a home audio format.

Since all three competing digital systems employ different areas of the filmstrip to record the digital soundtrack or time code, there was no reason that a film couldn't use all three formats at the same time. Fox did just that in 1995 for *Die Hard: With a Vengeance,* as have most films that have used digital soundtracks since then.

Just when I thought film sound couldn't get any better, the folks at Lucasfilm struck back. The THX division, in collaboration with Dolby Labs created the Dolby Digital Surround EX format for the Star Wars prequel,

Star Wars I: The Phantom Menace. Like with Dolby Stereo before it, Surround EX information gets carried along with the 5.1 soundtrack to the home video release. DTS offers a similar format.

Home Theater

Home theater combines the evolution of movies and surround sound with television and 2-channel hi-fi. In the late '70s, home video formats, like videotape and laser disc, became very popular with consumers. We enjoyed being able to watch our favorite movies on TV without commercial interruptions. Two other things happened as well. Televisions became large-screen video monitors that accommodated multiple video sources and made watching movies much more cine-matic. Also, stereo VCRs and television broadcasts were introduced, which inspired people to connect their hi-fi system to the TV. Movies and television shows sounded substantially better than listening through the television's lousy single speaker.

Dolby and some audio equipment manufacturers realized that con-sumers' home stereo equipment could take advantage of the Dolby Stereo theatrical format, which had been copied onto home video formats directly from the theatrical audio master recordings. The Dolby Surround processor was introduced and could decode the Dolby Stereo signal that had been recorded onto the stereo soundtracks of videotapes and laser discs. Initially, Dolby Surround could only decode the single surround channel, but Dolby Pro Logic was soon released and decoded the three front channels (left, center, and right) in addition to the surround channel. Home video releases were soon stamped with a Dolby Surround logo, indicating compatibility with the Dolby Stereo theatrical format.

Since then, nearly every advance in theatrical sound has migrated to the "small" screen. Dolby Digital and DTS were available on laser disc, and are now available on DVD, as is Dolby Digital Surround EX 5.1. Dolby Digital, and DTS soundtracks are also available from a number of digital cable and satellite channels and video games. Dolby Digital is the audio standard for the new high-definition television format. Numerous other advances have been made to consumer surround processing as well, and these are outlined in Chapter 6, "Command Central: Audio and Video Processors."

Anatomy of a
Home Theater
(Where to Start)

Assembling a home theater is much easier than you think—you only need a few basic pieces. For one, you need source components, which are components that play DVDs, CDs, and tune in TV programming. After all, without these things, what will you watch or listen to? You also need a TV and some speakers. The item that really takes the experience to the next level, though, is the surround processor. This decodes the audio signals into as many as eight different speaker channels. Setting up a home theater can be as easy as buying an all-in-one system or as adventurous as buying separate high-performance components and speakers tailored specifically to your needs for the ultimate experience.

Home Theater Equipment

Source Components

The first thing to consider for your home theater is what you want to watch or listen to. In many cases, this decision will determine the type of TV, speakers, or processor you need. Source components generate audio or video signals. Digital video disc (DVD) players and recorders certainly top the list for playing movies, thanks to their crisp, wide-screen picture and digital audio soundtrack. I'll also talk about digital video recorders (DVR), which are computer hard drives that act like VCRs but have much greater functionality. DVRs are so awesome that there's no point in talking about old-fashioned videocassette recorders (VCR). I'll do it anyway, but only about the newest digital version, called digital-VHS (D-VHS), that can record high-definition television signals.

Direct Broadcast Satellite (DBS) systems are replacing cable as a major source of television programming, but cable companies have made great strides with digital cable and CableCard. Either system can provide regular television signals but you should really look for digital television (DTV) and high-definition television (HDTV) capabilities. The digital TV format is an outstanding source of audio and video signals. I'll talk about these signals in great detail in Chapter 3, "Choosing Source Components: TV Programming."

Home theater implies movies, but don't forget music. I'll talk about multi-channel, high-resolution audio sources called Super Audio CD (SACD) and DVD-Audio, as they can take advantage of home theater's theatrical-style speaker system. In Chapter 5, "Choosing Source Components: Music," I'll also discuss music servers, just because they're new and cool and

Figure 1.1

Home theater consists of a TV, up to seven or eight speakers, a rack of gear, appropriate furniture, and lots of movies on DVD. (Image courtesy of Dolby Laboratories)

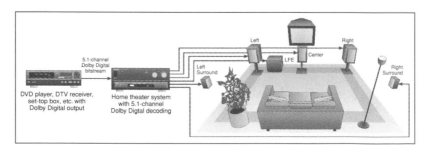

something you might want to consider. Other than leaving out antiquated sources like radios, tape decks, and turntables, none of which has much connection to home theater, the most noticeable omission is the CD player. The music server or DVD player replaces your need for a CD player. Even if you want a high-end CD player, you're better off getting DVD-Audio or SACD. There are so many disc player options available that you don't need to add yet another stand-alone CD player to your equipment rack.

This book is not about and doesn't cover video games, but you can (and should) consider games a viable source for your home theater. The three major gaming consoles—Nintendo GameCube, Sony Playstation2, and Microsoft X-Box, include some capacity for surround sound and widescreen video and can look and sound great on a home theater system. The X-Box can even output high-definition signals and 5.1 sound (I explain this term later) throughout the game. Just be careful when playing video games on plasma or large-screen CRT-based televisions. (See "Image Burn-in and Wear," on page 127 for more details.)

The Surround Processor

If you're on a budget or just getting started, you can connect all your source components directly to a TV. But if you really want to experience home theater, you need a surround processor. This is the central computer for your home theater and decodes the digital audio signals that come from your DVD player, VCR, DBS receiver, Digital TV tuner, or other sources into anywhere from six to eight channels of audio. Each channel provides sound to a different speaker. A 6-channel speaker system, usually referred to as a 5.1 system, uses three front channels (left of the TV screen, center, and right of the TV screen), left and right surround channels placed at the back of the room, and a separate subwoofer (the .1) for low-frequency or bass sounds.

Figure 1.2

Audio/video surround receiver, model STRDA3000ES, courtesy of Sony Electronics

In the early days of home theater, the surround processor was a separate component. Today, it's built into receivers, integrated amplifiers, and preamplifiers, or devices that are often called "controllers." In addition to surround processing and volume control, these components can accept the audio and video signals from all your source components and can route the signals to the output of the processor. They are, in a sense, the Grand Central Station of audio and video signals. Controllers may or may not include amplifiers, however, and amps are an integral part of this main control system. Each amplifier channel drives a particular speaker. If the controller is the station, then the amplifier is the locomotive that drives the system. If the controller doesn't have an amplifier, then you'll need to add one. Chapter 6, "Command Central: Audio and Video Processors," includes more information on controllers.

Figure 1.3

A surround receiver consists of multiple components built into one chassis. This includes an audio/video preamp, a surround processor, a multichannel amplifier, and an AM/FM radio tuner. An integrated amplifier is essentially the same thing, but doesn't have a radio. Many of the remaining components are available separately, as well.

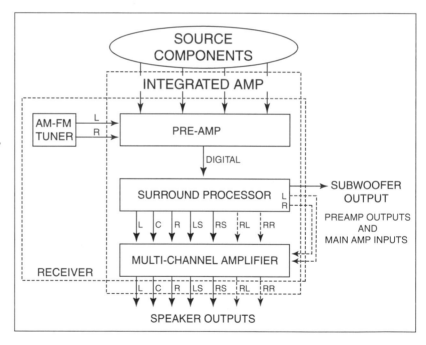

The configuration of your controller depends on the functions you want built into it. When the controller includes audio-video switching, an AM/FM radio tuner, surround sound processor, and a multichannel amplifier, the device is referred to as an audio-video (A/V) or surround "receiver," which is by and large the most common choice. The all-in-one approach makes it easy to configure and control the system. It is also cost-effective. Some receivers even come with a built-in DVD player, which is a good idea for many people.

Receivers are often confused with "integrated amplifiers." The only difference between receivers and integrated amplifiers is that an integrated amp lacks a radio, but it includes the switcher, surround processor, and amplifier. Technically, a receiver is an integrated amp (with a tuner) but an integrated amp should never be referred to as a receiver.

Another controller configuration is called the preamplifier-processor (or pre-pro, for short). This component includes the switching and surround processing functions of a receiver, and may even include a tuner, but lacks the amplifier section. You need a separate amplifier to power the speakers which increases the price, but improves performance and flexibility. The advantages and disadvantages of receivers, integrated amplifiers, and separate pre-pros and amplifiers are outlined in Chapter 6.

Speakers

The surround processor decodes the soundtracks of your movies, music, and television shows in a way that simulates a theatrical sound system or concert hall, but to hear the output you need at least six speakers, five main speakers plus a subwoofer. The surround processor provides outputs for three front speakers, which you should place left, near the middle, and to the right of your TV. These speakers anchor sounds to the on-screen action. An array of loudspeakers on the side and back walls of movie theaters reproduce ambient effects like rain, street traffic, or the echoes of a concert hall. You only need a pair of speakers at home, often placed at the sides and just behind the listening area, to re-create these ambient and directional effects. In some cases you can add one or two more surround speakers.

You also need at least one subwoofer and might even want to add more. The subwoofer provides warmth and richness to music and adds extra impact to movie and television soundtracks. A subwoofer also allows you to use smaller, less-obtrusive main speakers without sacrificing that big-speaker sound.

Figure 1.4

Multichannel speaker system, model System 6, courtesy of Paradigm

In Chapter 8, "Speakers," I'll talk about how many speakers you need, how big they should be, when you should choose a 5.1, 6.1, or 7.1 system, and how to set up everything so you get the best sound.

Video (TV)

Good movie theaters have huge screens. A good home theater also needs a big TV so you can watch movies in all their cinematic glory. In many cases, you don't need anything more than a big TV. You can use a tried and true direct view cathode ray tube (CRT) display, or rear-projection "big screen," or a space-saving plasma or liquid crystal display (LCD). Solid-state or digital TVs offer excellent quality in small form-factors and are becoming increasingly popular.

If you want to get adventurous, consider front or custom rear-projection systems to get a great big image. You need the projector and a separate screen and possibly an outboard video processor, though. In fact, the video processor, which enhances video signals, is a good idea for any video display. Whatever your style, I help you sort through all the options in Chapter 7, "TV and Video Monitors," page 123.

Figure 1.5
Plasma TV, model DU-50PZ60, courtesy of LG Electronics

Of course, you might already have a DVD player, surround sound receiver, some speakers, and a television. You can start from scratch or you can fit these or other pieces together to assemble an enjoyable home theater system. All you have to remember is that you need source components, a surround processor of some kind, speakers, and a TV. That's it. Everything else is just gravy.

Home Theater in a Box

There are complete, all-in-one packaged systems available that include a receiver, a 5.1 or 6.1 speaker system, and in many cases a DVD player. Sold as Home Theater in a Box, or HTIB, these systems are often incredibly inexpensive. (I've seen them as low as $100.) I don't talk about these systems specifically because they are made for convenience and aren't usually built with performance in mind. There are exceptions, however, and when you're on a budget or looking for convenience, an HTIB can be a good place start. You should know that all the comments in this book that apply to separate components apply to the components found in an all-in-one system.

Room Acoustics

Good room acoustics can improve the sound of any system. This is an important element to consider, even if there's little you feel you can do about it. Chapter 12, "Sound and Room Acoustics," discusses sound and the importance of room acoustics to give you a better idea of what's involved. Often there are just simple things you can do to help the system sound better in a particular room. If you don't want to change your room's acoustics, then by all means, put your money into the best components you can afford. However, it's entirely possible (and likely) that you'll get better sound from less expensive equipment if you can improve your acoustical environment, if even slightly.

2

Your Budget

The first rule to buying a home theater system is not to feel anxious or stressed, nor should you feel bullied into spending more than your budget allows. Audio and video components don't generate income or give you a return on your investment, and you have to go to a lot of movies before a home theater becomes economical. But when you watch movies at home, you don't have to deal with sticky floors or yapping patrons and there's an excellent chance you'll have a better overall experience. Plus with a good home theater you'll spend more time watching movies at home with your family, which—like a MasterCard commercial might point out—is priceless. Most of all, you're buying a home theater because it's fun.

Now that you've decided to buy a home theater, you need to determine how much discretionary income you want to spend, and ration it accordingly. You don't want to spend so much money that you can't afford to rent the movies to watch on your new system (let alone send the kids to college or save for your retirement). I don't believe there's a magic number that will give you the best performance for the money, at least not one that applies to everybody. The amount is different for each individual and for each product category. The cost to performance ratio might get steeper as you move up the curve, but generally speaking, the more you spend wisely—the better the performance. There are some guidelines to consider.

Figure 2.1

Many people assume there's some single, magic point where spending more money will result in incomparable improvements in performance.

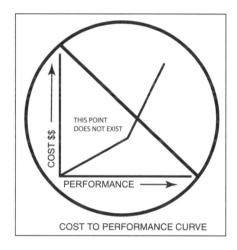

Figure 2.2

You can almost always get better performance from a home theater system as you spend more money. The curve may get steeper as you spend more, but how much you need to spend depends on your priorities.

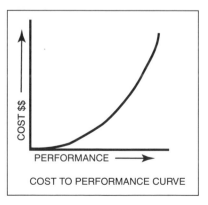

Average Consumer Spending, 2002

Food	13.5
Housing	32.6
Home furnishings and equipment*	(10)
Apparel and services	4.7
Transportation	19
Health care	5.3
Entertainment	5.1
Personal insurance and pensions	9.3
Other expenditures	10.5

*Note: Home furnishings and equipment consist of 10 percent of the total amount spent on Housing, not the total amount of all income spent.

Average consumer spending for 2002, courtesy of the Bureau of Labor Statistics

To get an idea of how much you should consider spending, find out what the average person spends compared to what enthusiasts pony up. Unfortunately the Average Consumer Spending table doesn't include a "home theater" equipment category, but the amount is likely divided between home furnishings, entertainment, and other expenditures. The average of these items, though, is between 5 and 10 percent of the after-tax income. Enthusiasts for whom music or home theater is a significant hobby—those who own thousands of CDs and hundreds of DVDs and read electronics magazines regularly—spend a much greater percentage on home theater equipment.

Your next step is to visit a few stores, particularly specialty stores that sell high-end equipment and have knowledgeable salespeople, and see what very little money ($300) and a whole lot of money ($30,000 to $150,000 or more) will buy. On the low end, you'll find an all-in-one system. On the high end, you should experience a top-notch system that's been carefully installed in a room engineered to sound great.

How much of a difference you notice, and what components you'll need to get there, will give you an idea of how much you need to spend.

Each chapter in this book outlines what you should look or listen for. In general, though, better systems should provide clear dialogue, rich, full-sounding music, enveloping surround effects, deep bass, and powerful explosions or other dramatic effects without making popping or huffing noises. You should hear a field of sound between a system's speakers, not the speakers themselves. Expensive video displays are often large and flat, but should be clear, detailed and vividly colored without seeming unnatural or exaggerated.

Allocate Your Funds Appropriately

How much money you spend might not be as important as spending the right amount in the right places. There's no magic answer, and the ratio can change depending on your purchasing strategy or budget. The overall objective is to make sure that all the components are complementary. That $1,000 DVD player might be terrific, but you're not likely to see or hear the difference if the rest of your entire system costs a total of $1,000.

However, there's always an exception isn't there? You could buy a relatively inexpensive total system now, and upgrade various components as time goes on. In this case, you might spend a larger portion of your budget on a particular component if you know that component is going to be part of your final system. Spending more money on one component, with plans to upgrade others later is particularly useful when spending money on speakers (particularly in-wall speakers that you don't want to replace later) or your TV. In other words, you could buy an expensive flat-panel TV with an inexpensive all-in-one audio system, knowing that you'll upgrade the audio system later as your budget allows. Or, if you're going to purchase an expensive entertainment cabinet to house the system, you could spend more on the TV now, knowing that it, and the cabinet will be with you long after you've replaced the rest of the equipment.

In general, you should spend the largest portion of your budget on the 5.1 speaker system and an HDTV. After all, these components convert the audio and video signals into what you see and hear. If the speakers or the TV can't reproduce the quality generated by the source components, all that additional quality is lost. These components are also the least likely to be replaced as time goes on.

You might also consider spending some time, effort, and money on room acoustic treatments. Adding absorptive or diffusive elements to the room is money well spent if you have enough money left over after you buy competent components. In a piece-by-piece scenario, you could start with room acoustic materials to provide a good backbone for the rest of your system. If you spend more than $10,000 on your system, you need to seriously consider some fundamental room acoustic treatment or design.

For equipment, a subwoofer will eat up a good chunk of your speaker budget. Your next largest expenditure should be the front three speakers. These speakers, combined, might cost more than the subwoofer, but individually will likely cost less. For example, you'll find a great subwoofer for $2,000, but could easily spend $1,000 for each front speaker. You can get by with small, inexpensive surround speakers if you're on a budget, but with full range 5.1 and 6.1 soundtracks available from DVD, satellite, cable, and even video games, the surround speakers should be comparable to the front speakers. Remember, you can always upgrade when you checkbook permits.

If you buy your system one piece at a time, purchase the surround processor and DVD player last. You can get by with less expensive receivers and DVD players for the time being. These components frequently change features, so you might as well buy them last after the next latest and greatest development has come along. Also, if your budget doesn't allow you to spend more than a couple thousand dollars on a 5.1 or 6.1 speaker system or your TV, it doesn't make sense to spend much money on the electronics. I have a $40 DVD player that works great for the system it's connected to. If I were spending $4,000 to $5,000 on a system, I'd buy a better DVD player.

Stretch Your Dollar

If the system you want is slightly out of your budget, or if you just want to build your system gradually, here are a few tricks to make your dollar go further.

For one thing, if you are buying a number of components at the same time, you can likely barter with stores and salespeople for a better deal. Most of us, however, don't have the luxury of buying as nice a system as we would like if we buy it all at once, so buying components piece by piece lets us assemble a high-end system over time. (Plus, you get to look forward to each new purchase.) You can start with a TV, add a DVD player, then a surround receiver and a pair of speakers, and so on; or you could purchase a TV and a home-theater-in-a-box, then replace components as you see fit. No matter what you start with, create a plan and a timeline and go from there.

Look for store sales or save money and buy components that have been discontinued. Most major, mass-market manufacturers come out with new models nearly every year. Last year's model likely has few cosmetic or feature set changes, yet will be priced lower once the new models are out. Each product category has its own caveats, though. New and still-in-the-box discontinued items might be a reasonably good buy. Demonstration models or "floor samples" can vary in reliability from one product category to another. Amplifiers and speakers, for example, are fairly good buys as long as the speakers don't show major wear (finger-poked tweeters, for example). These products are built to last and there have been few changes in amplifier or speaker designs in the last 20 years. Receivers, preamplifiers, and surround processors are also extremely reliable in terms of performance, but last year's models might not have the latest and greatest surround processing technique or input connection and might only be a good choice if you're trying to assemble a good system all at once.

I don't recommend buying floor sample DVD players given the wear and tear that can occur to the many moving parts. Discontinued DVD players may not garner much savings, either, considering how quickly prices have dropped and new features are introduced. Even if there's an unused sample available, at the rate things are going, last year's

DVD player might cost more even after the discount, and will likely have fewer features than the newer model.

Prices are also dropping quickly for flat-panel LCD and digital (microdisplay) rear-projection TVs, and you should be able to find some great deals on used or unused discontinued models. The displays should be fairly reliable in either case. However, LCDs and digital rear-projection displays use a high-powered light bulb that needs to be replaced every so often, so if you're buying a floor sample, make sure that the model you buy has a new bulb, or that the discount price covers the cost of a replacement bulb, which can be several hundred dollars.

Unused plasma and CRT TVs are fine to buy at clearance sales, but don't buy the floor sample models that have been used for in-store demonstrations. Both types of technologies wear out over time and are susceptible to a condition called "burn-in" (see "Image Burn-in and Wear," on page 127) where repeated viewing of a stationary (e.g., CNN logo) or semi-stationary (e.g., news and sports tickers at the bottom of the screen) image can become permanently imprinted into that portion of the screen. Also, the price of plasma TVs are dropping like rocks. The clearance price should account for the lower cost of the newer models.

Saving money on various products might help you spend less, or purchase more for the same money. Keep in mind, though, that when you buy new products from a knowledgeable dealer, he or she will help you find what you need. Plus, when you buy all your equipment from one dealer, they can help you solve any problems that might come up later. If you buy from multiple dealers and have a problem, each dealer will likely point the blame on one of the other dealers. The knowledgeable dealer can help you avoid bringing home otherwise great products that don't work with the rest of your equipment and can help you get your system installed and performing optimally. In almost all cases, I recommend shopping for a dealer first, then looking at what they have available. Even if a dealer doesn't carry all the premium brands, if the equipment he or she does sell works together, you're better off buying from them than purchasing high-end equipment from separate dealers, only to find the parts are not compatible. The dealer should be someone you get along with, who listens to your needs, and can patiently explain what they think would work for you. Above all else, the dealer should help you see how a home theater can be fun and should make you feel at ease. Below is a recap of some things to consider:

- Check out various systems—from the ridiculously cheap to the outrageously expensive to help determine what's available and how much you need to spend to get what you want.

- Set your budget before going to the store.

- Decide if you're going to buy a system all at once or piece by piece. If the latter, determine if one component requires a greater upfront expense (like in-wall speakers or an in-cabinet TV). Create a time-line for buying the other components.

- Know what's most important to you—great sound, large-screen viewing, and so on.

- Bring your own CDs and DVDs for product comparisons when shopping so you have a reference if you view or listen to different products in different stores.

- Shop around, compare prices, and don't be afraid to look for sales or discontinued merchandise if you're on a budget.

- Look for a knowledgeable, friendly dealer and stick with him or her.

- Have fun. This is entertainment, after all.

3

Choosing Source Components: TV Programming

Digital TV and HDTV— the Future of Television

For the last 50 years or so we've been watching analog TV created by the National Television Standards Committee (NTSC), and while it has served us well, change has arrived. In 1996 the Federal Communications Commission (FCC) adopted the new television transmission system developed by the Digital HDTV Grand Alliance (a consortium of manufacturer, education, and research groups) and documented by the Advanced Television Systems Committee (ATSC) and it's better than analog in nearly every respect.

The ATSC DTV standard uses a digital transmission scheme—the ones and zeros of computer code—to broadcast television signals. It's so revolutionary that the FCC allocated new channels for local broadcasters to transmit the new signals. Nearly all TV stations are already using both their analog and digital channels while consumers are purchasing new digital TVs and TV tuners. After 2007 (or 2009 perhaps), or when 85 percent of the population in a TV station's region can receive the digital signal, the government will pull the plug on the analog channels and broadcasters will transmit using only the all-digital system. Portions of the analog spectrum will subsequently be "repurposed" (e.g., auctioned off, and the proceeds will go to pay some of the national debt. No lie.)

Stay calm. All your analog NTSC televisions placed strategically around the house so that you can refill the Cheetos bowl without missing a play in the big game won't become instantly obsolete. In fact, the signal will go dark only for those who exclusively use rabbit ears (or a roof-top antenna) to receive terrestrial (AKA over-the-air) television signals. If, like most of us, you have cable or satellite, you'll still get a signal. But once everyone sees what DTV and in particular, high-definition television (HDTV) has to offer, you'll want it. HDTV is the perfect complement to your home theater system.

Figure 3.1

Plasma HDTV, model DU50PZ60, courtesy of LG Electronics

Advantages of Digital TV

The ATSC signal is digitally encoded with a compression scheme created by the Moving Picture Experts Group. This scheme is called MPEG2 and it stuffs much more video and audio data into the same channel as the analog broadcast system. The fact that the signal is digital means there's no degradation between the TV station's transmitter and your TV. NTSC signals use an analog system that is subject to noise, reflections, and interference. Tall, nearby buildings, for instance, can cause double or ghost images that blur the picture. A distant signal, or a signal blocked by trees, might be too weak and the images will appear with video noise or "snow." With analog signals, the farther you are from the transmitter, the worse the picture will be. With the digital system, if you can receive a strong signal then trees, buildings, or video snow won't affect it. The picture quality will be as good as it is at the TV station.

This digital clarity, however, is only an improvement if you currently receive analog terrestrial TV signals. If you are one of the millions that get digital cable or a satellite TV signal, you already know the benefit of digital transmission. But there are many other benefits to digital TV.

Multicasting

Broadcasters can use the ATSC system's extra data capacity to transmit as many as five different subchannels, (called multicasting), with picture and sound quality similar to what you get from a DVD, or stations can use the bandwidth to transmit one or two high-definition signals in the same 6 MHz channel.

How many channels broadcasters can fit into the available space depends on the number of digital bits used for each channel or subchannel. Generally speaking, more bits are needed for higher-resolution images like HDTV. All NTSC signals, whether they come from your VCR, rooftop antenna, analog cable box, standard definition satellite receiver, laser disc, or DVD player are delivered with a specific interlaced vertical resolution or scan frequency known as 480i. The actual horizontal resolution is determined by the source (see "Resolution," page 20). Higher capacity sources like DVD have better horizontal resolution.

Resolution

Resolution is a measure of detail in an image and is measured both vertically and horizontally. The higher the resolution in either dimension, the more defined the image. Poor resolution can turn what was a smooth diagonal line into a series of steps resembling a Mayan pyramid. Good resolution can make each petal visible in a bouquet of flowers. With HDTV, you can see water droplets on the petals.

Figure 3.2
A CRT draws scan lines in one continuous motion, starting from the top left of the screen, moving horizontally to the right. The electron beam goes dark as it travels back and down to the left to start the next line.

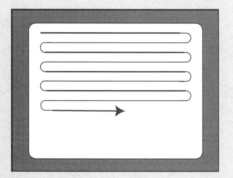

In both analog and digital TV formats, the vertical resolution determines whether the source is compatible with an analog display. NTSC, for example, has 480 active interlaced lines (see "Interlaced vs. Progressive," page 22). An NTSC TV must be able to draw 480 lines to be compatible with the system. By comparison, a digital TV must draw 720 or 1,080 lines to be compatible with HDTV.

Horizontal resolution, on the other hand, measures the number of black to white (or white to black) transitions in each horizontal scan line and is often described in analog formats as "lines per picture height" (pph), which equates to a per square area or density factor. Some manufacturers describe their TV's resolution capability across the full screen width, which falsely increases the measurement. (DTV systems are measured across the full picture width, though.) "Lines" refers to the results of a test pattern used to measure the specification that draws a row of ever-shrinking vertical lines on screen. The point where the vertical lines blur together is the limit of the horizontal resolution. With analog systems, the horizontal resolution is dependent both on the source and the TV. Older devices have very little horizontal resolution. VCRs output approximately 240 "lines" pph; broadcast analog TV has about 300 lines. Laser disc, an old 12-inch disc format, was the resolution leader with about 430 lines before DVD came out. DVD has a horizontal resolution capability of about 540 lines.

Resolution *(continued)*

Digital TV offers a number of resolutions that broadcasters can use depending on what makes the most sense for the signal, the program's time slot, or the TV station's budget. The image is divided into a grid of individual pixels, which are described horizontally then vertically. For example, a standard definition television signal can have 704 horizontal and 480 vertical pixels for a total of 337,920. This resolution is usually listed as 480i. SD is also available as either a normal or wide-screen image. The pixel count stays the same, though. Enhanced definition television (EDTV) offers the wide-screen SD signal as 480p, which is a progressive image. HDTV starts at 1,280 by 720p, or 921,600, which is almost three times the resolution of EDTV and is referred to as 720p. A second interlaced HDTV format, called 1080i, has a resolution of 1,920 by 1,080i, or nearly 2,073,600 pixels. That's a lot of pixels. Both 720p and 1080i images look great.

Digital TV, however, isn't restricted to one vertical scan frequency or horizontal resolution. If a broadcaster wants to pack a number of subchannels into their frequency space, they can transmit those subchannels as standard definition digital television (SDTV), or 480i. The SD picture can have as much horizontal resolution as a DVD and can even come in a wide-screen image. Many independent local TV stations will offer SDTV until there's a backlog of high-definition programming. Stations can pack fewer channels with better quality using EDTV, or enhanced definition digital television. EDTV refers to signals broadcast in a 480p format. The 480p resolution is progressively scanned and is noticeably better than 480i, though it requires more bandwidth (see "Interlaced vs. Progressive," page 22). EDTV offers a wide-screen image as well. PBS and Fox have used 480p for a number of specials and prime-time Fox TV programs. By the time you read this, however, even Fox will have upgraded to high definition.

NOTE High definition is the pinnacle of digital TV. Defined loosely by the ATSC, HDTV is any image with twice the vertical and twice the horizontal resolution of our current system, presented in a 16:9 aspect ratio with 5.1 channels of audio. There are two broadcast formats that fit into this description, the lowest of which, 720p, still has three times more vertical detail and twice as much horizontal detail as DVD. ABC, Fox, and ESPN all transmit their high-definition signals in 720p. Most broadcasters use an interlaced HDTV format called 1080i, which contains twice the vertical resolution and more than three times the horizontal resolution of regular television. In fact, few displays can yet take full advantage of 1080i's full horizontal resolution.

Interlaced vs. Progressive

Everyone has seen an interlaced image. It's the NTSC signal you currently receive and it's called 480i (the "i" stands for interlace). Each video frame is divided into 480 horizontal lines and 30 frames are shown per second. To decrease the size of the signal, each video frame is split into two fields, making 60 fields per second. Each field contains every other line of the original video frame. If you numbered the lines of each frame from top to bottom—from 1 to 480—the first field of each frame would contain the odd lines (1, 3, 5 … 479) while the second field would contain the even lines (2, 4, 6 … 480). Each field is displayed so quickly that if there's no motion between them, persistence of vision will blur the two fields together into one frame; 1080i works the same way, there are just more lines per field.

There are problems with interlaced signals when there is a difference between two fields. This happens often when movies shot on film are transferred to video. Film's 24 frames per second rate needs to repeat every fourth field in order for the film to keep the same time as video's 60 field per second rate. Film frame 1, for example, is split into fields 1A (odd lines) and 1B (even lines). Frame 2 becomes fields 2A and 2B, but then repeats field 2A again. Frame 3 now starts with field 3B (even lines have to follow odd lines), then 3A. Frame 4 continues the pattern with 4B, then 4A, but then repeats field 4B, which brings the cycle back to the beginning.

Interlaced vs. Progressive *(continued)*

Figure 3.03

Film's 24 frame per second rate is converted into 60 interlaced fields for video playback. The viewer perceives a 30 frame image, though some of the interlaced fields don't always match up.

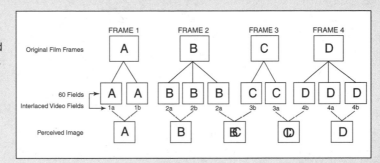

When fields 2A and 3B contain different picture information, the effective resolution will be only 240 lines for each field. If there are slight differences between the fields, the areas that are different lose resolution. Even if the fields all match, but there's vertical motion in the image at just the right pace, the line structure is readily apparent. If you sit too close to a large image you'll also notice the line structure. This is especially true with a 480i signal on a 36-inch TV if you sit closer than 9 feet from the screen. Note that all of these problems can go away if the signal is properly upconverted to 480p (the "p" stands for progressive). Upconversion, also called de-interlacing or "line-doubling" is discussed in greater detail in Chapter 6, "Command Central: Audio and Video Processors."

Progressive signals, first used in computer displays, draw every line successively, from top to bottom, in each field or frame. With a 480p signal, there are 480 lines drawn in every field. If the signal originally had 30 frames, every frame is duplicated to maintain a 60 "field" rate. Subsequently, progressive scan images have more apparent resolution and fewer image distortions, especially during fast-motion sports programming, than would otherwise be present in a similarly interlaced signal. Progressive signals take up twice as much space to broadcast, though and can only be shown on TVs with scan rates that are twice as fast as regular televisions. 720p requires a TV that scans three times faster than a regular TV.

In a perfect world, there wouldn't be interlaced signals. Unfortunately, the world's not perfect and interlace is a fact of TV life. Interlacing works fine the majority of the time, and it makes sense as a broadcast format because it has less bandwidth than a progressive signal. For users, it's relatively easy to find a de-interlacer that can convert interlace broadcast signals into progressive images. Many HDTVs have built-in de-interlacing circuits for 480i signals.

Datacasting

A side benefit of the ATSC format is that in addition to offering multiple TV channels, a station can opt to transmit data. At its 19.4 mbps (megabits per second) broadcast rate, DTV offers Internet download speeds approximately 340 times faster than a 56 kbps dial-up modem. In theory, you could download the entire Sunday edition of the *New York Times* or the complete *Encyclopedia Britannica* within seconds. The ATSC has standardized a data broadcasting system that is being used by some public television and commercial stations as a value-added service along with their HDTV signals. A company called USDTV is using the extra bandwidth to transmit cable television-like service through terrestrial signals, but only in select markets.

Wide screen

In addition to the high-resolution picture, DTVs offer a wider screen image (and it's required for HDTV). DTV's wide aspect ratio, or ratio of image width to height, is 16 units wide for every 9 units high. This is expressed as 16:9 or 16 by 9 but can also be referred to as 1.78:1. (This ratio is just simple math; 16 divided by 9 equals 1.78.) Regular TV images of the same height would only be 12 units wide (12:9 or 4:3, AKA 1.33:1). SDTV images can still be 4:3, but HDTV images must be 16:9. The HDTV image gives the digital TV viewer a much wider land-scape and matches more closely with human vision, which is attuned to seeing a wide field. The wide image is also closer to the aspect ratio used for most movies. When movies are played on an HDTV they will usually not have to be cropped or letterboxed much to make the image fit the screen. TV shows recorded and broadcast in high definition, however, fill the screen entirely.

Color and dynamic range

HDTV signals also have improved color and dynamic range. The color palette with high-definition signals is much wider than with regular TV signals. Reds and greens are much deeper and more saturated, which gives the image a much richer and more vibrant appearance.

Dynamic range, or the difference between peak white and pitch black, is also slightly improved. This means that gradations from light to dark are smoother. The combination of color and dynamic range and the increased resolution make HDTV look great.

5.1-channel Dolby Digital audio

DTV is more than just great images. The audio that accompanies the video is equally impressive. The same Dolby Digital (AC-3) soundtrack heard on DVD and in the best movie theaters is now potentially available with all your favorite TV shows. This soundtrack includes left, center, right, left surround, and right surround channels as well as a low frequency effects channel (the ".1") for a completely enveloping audio experience. Dialogue stays anchored to the screen while other sound effects travel around the room. Ambient sounds from the two rear speakers immerse you in the middle of the action of a scene or sporting event while the subwoofer fills in ultra-low frequencies, making the sound rich and full-bodied. The full 5.1 soundtrack might not be used for all DTV broadcasts, or might not be passed along by your local station, but when it is available and your audio system can accommodate the audio, you'll hear the difference.

Program specific information protocol

OK, so maybe this doesn't sound as sexy as "12 kajillion dots of diagonal detail" or "360 channels of surround-encoded sound," but I'll bet that program specific information protocol (PSIP) will be as important to your use of HDTV as anything else. PSIP is really just a techie way of saying "built-in TV Guide," but it also includes some nifty features. Along with the audio and visual information, the DTV system transmits data about the program itself, and your TV creates its own interactive, on-screen channel guide, complete with show data, times, content descriptions, and more. Everything you've come to expect from advanced program guides available from satellite and digital cable are also possible with DTV.

One of the other nifty features of PSIP lets the broadcaster identify the DTV channel with the same ID as their analog channel. In Los Angeles, for example, KCBS, the local CBS station, broadcasts their analog signal on Channel 2. KCBS's digital signal is available on Channel 60. The station's PSIP information automatically tells your DTV tuner to re-map the channel as channel 2-1 or 2.1 so it's in the same place in your TV channel lineup as their analog station.

Tuning In to Digital TV

Changing over from regular TV to digital TV is a bit more involved than just buying a new television set, but the result is well worth it. First, find out what programming is available because not all channels are recorded in high definition and ones that are nationally broadcast might not be available locally. Networks break down into two groups: broadcast HD networks (CBS, ABC, NBC, Fox, UPN, and the WB) are generally available from local TV stations and digital cable, while premium networks (HBO, ESPN, Discovery, etc.) are available from satellite and cable services. (I'll talk about these and the exceptions in the sidebars on satellite and digital cable.) You need an HD-enabled terrestrial, digital cable or satellite tuner to receive the premium channels, which I'll talk about later in this chapter. Last but not least you need an HD-capable display. I discuss displays in Chapter 7.

What TV shows are recorded in HDTV?

The first step in the quest to upgrade to HDTV is to determine if your favorite programs are recorded in HDTV (or at least EDTV). Check out my magazine's website (www.dtvmag.com) and go to the HDTV Programming Weekly Schedule for an updated list of regularly scheduled HD programs. The list includes only shows that appear at the same time every week. Some networks broadcast HD programming all the time, but the network's schedule changes weekly.

Figure 3.4

The HDTV weekly programming grid found on the www.dtvmag.com website.

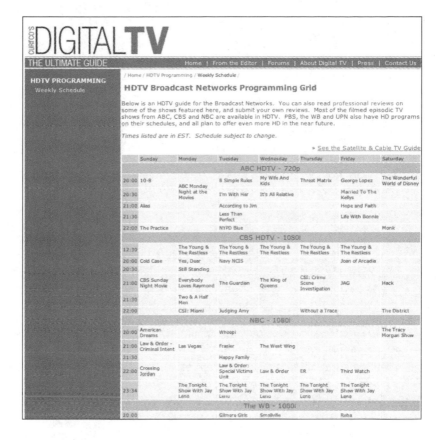

Each of the five major broadcast networks record and transmit most of their scripted prime-time shows (comedies, drama, and action) and special events like awards shows and major sports championship games in HDTV. HD News shows are rare, as the cameras are expensive. Sorry, no reality-shows are broadcast in HD, yet.

There are a number of premium networks that offer an HDTV channel with HDTV programming, including HBO, Showtime, Cinemax, Starz!, Encore, The Movie Channel, Discovery HD Theater, ESPN HD, TNT, NBA-TV, INHD, HDNet, Bravo HD+, Playboy, and others. The list of networks gets longer nearly every week. Check the recently updated HDTV Networks List under the Programming Highlights at www.dtvmag.com. Each network offers some HD programming, be it movies or original programs or special events.

When Digital TV Isn't Really "Digital"

You might have digital cable or satellite TV service, in which case you're already watching "digital" signals. Unless specified as HDTV, these signals are just a digitized version of analog signals and while hundreds of channels can be broadcast instead of just dozens, the signals aren't high definition. The image might be slightly cleaner than analog TV or cable images—though, in some cases the additional compression can make them considerably worse—but the signal still originates from an analog recording, not a digital or high-resolution recording.

Also, local digital TV broadcasters upconvert signals to fill the time between true HDTV programs. As with digital cable, these signals originate from NTSC analog recordings and are upconverted to HDTV so that they can be broadcast on the same channel. Upconverted shows don't necessarily look better on a digital channel than on a regular channel, but at least you don't have to switch back and forth between channels when true HDTV programs aren't being broadcast.

Make sure the service provider (particularly with cable companies) specifically offers HDTV, including programs either recorded in high definition or recorded on film and transferred to high definition. Programs recorded in high definition typically look better than programs transferred to high definition, but both qualify as true high definition. Most scripted HD television shows are actually shot on film and transferred to high definition.

What HDTV shows are available

Just because NBC records *The Tonight Show with Jay Leno* in high definition doesn't mean your local NBC station has a digital channel to broadcast the high definition signal. If a digital channel isn't available, you won't see Jay in ultrafine detail from an antenna, cable, or satellite. You need to find out what digital channels are available locally.

Go to www.antennaweb.org. This site asks for your street address (don't worry, the site doesn't record any personal information). The site then lists all the local broadcast TV stations available in your area, including analog and digital channels. The site will often mention when as-yet-inactive stations are expected to go digital. Stations listed with an asterisk or the letters *DT* added to the call sign already broadcast digital signals.

Figure 3.5

Find out what digital stations are available and what kind of antenna you need to receive them at www.antennaweb.org.

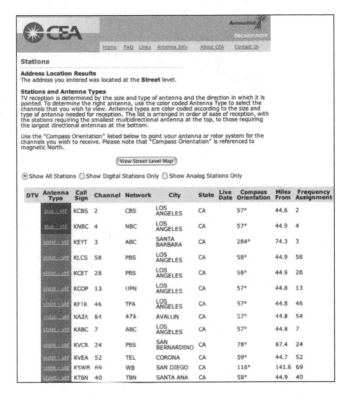

Premium HD networks, on the other hand, are available from either digital cable or digital broadcast satellite (DBS). The only way to know which premium HD networks are available from each service is to check your cable or satellite company's website or call and ask them. They add networks all the time.

Receiving HD signals

Your best bet for receiving terrestrial digital channels is either with an antenna or through a digital cable service. If you're willing and able to install an antenna on your roof or attic, the reception looks great, the signals are more abundant than from cable or satellite, and are free. You can tune the signals with either a terrestrial-only HD tuner (external or built into an integrated HDTV), or with the off-air ATSC tuner found in most HD satellite receivers. Make sure the installer has experience installing an antenna (and has a piece of test equipment called an RF spectrum analyzer), and he should be able to get you set up quickly.

If you can't receive many HD stations using an antenna, you'll have to call your local cable company to see if they offer local channels in HDTV. Some cable companies are better than others. HDTVs labeled as "Digital Cable Ready" are equipped with CableCard and can receive premium digital cable signals, including HDTV, without a cable box (but you'll still have to pay for the service and you need a credit-card-sized access key from the cable company for the TV).

Unfortunately, while some satellite services offer local channels, they don't yet offer these channels in high definition. Dish Network and DirecTV offer a national feed of CBS's HD programming (from the Los Angeles or New York affiliate). DirecTV also offers a national feed of NBC and may soon offer local HDTV channels in major markets.

Laws Regarding Antenna and Satellite Installation

Your landlord or homeowners association may have told you that you can't put up an antenna or satellite dish. Even though you signed the homeowner's agreement, federal law prohibits such restrictions. The FCC specifically allows the installation of small dishes or antennas on property you own or have exclusive access to including separate patios and balconies, but doesn't include shared areas, like a joined patio or the roof. The only exception is when the landlord or homeowner's association makes a communal signal of comparable quality available to everyone in the complex. (Check the FCC website at www.FCC.gov/cgb/consumerfacts/consumerdish.html.)

Your landlord cannot require you to get permission or pay an extra security deposit to install the antenna or dish (unless you have to drill holes in the walls). If you have any problems with your homeowners association or landlord call the Federal Communications Commission at 888-225-5322. Of course, if your balcony doesn't face the direction it needs to in order to receive the satellite or terrestrial signal, the law doesn't help much and you're back to negotiating with the landlord or homeowner's association.

Receiving premium HD networks from satellite or cable signals is fairly straightforward. Call the cable or satellite company and ask them to install the service at your house. Unfortunately, there's no easy way to know which TV service you should subscribe to. Digital cable has the most promise as an all-in-one provider of both local and premium HD networks, but few digital cable companies have seized the opportunity to do so, assuming they ever will. They also need to overcome their failing customer service records, as well. If you can use an antenna to receive most or all of your local channels and add satellite (or digital cable) to get premium networks, you'll probably receive most stations available in your area. If you can't or don't want to use an antenna, you'll need to make some choices and trade-offs.

Terrestrial Digital TV Tuners

Terrestrial tuners receive local digital TV signals from an antenna and are available as stand-alone devices, are included with HDTV-enabled digital satellite tuners, and are built into integrated HDTV displays. Some manufacturers even make digital cable boxes that include a terrestrial tuner. I'll talk more about satellite and digital cable services later in this chapter.

While most people use or augment their local channel reception with satellite or cable signals, there is still a market for local-channel-only terrestrial tuners. Adding an antenna is worthwhile, but since the terrestrial tuner is included with most HD satellite receivers, there's little point in buying an additional external tuner. If you subscribe to digital cable, on the other hand, and your cable system doesn't offer high-definition local channel service, buying a terrestrial tuner makes sense. It also might be worth getting a terrestrial tuner if you have a second HDTV and don't want to spend the money for the additional satellite or cable receiver. Keep in mind that the features described here also apply to any component or TV that comes with a terrestrial digital tuner.

Figure 3.6

Digital TV tuner, model LST3100A, courtesy of LG Electronics

What to Look For

Price

Prices on digital tuners vary according to features, most notably DVR recording and the amount of storage included. A basic terrestrial DTV tuner might cost a few hundred dollars. Add HD-DVR functionality and satellite reception and you can easily spend a thousand dollars or more. If you opt for interactive HD service through a digital cable company, the box might be provided by the cable company for nothing or as little as $10 a month. There's no easy or exceptional cost-saving recommendation. It comes down to what functions you want and can afford.

Connections

Your terrestrial tuner should have outputs that match the inputs on your TV, plus as many additional outputs as possible to accommodate future upgrades. The best connection to transfer HDTV signals from the tuner to the display is HDMI (high-definition multimedia interface) and FireWire. Both outputs carry the digital audio, video, and control signals from the tuner to the TV. An HDMI sends the decompressed signals to the display. FireWire transports the undecoded signal to your Digital-VHS recorder or integrated display. In the future, more digital products will be available, like hard drive or disc-based recorders that will accept the FireWire signal.

 HDMI is a backwards-compatible replacement for DVI (digital visual interface), which only carried the decompressed video signal. An adapter will connect HDMI and DVI components, but cannot carry the audio or control signals.

If your existing HDTV display lacks digital video inputs, be sure the tuner has an analog video connection, like component (YPrPb) or RGBHV, that match the TV's connection. You'll also need to send the tuner's audio signal to a 5.1 surround controller and need a digital audio connection (either optical or coaxial) that coincides with the inputs available on the controller.

Another handy connection feature outputs NTSC signals (composite, S-Video, and RF) simultaneously with the ATSC or HDTV image. Some inexpensive tuners require that you select the active output with a switch, which disables the NTSC outputs and prevents you from sending the NTSC signals to older, non-HD-capable TVs.

Output rates

Since there's no single signal resolution defined in the ATSC system, TV broadcasters use different formats. Fortunately, most displays accept any scan rate and internally convert the signal to whatever the TV needs to display a picture. Not all TVs have this capability, though, particularly earlier CRT-based TVs that can't accept 720p signals. Most tuners offer the ability to convert any incoming signal to a desired output rate, but again some don't. Check your TV owner's manual and make sure your TV doesn't have any of these restrictions. If it does, or you just want to be on the safe side, get a tuner that is capable of working around the restrictions.

Digital video recording

Using a digital video recorder (DVR) is one way to time-shift HDTV programs, and they're way cool (the other is D-VHS and it's much less cool). If you've never used a DVR (think TiVo), it's like a VCR, but it stores the audio and video information on a built-in computer hard drive, which gives you enormous flexibility. Once you've used a DVR, you'll never understand how you lived without it. The biggest issue with HDTV is that the format requires approximately 10 GB to record a single hour of TV. So buy as much storage as you can afford, and make sure it's easy to offload content from the hard drive onto a D-VHS or other FireWire-based device. Some Satellite HD-DVRs use the TiVo service, which is easy to use, but most stand-alone HD-DVRs rely on the PSIP, or the program specific information protocol. Check out the section on stand-alone DVR recorders later in this chapter for more general information.

Satellite or digital cable

Many HDTV tuners that include terrestrial reception also include HD-enabled satellite or digital cable reception. Either service is a great combination with terrestrial TV reception. You get your local digital broadcasts through the terrestrial tuner and get premium channels like Discovery HD, ESPN-HD, or HBO-HD through the satellite or digital cable service. See the sidebars on satellite and digital cable in this chapter for more information.

Digital Broadcast Satellite

Tired of lousy cable signals? Check out digital broadcast satellite TV. Satellite is a popular option for TV service because the picture quality is generally excellent, there's loads of programming available—including a number of HDTV channels—and the interactive program guide makes it easy to sift through several hundred channels. Plus, no matter where you are, if you have a clear view of the Southern sky, you can probably get satellite TV. Cable TV, on the other hand, isn't always available in rural areas and their customer service had declined substantially until satellite came along. Analog cable is limited in the amount of programming available, lacks an interactive program guide, and the picture quality ranges from poor to mediocre. It's no wonder satellite has become one of the fastest-growing consumer electronics products.

If you're old enough to remember the 12-foot BUD (big ugly dish) satellite systems of the '80s, you'll appreciate the low profile, pizza-sized dish used with digital broadcast satellite (DBS). Satellite offers a pure digital signal, which means that so long as you can receive the signal, it comes in clean and clear. You also get hundreds of channels, which include nearly all of your favorite premium networks, dozens of pay-per-view movie channels, dozens of digital music channels and in most major markets, you can even get analog local broadcast channels (but not local digital channels, yet). A number of movie and pay-per-view channels even include Dolby Digital 5.1 soundtracks. There are three major national satellite providers: DirecTV, Dish Network, and relative newcomer Voom. All have the same basic core services mentioned above, with some subtle differences between them.

DirecTV

DirecTV was the first company to introduce digital satellite service and has been the leader ever since. The system uses a single round or oval-sized dish depending on what channels you want to receive. The oval dish picks up many foreign language and HDTV

Digital Broadcast Satellite *(continued)*

channels. In addition to a full suite of movie networks and movie pay-per-view channels, DirecTV offers one of the most comprehensive suites of sports packages including things like NFL Sunday Ticket, which lets you see a huge selection of NFL football games, some of which are broadcast in HDTV. Similar packages are available for baseball, hockey, basketball, and college football games. Prices for programming depend on channels included, but range from $40 to $90 per month.

DirecTV's HDTV lineup has been somewhat average and expands rather slowly, though it promises to increase the number of channels dramatically next year. There's a good chance it added channels since this book was published. As I write this, DirecTV offers HBO and Showtime HD channels when you subscribe to either HBO or Showtime movie packages. A separate HD package provides ESPN-HD, Discovery HD Theater, HDNet and HDNet movies for $10.99 per month. DirecTV recently added Bravo HD+, as well. A single pay-per-view HD movie channel, which offers adult HD programs from Playboy, late at night, is also available. DirecTV includes a national feed of CBS and NBC in HDTV, but the channel's are only available in certain markets. Check with DirecTV to see if it's available in your area.

You used to be able to receive DirecTV with satellite tuners from several different manufacturers. By 2005, the company will have eliminated this option and will brand its own reception equipment. Your basic packages usually come with free equipment and installation, so long as you commit to a year or more of service. Additional receivers, which allow you to watch different things in different rooms, cost about $5 extra per receiver per month.

If you're interested in HDTV, you'll have to pay for an HD-enabled receiver. Fortunately one receiver option includes the TiVo DVR service. HD receivers without the DVR are also available, but I'm not sure why you'd want one. Get with the times and get a DVR. You'll need an HD-capable dish (the oval one with three LNB, or low noise blockers) to receive the extra HD channels. If you don't have an HDTV, get a receiver with at least the standard definition TiVo DVR and a digital audio output so that you can take advantage of the Dolby Digital soundtracks. TiVo costs a few bucks extra a month, or has a single "lifetime" fee, but it's worth it.

Figure 3.7
DirecTV HD-DVR satellite receiver, model HR10-250, courtesy of DirecTV

continues on next page

Digital Broadcast Satellite *(continued)*

Dish Network

Dish Network is the nation's second-largest satellite provider and is rapidly closing on DirecTV's lead. While most of the programming, equipment, and features available with DirecTV are available with Dish Network, there are a few differences. For one, Dish Network provides local analog channels to 45 percent more markets. You'll also receive at least one additional premium HD channel with Dish Network (currently TNT-HD) and have access to more than 60 foreign language channels in 25 different languages. Last but not least, Dish Networks programming packages, costing from $25 to $85, are a bit less expensive than DirecTV's.

Dish Network has almost always sold Dish Network-branded reception equipment, which means, like DirecTV, your options are limited. In most cases you only need one dish, but for some international or local programming you'll need a second one pointed in a slightly different direction. Basic reception equipment is available free with free installation and can be used to deliver signals to multiple rooms. Dish Network has some trick technology though for providing multiroom options that don't require the extra fee for the extra receiver. Otherwise it's $5 per receiver per month. Dish-branded DVR service is also available, and is one of the most popular DVRs on the market. All receivers include digital audio outputs to send Dolby Digital signals to your surround processor.

Dish Network offers some unique HD equipment options. They have two separate receivers, one of which includes an HD-DVR with a great deal of recording space. Both receivers are available as a package with Dish Network-branded HDTV displays (built by RCA). The total cost for the combination is $1,000 for either TV with the basic HD receiver model and $1,600 for a TV and the HD-DVR receiver. These are some of the best values in HDTV anywhere.

Figure 3.8

Dish Network HD-DVR satellite receiver, model DVR-921, courtesy of Dish Network

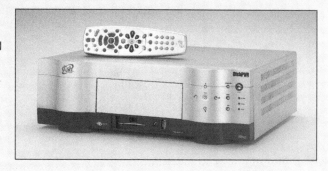

Digital Broadcast Satellite *(continued)*

Voom

Where DirecTV and Dish Network offer a handful of HDTV channels, Voom, a division of the Comcast Cable's Rainbow Media, provides more than 35 HD channels including HBO, Showtime, Discovery HD, ESPN, Cinemax, Starz!, The NFL Network, Spice (adult) TMC, and more, plus 21 HD networks that are exclusive to Voom. HD is obviously a major focus for the fledgling satellite company and it will be a while before the other companies catch up. Voom provides more than 80 major networks in standard definition as well. The only thing Voom doesn't offer is local analog reception. For that, Voom provides an antenna and a terrestrial and digital TV tuner with the system installation, which is usually a better option anyway. If you are not able to receive digital over-the-air signals, you might have to find another way to get your local TV channels.

Voom currently offers one HD receiver. Installation is free, the equipment costs a few bucks a month and programming packages run between $40 and $80. By late 2004, Voom should have the first networked HD-DVR, which should let you to watch and/or record a show in one room, and transfer the recording to another receiver in another room so you can watch TV without missing a second of a program. If Voom continues to improve its basic channel offerings and maintain its leadership position in HD programming, they will become a serious contender in the satellite industry.

Figure 3.9
Voom HD satellite receiver, model DSR-550, courtesy of Voom

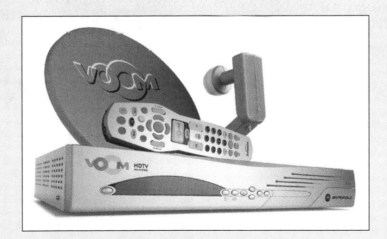

Digital Cable

If you're like 70 percent of the U.S. TV-watching public, you probably have cable. If you have analog cable I feel your pain. Digital cable, on the other hand, has the potential to knock satellite off its lofty perch. I say "potential" because some cable companies use digital technology to do nothing more than compress their lousy analog signals. There are just more signals. Digital cable can, when done right, provide the same number of programming options and interactive services as satellite TV, if not more.

Digital cable can offer local broadcast HD channels, in addition to the premium HD Networks. They might even offer regionally available sports channels like the Madison Square Garden Network and Comcast SportsNet, or their own pay-per-view movie channel like iNDemand. You'll find a listing of cable HD offerings at http://www.ce.org/publications/books_references/dtv_guide/default.asp, but it's not updated often. Contact your local cable company to find out if it offers digital cable (it's not available everywhere) and what services it includes in your area. The cable company provides a digital cable receiver, which can also include DVR functions, though you might have to ask specifically for an HDTV-enabled receiver. They'll provide only the receiver, however, if you actually have an HDTV.

One recent advance in cable (and DTV) that sets digital cable apart from satellite is an agreement between TV manufacturers and cable companies called CableCard. Technology is being built into the next generation of DTV-ready TVs that allows you to connect your digital cable signal directly to the TV and receive one-way digital cable service (including HD programs and other premium services) without a cable box, much like you did with analog cable. These displays, and the next generation of digital cable boxes, will also include FireWire connections so that you can record digital content onto a D-VHS VCR or external DVR. You need to contact the cable company, subscribe, and ask for its security access card. You'll need a separate cable box if you want two-way services like pay-per-view or an interactive service guide, but eventually a similar agreement will include these services as well.

Aspect ratio control for 480i DTV channels

For who knows what reason, too many TV tuner manufacturers fail to provide the ability to change the aspect ratio of 480i programs received on digital channels. I don't know if they forgot that these signals could come in either 4:3 or 16:9 or if they assume the aspect ratio control will be built into the TV. And while wide-screen TVs do have aspect ratio control for NTSC signals, the function is often not available for digital channels of any type. It's likely that at some point in the future, your local digital broadcaster will use 480i for some signals, so make sure you can control the signal's aspect ratio somehow, preferably through the tuner.

Sorted digital and analog channels

It's particularly handy to have the tuner sort all the digital channels and analog channels together in the same channel list. Some tuners separate digital from analog channels and require that you cycle through the analog channels first before getting to the digital channels. Sure, the analog channels should go away at some point, but until then, if you can't get everything on a digital channel, it's more convenient to channel surf through all the available channels in sequential order.

Remotes

The remote control should be easy to use and preferably backlit so that you can see it in the dark. In Chapter 9, I talk about universal and automation remotes and the advantages of having one. If you're spending more than a couple thousand bucks on a system, an automation remote, usually purchased separately, should be part of that package. The DTV tuner remote should have separate buttons for Power On and Power Off to make it easy to program the automation system.

Getting Started

Step 1: Install an antenna

Installing an antenna is fairly simple and straightforward. In some cases, you can probably use the modern equivalent to rabbit ears. (See **Figure 3.10**). Antennas are cheap and worth trying. To find out what kind of antenna works in your area, go to www.antennaweb.org and type in your address. The website will tell you what type of antenna you need, which direction to point it, and whether or not you'll need a signal booster to receive certain channels. Small antennas can receive signals from nearby stations in various directions, but can't provide as strong a signal as you need for a good picture and don't reject ghost signals that are reflected off nearby mountains or buildings.

Large antennas provide strong signals from distant stations, do a better job of rejecting ghost signals, but might have trouble picking up signals from two stations that are in slightly different directions. If you're able to hide the antenna in your attic, get an antenna larger than antennaweb.org says you need or add a signal booster (called an RF Preamp or RF Amp). This will compensate for the signal loss through the roofing material. Radio Shack and Home Depot sell antenna and mounting hardware for about $40 to $100.

If you live between two major cities, you'll find that the TV stations broadcast from different locations. If you can't receive all the channels you want with a fixed antenna, you might need a rotor. The rotor is a small rotating motor that, depending on what channel you want, spins the antenna in the right direction.

Just mount the antenna and route the wire to your TV tuner. Most DTV tuners have a built-in signal strength meter to help you make sure you have the antenna pointed in the right direction. If your tuner doesn't, you can probably use any analog TV tuner (like a small TV).

The strongest analog signal generally provides the clearest picture and analog signal strength usually coincides with digital signal strength. Fine-tune the antenna's direction so that you get the strongest signal from as many stations as possible. If you're not handy with a hammer or drill, hire an installer. Some installers will even have technician-quality signal strength meters.

Figure 3.10

Indoor terrestrial antenna, model HDTVi, courtesy of Terk

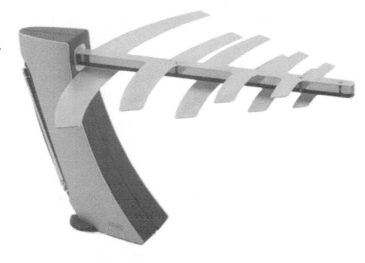

Figure 3.11

Outdoor terrestrial antenna, model CM3017, courtesy of Channel Master

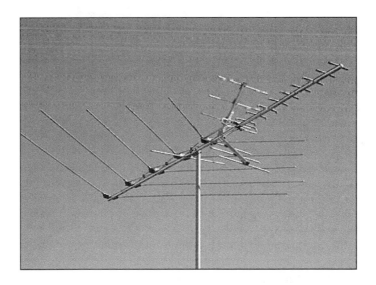

Step 2: RF distribution

Chances are before you connect the antenna signal to the tuner you'll need to split the signal to several TVs, VCRs, or other components. This is easy to do, even though most people don't do it correctly, which can result in poor quality analog reception and sometimes no digital reception at all. The goal is to always maintain the signal level above the threshold that an analog TV needs to create clear and clean images or that the DTV tuner requires to lock on to each channel quickly and decode the signal without the signal breaking up every time a bird flies by.

Start by checking the signal level at the point where the antenna or cable signal enters the house and before any splitters are added to the line. Use a DTV tuner (if it has an on-screen signal level meter) or a small analog TV. If the signal isn't clean and clear at this point, you need a larger antenna (to pull in a stronger signal), or a preamplifier (to boost the signal if there's a long cable run to the antenna). If you have cable TV service, call the cable company, as there's probably not much you can do. Adding an amplifier to an already lousy signal just makes it extra lousy.

If the signal is clean, though, check the signal in other rooms in your home. Small cables used over long distances (over 100 feet), splitters, and taps degrade signal levels. If the signal level drops below an acceptable threshold, analog picture quality suffers and digital reception becomes difficult if not impossible to achieve.

Cables labeled RG-59 are cheap and pliable but lose more signal strength than RG-6, which is a bit thicker and stiffer. At the very least, use RG-6 behind the wall and use RG-59 only to connect the TV to the wall jack. Splitters lower the signal level about 3 to 4 decibels (dB) at each output, more so with multiple outputs. Splitters may be necessary, but consider using taps or some combination of the two, instead. Taps are like splitters but the signal level drop is disproportional between the two outputs. One output might lose only 1 or 2 dB. Taps are good for daisy-chaining the signal from one TV to the next. The output with the greatest loss feeds the local TV while the output with the least loss feeds the rest of the line.

If needed, add a big enough amplifier at the signal's entry point to maintain a good signal at the end of the line. If you have three splitters and 200 feet of cable from the beginning to the end, you'll probably need about 15 to 18 dB of signal boost at the beginning. You might need to reduce the signal level at TVs that are close to the output of the amplifier to prevent the TV from overloading. Overloading will add sparkles and herringbone-like noise patterns to analog TV signals and can prevent digital tuners from locking on to the signal. If you use splitters, you might need to add signal level "pads," which cut the signal level down, usually in 3 dB increments. Taps have pads essentially built in. If you have an 18 dB amp, you might want a tap with a -12 to -15 dB output for the first TV or tuner. Again, the output that sacrifices 1 to 2 dB of signal will feed the line to the next TV. Use a -9 to -12 dB tap for the second TV, and so on. Follow this procedure with every TV throughout your house (the farther from the amplifier you get, the less signal cut you need) and you'll have consistently strong and clear signals.

Step 3: Connect tuner to the TV or A/V controller

Depending on how you configure your system (see the Appendix), connect the DTV tuner to your HD-capable display or audio/video controller. Use the best signal connection possible. In descending order of preference, start with HDMI; DVI or FireWire; then Component or RGBHV. Connect S Video or Composite signals as a backup or to send down-converted signals to other non-HDTVs. If you use the analog video signals (component or RGBHV), make sure you also connect the digital audio signal to the surround processor. If not, make sure the analog audio connections accompany the DVI or analog video connections.

Step 4: Configure surround processor

If you don't route the DTV tuner's audio or video signals through your surround controller, skip this step and go straight to A 5.1 (or Better) Audio System under "Secrets" that explains why you should upgrade.

The most difficult task when installing a new home theater system is finding the setup menu for your surround processor. Many receivers access an on-screen installation menu with a display or setup button, others use more cryptic approaches, like holding down the menu button for several seconds. Check your owner's manual for details.

The inputs on the back of most newer receivers and preamps no longer directly correspond with the source buttons on the front panel, particularly for digital audio and component video signals. You have to tell the surround processor which inputs to use. Make a note of which ones you use. Then, when you enter the setup menu and find the submenu for the TV input, you can tell the processor where to find the DTV tuner's audio and video signals. These signals might be HDMI 1, or digital audio input 3 and component video input 2, for example. You might also be able to select default surround modes for that particular input, which I'll cover in the surround processor chapter (see Chapter 6). In some cases, the processor can't collect the information for each source in one submenu and will instead configure the information for each signal type. In other words, you'll have to enter the submenu for digital audio inputs, find input 3, and assign it to the TV source button. You'll have to do the same for the video signal.

Step 5: Run a channel scan

At this point you should be able to route the signal through the surround processor, where available, and see an image on the screen. The last thing to do is to run a channel scan and let the tuner search the airwaves for digital signals. If all went well, the tuner will find everything that's available in your area. If a few channels don't show up, make sure they're broadcasting signals at the time you run the channel scan. Some stations figure not too many people are watching, and might turn off or at least lower their transmitter power to save energy when they're not showing actual HDTV content.

If the stations are up and running and you still can't receive them, you might need to fine-tune your antenna installation. In some cases, minor directional changes will make the difference between receiving some channels or not. This might lower signal levels for other channels, but so long as all of the channels come in, you'll be fine. If there are nearby buildings or mountains, you might need a larger antenna, which will reject reflected signals that otherwise confuse the tuner. You can always consult with an installer if you need help.

Secrets

Adjust the screen type for your TV

Most non-HDTV shows, particularly on satellite or cable are presented in a 4:3 aspect ratio. HDTV programs are presented in the wide-screen, 16:9 aspect ratio. (See "Anamorphic Explained, or Why Movies Need Black Bars" in Chapter 4, page 57 for more information on aspect ratios.) Depending on the shape of your TV, you need to select how the nonstandard signals fit the screen. For example, if your TV is wide screen, there will likely be a menu function in the tuner that allows you to crop, stretch, or letterbox 4:3 signals to fit the screen. In this case, a "letterboxed" 4:3 signal will appear with gray or black bars on the sides of the active image area. The opposite is true if you have a 4:3 TV. The tuner should have a menu setting that either crops, letter-boxes, or squishes wide-screen material into the screen shape and will make images appear tall and thin. Which setting you use is up to you, but most tuners default to the letterboxed options in either case, which you may or may not want.

Eliminate gray bars

If you choose to preserve the signal's original geometry and aspect ratio, you will have gray bars on the screen at one point or another (see above). Service providers use gray bars to keep unused portions of the screen illuminated to prevent the signal from causing uneven wear on a picture tube or plasma display. (See Chapter 7 for more details.) If your TV uses newer technology, like LCD, LCoS, or DLP, it's not susceptible to burn in, and you can turn off the gray bars using the advance settings in the tuner's setup menu. Don't turn off the gray bars if you have a tube or plasma TV.

Add FireWire to your DirecTV satellite system

Currently, DirecTV and Dish Network don't offer FireWire outputs on their satellite receivers, which would make it possible to record the digital signal to a D-VHS. The FireWire output is one reason digital cable has the potential to steal market share. That said, there is at least one website, www.169time.com, that modifies certain HD-enabled

DirecTV receivers to output a FireWire signal. The procedure is not cheap by any means, and might not be possible with future generations of receivers, but provides some existing users the ability to time-shift or archive some good HD recordings.

Repeat channel scans often

Repeat your channel scan from time to time if all your local TV stations aren't available digitally when you assemble your system. Repeating the scan helps pick up any new stations that recently converted. The www.antennaweb.org website will give you a rough idea when these stations will be on the air, but don't be surprised if they're delayed.

You might also find that stations you currently receive will change channels, particularly if they were on the wrong channel to begin with. Most stations are learning how to assign their PSIP information and start out on their broadcast channel, which might be something like UHF 60, but will convert to correspond with their analog channel.

Radio frequencies

FM radio station frequencies are broadcast between channels 5 and 7. If your antenna is capable of receiving these TV channels, you will probably get excellent radio reception as well. A simple dividing filter, available from any decent electronics parts store for a few bucks, can split the TV signals from the radio signals, and allow you to send the signal to the AM/FM radio in your receiver.

A 5.1 (or better) audio system

Just as HDTV is inherently wide screen, it also includes a 5.1 sound-track. Many DTV programs include 5.1 channels of audio that are comparable in sound quality and effect to the sound you hear in the best movie theaters. Not only that, but a number of non-HD channels on satellite and digital cable systems include 5.1 soundtracks as well. To unleash this potential you need a 5.1 or better sound system and a digital audio connection between the tuner and the surround receiver. If not, if you're still listening to DTV programs on a pair of speakers, or worse, through the speakers in the TV, you haven't even begun to tap the potential of your DTV system's performance capabilities.

Digital Video Recorders

Charleton Heston would probably give up his rifle before giving up a digital video recorder. They're that cool. But it's really difficult to explain how cool digital video recorders (DVR) are, which is why companies like TiVo and ReplayTV have had such a difficult time selling them. I highly recommend you give one a try. Once you get used to using it you'll realize, like nearly all DVR users do, that you can't live without it. And it doesn't matter if you watch TV a little, or a lot.

Digital video recorders store audio and video signals on a computer hard drive. They're like a new-age VCR. But the DVR has much greater potential. For one, nearly all DVRs include a buffer that records whatever you're watching. You can "pause" the program if you need to answer the phone or use the bathroom and the DVR will continue recording. When you return, press play and watch the recorded program from where you left off while the DVR continues to record the end. You can then fast-forward through commercials until you catch up with the live program. You can't do that with videotape.

Better yet, you can set the DVR to record a program while you're out, like you can with a VCR. If you come home early, though, you can start watching the recorded show from the beginning, while the DVR is still recording the end. The DVR can record a TV show every week, from now until the end of time, without you ever worrying about a tape being rewound, and if so instructed, it can store just the latest, newest episodes (not repeats), erasing earlier recordings as space is required. Even VCR Plus, the process of looking up codes in your local TV listings and typing them into your remote control to program the VCR timer is more complicated than setting a DVR to record. Simply select a program from the on-screen channel guide and press the record button. That's it. Some DVRs will even note what programs you record and recommend similar programs you might not know about. The list of DVR features goes on and on.

The end result is that you no longer have to pay attention to what's on, or when. You just set up the DVR to record, or let it pick programs for you, then, when you have time, you can watch all your favorite shows. If you're like me, TV may not be that big a deal, and you might not care if you miss a certain episode of something, but you like to watch something interesting from time to time. The DVR becomes your own personal network channel that's always playing the shows you like, whenever you're ready to watch.

DVRs come in several different forms. I've focused on stand-alone units, but hard drives are finding their way into any number of devices that include a programming guide, like terrestrial digital TV tuners, satellite receivers, cable boxes, and even some televisions. Hard drives are also being included in recordable software products like VCRs and DVD recorders. In most cases, I recommend the built-in variety, as they typically record the digital audio and video stream directly from the source, be it terrestrial DTV, satellite, or cable.

If you have analog cable or use an off-air analog tuner, however, a stand-alone box is a good choice. Most of the features discussed here also apply to terrestrial digital TV, satellite, and cable tuners as well.

Figure 3.12

Digital video recorder, model 5500, courtesy of ReplayTV

What to Look For

Price

Some of the best DVRs come with your satellite or cable receiver boxes, though you'll also find stand-alone DVRs for terrestrial HDTV. For satellite and cable DVRs, there's often no extra cost for the hardware, though you may have to pay around $5 a month for the DVR service. In some cases, like with TiVo, you can get a discounted rate if you pay yearly or can pay a "lifetime" fee of a few hundred dollars. In cases where you have to buy hardware (you already have satellite service and are purchasing a new box or your buying a stand-alone DVR), prices start at a few hundred bucks and will increase with the amount of storage available. As I'll explain in the Storage section, get as much as you can afford.

Broadband connection

Stand-alone, standard definition DVRs obtain their programming guides through either a dial-up or broadband connection to the company's main server. Terrestrial HD-DVRs create a program guide from the channel PSIP information (make sure your local channels actually program their PSIP information). For standard definition models, the box connects to the service regularly and receives the new guide information. If you don't have a broadband connection, you'll need a phone jack near the DVR. First-generation models sometimes had trouble dialing out and receiving their guide information. Without the guide, most of the DVR functions don't work. A broadband connection allows the DVR to connect and download information through the Internet, which makes the download nearly foolproof.

Programming guide

The hard drive alone does not make a DVR, which is a combination of digital recording and interactive program guide. There are numerous features, like searching for programs based on actors, directors, or key words in the description, that are a result of the program guide. Several companies make DVRs, like TiVo and ReplayTV, and other companies provide program guides, like Gemstar and every satellite and digital cable company. You can even get TiVo-powered satellite receivers from DirecTV. If possible, make sure you check out how the programming guide works before you commit. Accessing the program guide should be nearly idiot-proof, even if you consider yourself a total neophyte in the world of audio and video. After all, that's part of the point of the DVR, right?

Storage

As you get used to your DVR, you'll find that you store more and more stuff. It doesn't mean that you watch all of it, but you discover programs you think you might want to watch, then want to keep them around just in case. After all, it's not like you're eating up videocassette tapes with this information and you can delete it at any time. For HDTV, you'll need about 10 GB per hour of storage. The point is: Get as much storage as you can afford.

Network capability

Several DVRs now come with an Ethernet jack that can connect to your home computer network. If you don't have a computer network, you can create one for less than $100. You can then link together two networked DVRs and transfer programs from one to the other. If you record *The Daily Show with Jon Stewart* in the living room and decide to go to bed, you can transfer the recording to the bedroom DVR and watch it from there.

The network connection also provides some interaction with your PC. With appropriate software on the PC you can transfer images from your digital camera to the DVR and play them back on the TV, creating your own family slideshow. Check out TiVo's multimedia option for an example.

Easy offloading

If you're a TV show pack rat, you can offload content stored on the DVR's hard drive to a VCR or DVD recorder. In fact, unless the DVR is HD capable, I don't see any reason not to get a DVR with DVD recording.

Some models even include TiVo. See the section on DVD recorders in Chapter 4 for more information. Either way, check out how easy it is to offload content before you buy. TiVo makes it pretty easy. Other independent services may not be as adept.

Getting Started

Step 1: Install a DVR

Installing a DVR is fairly simple. First, connect the analog cable or antenna signal to the recorder's RF input. If you have digital cable or satellite, you can connect the S-Video and stereo audio outputs from the receiver to one of the audio-video inputs on the DVR. Then connect an IR output from the DVR back to the receiver to allow the DVR to control the receiver. The DVR's setup menu should allow you to assign each input according to the type of signal. For example, if you have an antenna and satellite, assign the RF input for terrestrial, not cable, signals and assign the DVR's video input 1 or 2 (depending on which one you used) to satellite. The setup menu should step you through various selections that determine which satellite or cable service you have and make appropriate internal changes.

Step 2: Connect DVR to your TV

If your TV is archaic and has only an RF input, you can use the DVR's RF output. The DVR signal will convert to channel 3 or 4 so that your TV can receive it. Preferably, you can connect the composite or S-Video and stereo analog outputs of the DVR directly to the TV's external video inputs or through an outboard surround processor and then to the TV.

Step 3: Setup menu

Once everything is connected, go through the setup menu, let the DVR download the programming guide and start recording.

Secrets

Recording quality

DVRs built into DTV, satellite, or digital cable tuners record the digital bitstreams as they come from the source. Stand-alone DVRs, however, have to convert analog signals to the digital domain and typically have three different quality levels to do so. The lowest level, which provides the most recording time, is equal to videotape quality. The highest level is practically indistinguishable from the source, but eats up a good deal of recording space. I've found that the midlevel is a good compromise. If you want to save as much space as possible without losing any sound or image quality, midlevel is the best setting.

Upgrade the hard drive

Americans have an odd fascination with hot-rodding stuff and DVRs are not immune. Thanks to the Internet and a number of tech-savvy enthusiasts, you can upgrade the hard drive in your DVR, particularly if it's based on the TiVo service. Numerous websites describe the procedure, which requires that you disassemble your DVR, remove the hard drive, and connect it to a PC, copy the formatting information to a second or replacement drive, then re-install the first, second, or both drives back into the machine. The gains in recording time can be substantial, but the procedure is not for the faint of heart, and will almost certainly void your warranty. At least one site, www.weaknees.com, will do the work for you, or sell you an already modified DVR.

4

Choosing Source Components: Movies

DVD Players and Recorders— Small Disc, Big Experience

Movies are the essence of home theater, and, for the foreseeable future, the most popular way to play movies at home is with a DVD (digital video disc, though some people call it the digital versatile disc. Take your pick). The 5-inch, CD-sized disc can store a full-length motion picture with superb video quality and up to 5.1 channels of awesome digital sound. We have adopted the DVD faster than any other consumer electronics product—ever—partly because you can use a DVD player with nearly any TV, no matter how old it is. Even better, you can upgrade your system and glean even better performance from the DVDs you rent or purchase.

Figure 4.1

DVD player, model DVD-5900, courtesy of Denon Electronics

Using a DVD Player with a Really Old Television

Older TVs use only antenna or cable-type input connections. DVD players don't have an RF or cable-type output. An RF connector is a round, threaded plug that accepts the cable or TV-antenna signal and is also used on VCRs.

Figure 4.2

If your TV has only an antenna or CableTV-type RF connection like this, you'll need an adapter (or a new TV) to connect a DVD player, courtesy of Mitsubishi Electronics.

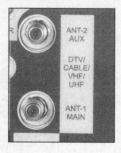

If your TV only has an RF input, you need an adapter to connect the two components. The adapter takes the analog audio and video signals from the DVD player and converts (or modulates) them into a TV channel, usually channel 3 or 4. Connect the output to the TV, tune the TV to channel 3 (or 4), and you'll be fine. The converter is built into most VCRs. You can connect the DVD player's audio and video outputs to the VCR, then route the VCR's RF connector to the TV, but sometimes the VCR won't pass the DVD's copyright-protected signal through to the TV. Unfortunately, the only way to find out if it works is to try it. No matter how you connect your DVD player, you should definitely plan to buy a new TV. The picture will look better using the separate audio and video connections, and a TV without these connections doesn't take full advantage of DVD's resolution capabilities.

What to Look For

Price

Thanks in no small part to DVD's phenomenal popularity, the price of a DVD player has dropped like a rock since the format was introduced. I recently bought a perfectly good, off-brand DVD player with basic features from Wal-Mart for $40. While it doesn't have the fancy front panel or all the features of its high-priced competitors, it performs as well as any number of high-end players that I've reviewed for magazines. If you just want to play movies, don't care about frills, and want to save money on at least one component, the DVD player is it. There are, however, some worthy features that add to the cost, but might be right for you. Read on, I've listed some of the features you might want to add.

Ergonomics

Test the DVD recorder in the store before you buy. Can you put a DVD in the drawer and play or record on it, easily switch from one audio track to another, or skip to a particular scene in the move without consulting the manual (or your 9-year-old)? You'd be surprised how different players can be, and how few people actually test drive them in the store. If you can't get the DVD player to work, you'll be less likely to use it when you get it home, or you'll be frustrated every time you try. Make your life easy, and even if it costs a few extra bucks, find the one your in-laws can use with little instruction.

Remotes

Just like player ergonomics, the remote control should be easy to use and preferably backlit so that you can see it in the dark. In Chapter 9, "Remote Controls," I talk about universal and automation remotes and the advantages of having one. If you're spending a couple thousand bucks on a system, an automation remote, usually purchased separately, should be part of your system. With that in mind, separate buttons for Power On and Power Off on the DVD player remote will be handy when you start to program the automation system.

Performance

There are performance differences between DVD players, though some of these differences depend on how your system is set up. For instance, many DVDs are recorded in what's called an anamorphic format. (See "Anamorphic Explained, or Why Movies Need Black Bars" page 57.) If you don't have a 16:9-shaped TV, you can set up the DVD player to automatically convert the image to fit a 4:3-shaped screen. Be aware though that converting the image to 4:3, will throw away some resolution and the quality of the conversion process can vary greatly from player to player. Some DVD players create sharp pictures, but induce wavy horizontal lines and jittery diagonals on scenes with smooth vertical pans. Other players tend to soften the overall image. A camera pan over a Gothic building can demonstrate how well a player performs. Of course, if you have or get a wide-screen TV, conversion isn't an issue.

I use Chapter 8 in the movie *Tomorrow Never Dies* to test DVD player down conversion. Set up the DVD player to output a "4:3" image, then select the wide-screen version of the movie.

Resolution is an issue with any TV, and there are resolution differences between players. The differences are subtle, especially if you compare DVD players and say, videotape. Use any bright, complex scene from a recent blockbuster movie to test a player's resolution capabilities. Make sure you compare the DVD player using the same TV. Just remember, even a $40 DVD player's output looks pretty sharp.

You might notice a greater difference between the analog audio outputs of various DVD players than you'll notice between their video outputs. It's much more difficult, though, to test the audio quality of different players in a retail store. As the automatic 1.78 to 1.33 conversion only matters with 4:3 TVs, the difference in audio performance between players is only a major issue if you use the analog audio outputs. If the player has multichannel high-resolution audio, which I'll get to in Chapter 5, you won't notice a difference at all if you connect the digital audio output to a separate surround processor. The surround processor will have a greater impact on sound quality. If possible, bring some audio CDs and listen to various DVD players on the same audio system, matching the volume level for each player. Or, better yet, just buy a surround processor and don't worry about it.

Anamorphic Explained, or Why Movies Need Black Bars

DVD solves an inherent dilemma in home video. Movies have extremely wide images when shown in the theater. TV screens aren't as wide as theater screens. Until DVD, there were only two ways to fit a wide-screen movie into a TV screen: pan and scan or letterbox.

Pan and scan involves cropping the sides of a wide-screen image to fit the TV and then electronically panning across the image to center on the action (assuming it's not in the middle of the scene). This technique utilizes the entire video frame and TV screen, but sacrifices information at the edges of the original image and creates undesirable motion as the video now has additional pans that were not a part of the original movie. At the end of the spaghetti Western *Silverado*, Scott Glen (the good guy) and Brian Dennehy (the bad guy) shoot it out. In the theater, you see both men draw their pistols, only Glen draws faster and Dennehy goes down. In the pan and scan home video release, you only see Glen draw, then the video pans to Dennehy as he falls to the ground. It's just not as dramatic.

Letterboxing shrinks the wide-screen image so that the entire picture fits the 4:3 TV screen horizontally, but leaves blank space (or black bars) above and below the image. The film's original aspect ratio is maintained, but image size and resolution (fewer lines are used to draw the active part of the picture) are sacrificed in the process.

Figure 4.3

Wide-screen images (16:9 or 1.78:1 aspect ratio) can be: a) letter-boxed to fit a 4:3 image with black bars above and below the image; b) cropped at the sides to fit the 4:3 shape; or c) anamorphically squeezed to fit wide-screen TVs. The latter option preserves the most image area and resolution.

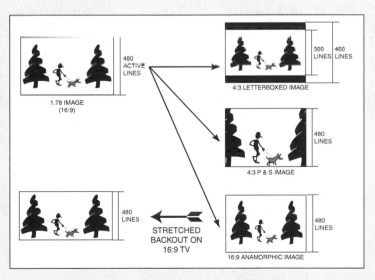

continues on next page

Anamorphic Explained, or Why Movies Need Black Bars *(continued)*

DVD can utilize either of these methods but adds a third technique called an anamorphic squeeze. This is an electronic process that squeezes a wide-screen, 1.78:1 (16:9) aspect ratio into the 1.33:1 (4:3) shape of the disc's video frames. If you play the anamorphic image back, unaltered, on a normal, 4:3-shaped screen, the objects in the picture appear tall and skinny. A wide-screen TV stretches the image back to the 1.78:1 shape (A 4:3 TV with a 16:9 mode squeezes the image vertically to achieve the same result) and correct geometry. Since the entire frame is used to record the image, 25 percent more vertical resolution is preserved compared to letterboxing the same image down to fit a 1.33:1 shape.

 NOTE Movies are filmed with aspect ratios greater than 1.78:1 and may be cropped or letterboxed, albeit only slightly, to fit the DVD's 1.78:1 frame before being anamorphically squeezed down to the 1.33:1 size. So even though a DVD might state that it's anamorphic, it still could display some black bars on screen if the movie was much wider than 1.78:1.

Video

DVD recorder

DVD recorders are the latest new trend and can completely replace your VCR, but this is one of the features that adds quite a bit to the cost. The problem is that there are at least five different recordable DVD formats (DVD-R, DVD-RW, DVD+R, DVD+RW, and DVD-RAM), none of which is compatible with *all* DVD players. If you regularly send recorded discs to your family and friends it is important to know which format is compatible with their system. If you plan to make discs only for yourself, it doesn't really matter which format you use; but you should check to see if a particular format is compatible with any DVD players you already own. Short of making recordings on each of the different types of recorders in the store then testing the recordings on your home DVD player, here's a quick rundown of what you'll probably find.

DVD-R is the original "recordable" write-once format and creates discs that are compatible with 90 percent or more of DVD players. The –R discs cost less than other formats, as well. +R is also a write-once format, but the +R discs are compatible with only 85 percent of players. Write-once means you can't record over any data on the disc, so if you make a mistake, you might as well use the disc as a plastic drink coaster. With DVD+R recorders, you can record programs until the disc is full or until you go through a process that essentially formats the DVD called finalizing—that takes up to 10 minutes with –R discs, and roughly a minute with +R discs. Once the disc is finalized, you can play it on other DVD players, but you can't record any additional data on it.

DVD–RW, +RW, and -RAM are rewritable formats, which means you can re-record over any information on the disc 1,000 times or more (100,000 times with RAM). Rewritable discs are much less compatible with other players, particularly DVD-RAM, which will only play in DVD players that are specifically RAM-compatible. DVD-RAM, acts much like a computer hard drive and can record bits and pieces of a program in blank sections or over old programs throughout the disc. With –RW discs, you can only record over old information that's arranged sequentially. This means that if you want to record a two-hour show, you need to have a two-hour chunk of consecutive space on the disc. +RW discs can be recorded with CLV (constant linear velocity) or CAV (constant angular velocity). CLV records sequentially, like -RW, and creates more compatible discs while CAV records more randomly, like RAM.

There are a number of so-called universal recorders. Unfortunately, the phrase is politically motivated and not entirely accurate. Most "universal" DVD recorders are compatible only with –R, -RW, and RAM formats (which are all sanctioned by the DVD Forum), other players can handle –R, -RW, +R, and +RW, but rarely will a "universal" recorder actually record in all five formats.

Digital video recorders

Digital video recorders (DVRs) combined with a DVD recorder are a match made in heaven. If you've never used a DVR (think TiVo), it's like a VCR, but stores the audio and video information on a built-in hard drive. The flexibility a DVR offers is amazing and can help you from turning too many –R discs into coasters. Once you've used a DVR, you'll never understand how you lived without it. Basically when buying a DVR, look for as much storage (the largest hard drive) as possible, and make sure you can easily offload recorded content from the hard drive onto the recordable DVD. Some DVRs use the TiVo service, which is pretty cool, but you must subscribe to TiVo, which costs money. Other DVR service guides have less functionality, but don't charge additional fees. Check the section on stand-alone DVR recorders in Chapter 3, page 47, for more details.

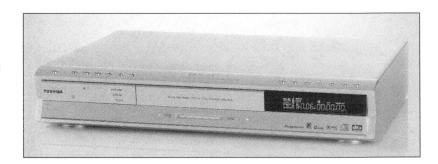

Figure 4.4

DVD-Recorder with built-in digital video recorder (DVR), model RD-XS32, courtesy of Toshiba

Outputs

An analog component output should be at the top of your wish list of video connections. The analog output consists of three plugs or wires, labeled Y, Pr, and Pb. (You might also see the connections labeled Y, Cr, Cb or Y, R-Y, B-Y. On consumer equipment, these labels all mean the same thing.) Each wire carries a different portion of the video signal. Your TV must have a similar connection and most displays made after 1998 probably will. The component signal offers the best image with more color detail and no color compression artifacts of any analog output. Some inexpensive players disable the S-Video (two wires wrapped into one, with a round 4-pin connector) or composite video (a single wire with a single-pin connector) outputs when the component video outputs are being used. If you need to use more than one output, make sure the player can run them all at the same time.

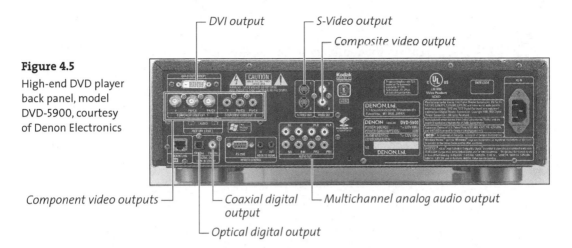

DVI output

S-Video output

Composite video output

Figure 4.5

High-end DVD player back panel, model DVD-5900, courtesy of Denon Electronics

Component video outputs

Coaxial digital output

Multichannel analog audio output

Optical digital output

Second on your list should be a digital visual interface (DVI) or high-bandwidth digital multimedia interface (HDMI). These connections output an uncompressed digital signal to the TV, assuming the TV is similarly equipped. Only newer digital TVs have one of these connections. DVI and HDMI have essentially the same video signal. They have different connectors, however, and HDMI carries digital audio and control signals, as well. Any player with an HDMI output can connect to a TV with a DVI input, and vice versa. You only need an adapter cable, and you will have to route the sound separately. The picture quality through the DVI output of a budget player is as good or better than the picture quality from a high-end player's analog component output.

Better players also offer dual composite and S-Video outputs. Though these outputs aren't the best way to get an image from a DVD, it might be your only choice depending on your TV. Players with multiple outputs give you more flexibility when you're setting up your system.

If you don't opt for DVD-Audio or SACD, you need at least an optical or coaxial digital audio output to send the Dolby or DTS 5.1 channel digital audio signal to the surround-sound processor. Which one you need depends on which connectors are available on your surround processor, but having both optical and coaxial outputs gives you more flexibility when you set up your system. While all players output a Dolby Digital signal, first-generation players don't pass the DTS signal. At this point, however, most newer players can pass the DTS signal.

Progressive scan DVD

One of the most highly touted, expensive, and often unnecessary features of many DVD players is progressive scan output. To understand the difference between interlace and progressive scanning, see the Interlace Vs. Progressive sidebar in Chapter 3. A progressive DVD player uses advanced video processing within the player to extract a progressively scanned, 480-line analog component signal from the digital image stored on the disc instead of the typical 480-line interlaced output. The 480p image from a progressive DVD player can be excellent, but the TV must meet certain criteria for you to enjoy 480p's benefits.

For one, you need a TV with a progressive or 480p component input. Analog-only TVs don't have progressive scanning but most DTVs do. The 480p input should also have aspect ratio control for 480p signals, otherwise the images from nonanamorphic DVDs will appear short and fat. TVs that are compatible with 480p usually have a built-in line doubler or video processor of their own, though. Therefore, the DVD player's video processor must do a better job of de-interlacing the DVD signal than the TV's built-in processor. Even though the TV's processor is using an analog signal at the input and the DVD player's processor gets the digital signal directly from the disc, the TV's processor might still create a better image. If the TV converts the incoming signals to something higher than 480p—say 720p or 1080i—then you lose some though not all of the benefit of the progressive DVD player. (These conditions are all true for front projection systems that use external or internal video processors, as well.)

As a rule, the output from the majority of progressive DVD players looks really good, while the output from most processors in TVs might not. The more expensive the video display, the better the video processing , and the less benefit you'll reap from a progressive DVD player. The best picture might come from a DVD player with a digital video output that's connected either directly to the TV or to a good quality external video processor.

You have to take progressive scan on a case-by-case basis and unfortunately, you may have to try it to find out if it's worth the extra cost. On the positive side, though, prices for progressive DVD players continue to fall.

High-definition DVD

Currently, your DVD player must be compatible with Microsoft's Windows Media 9 Series format (WM9) in order to get high-definition video quality from a disc player. Microsoft's system is a compression algorithm that substantially shrinks the large high-definition file down to fit onto a DVD. The format is typically used in computers and the DVD won't play on regular DVD players. A couple players, initially from V Inc. and Apex will be available in late 2004 that will play back newer WM9-encoded discs that don't require online license delivery. Older discs require an Internet connection to confirm that the user is licensed to view the content. The ability to play back WM9 DVDs may be worth considering if you own a high-definition TV.

Other high definition on small disc formats are in the works. One, called Blu-Ray is being developed by a consortium of nearly every major consumer electronics manufacturer. Blu-Ray is a completely new format and uses advanced technology to store five times more data than a regular DVD disc onto one side of a DVD-sized optical disc. HD-DVD, supported by Toshiba and NEC and adopted by the DVD-Forum, is a competing format that uses more compression than Blu-Ray (or DVD) to fit three times more data than on a regular DVD, and is reportedly easier for existing manufacturers to produce. Neither format will be available in great quantities for another year or two. With the uncertainty of knowing which format to go with and the low cost of current DVD players, I don't see any point in waiting.

Audio

CD-R and CD-RW

Older DVD players had trouble reading regular, noncompressed music recorded onto write-once (CD-R) or rewritable (CD-RW) recordable discs. Check the DVD player's feature list in the manual to make sure it can play back recordable CDs. These days, there's no reason it shouldn't.

MP3 (WMA and AAC) playback

If you haven't heard of MP3, find a teenager and ask about it. MP3 is the format that everyone under 30 is using to download music off of the Internet and store it on their iPod. The 2-channel system compresses the audio signal into smaller files that can be downloaded faster and saved on your computer's hard drive (WMA, or Windows Media Audio and AAC, or Dolby Lab's Advanced Audio Codec are alternate compression formats that are also popular). Many DVD players read MP3, WMA, or AAC files directly from a recordable CD or DVD. The result of the compression is a DVD disc with thousands of hours of music. If you or anyone in your household is an avid music download fan, get a DVD player that can play back these formats.

DVD-Audio and SACD playback

A number of players are compatible with two new types of multi-channel, high-resolution audio disc formats. DVD-Audio (DVD-A) and Super Audio CD (SACD) are competing systems that take advantage of a DVD's additional data capacity and use it to store up to six channels of pure, high-resolution audio. The DVD player will either have a 6-channel analog output (see **Figure 4.6**), or have a high-bandwidth digital multimedia interface (HDMI) or FireWire (IEEE-1394) digital output. The SACD or DVD-Audio signal doesn't come through the optical (Toslink) or coaxial digital audio connection. To hear the 6-channel signal, you'll need a comparable input on your receiver or surround processor. Unfortunately, neither format has been widely adopted and the feature adds to the cost of a DVD player. Currently only a few thousand titles are available in either format, and even they are hard to find. Fortunately, though, you can now get a player that accepts both formats (there's no point settling for just one anymore) without compromising DVD performance. Recordings made using either system sound absolutely fantastic. It's worth getting a demo. If you like what you hear, or if you're a serious music buff, spend a few extra bucks and get a universal high-resolution audio player. Eventually, all players will offer one or both formats, anyway. Multichannel audio players also internally decode and output the Dolby Digital signal via the 6-channel analog audio connection or will pass the undecoded digital signal via the HDMI or FireWire port. For more details on SACD and DVD-Audio, see Chapter 5.

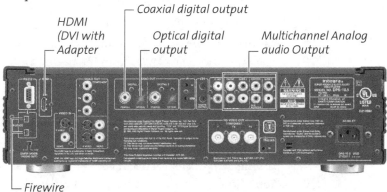

Coaxial digital output

HDMI (DVI with Adapter

Optical digital output

Multichannel Analog audio Output

Figure 4.6

DVD-Audio/SACD "Universal" DVD player, Model DPS-10.5, courtesy of Integra

Firewire

Getting Started

To explain how to set up every DVD player in every system would take a book the size of the Gideon Bible. I've made a rough outline or checklist of the steps you'll want to go through to make sure you're getting the maximum performance from your system.

Step 1: Connect DVD player to the system

Check the signal flow diagrams and descriptions in the Appendix to see how your systems should be connected. Ideally, you should use the best video signal possible. In descending order these signals are: HDMI or DVI; component; S-Video; or composite. If your TV doesn't have any of these inputs, see "Using DVD Players With Really Old Televisions," page 54.

Connect the DVD player's audio signal directly to your surround processor. If you have a DVD-A/SACD player, connect the 6-channel analog connectors, or the HDMI or FireWire digital audio signals. If you don't have SACD or DVD-Audio, you'll only use the digital audio connection. If you don't have a separate surround processor, then you'll probably just connect the left and right analog audio output directly to your TV.

Step 2: Configure the DVD player

The next step is to configure the DVD player for your system. First, you must access the DVD player's setup menu, which is likely the most confusing part of the entire process. Finding the menu can be as simple as pressing the "setup" button on the remote, or you might have to remove any DVDs from the player, and then press the menu button. Check your DVD player's manual for more information if you need help finding the menu.

Once you've found the menu, select the video output setting that's most appropriate given the aspect ratio of your TV. If the TV is 4:3 only, set the DVD player for 4:3 (most new players default to this setting). You might see two 4:3 options; one for pan and scan (which might also be called "normal" or "small") and one for letterbox. It doesn't really matter which one you pick.

DVDs were supposed to have a built-in feature that allows you to decide how they want to fit wide-screen movies onto regular, squarish screens. The system never worked. Most studios either create two versions of the movie—a pan and scan version and a wide-screen version, or just one.

If you have a wide-screen TV or projection system, select the DVD player's 16:9 (AKA "wide screen," "anamorphic," or "full") output setting. If you have a newer 4:3 TV or projector, it might have a 16:9 mode, which means the TV will take a 16:9 image, and reduce the size of the TV's raster vertically so that the entire image appears in the middle of the TV screen. This process preserves the extra resolution of an anamorphic recording without requiring a wide-screen TV. In this case, you should also set the DVD player to output a 16:9 image. Once you've set the output of the DVD player, you won't need to change this setting unless you buy a TV with a different shape. If you need to change the aspect ratio of the image, you should be able to do it with the TV's remote control.

Next you need to set the digital audio output. If you're using a separate surround processor, set the audio output to "bitstream." Don't select PCM or MPEG, unless you live in Europe or have a really old processor that doesn't have Dolby Digital. If the DVD player has a menu option for default soundtrack, choose 5.1. If you don't have a separate Dolby Digital processor, you can select the "two-channel" audio output, and then select the Pro Logic or matrixed default soundtrack, which is most likely the default setting from the manufacturer. But really, get a Dolby Digital processor.

Step 3: Configure the surround processor

Skip this step if you're not routing the audio or video signals through a surround receiver or preamp.

The second most-difficult task when installing a DVD player is finding the setup menu for your surround processor. Many receivers access an on-screen installation menu with a display or setup button, others use a more cryptic approach, like holding down the menu button for several seconds. Again, check your owner's manual for details.

The inputs on the back of most receivers and preamps no longer directly correspond with the source buttons on the front panel, particularly for digital audio and component video signals. You have to tell the surround processor which inputs to look for. Check the back of your receiver or preamp and make a note of which inputs you use. Then, when you enter the setup menu and find the submenu for the DVD input, you can tell the processor where to find the DVD player's audio and video signals. These signals might be digital audio input 3 and component video input 1, for example. You can also select default surround modes for a particular input, which I cover in the Secrets section of Chapter 6, "Re-assign the Default Surround Modes." In some cases, the processor doesn't collect the information for each source in one submenu and instead configures the information for each signal type. In other words, you have to enter the submenu for digital audio inputs, find input 3, and assign it to the DVD source button. You'll have to do the same for the video signal.

If you have a DVD-A or SACD player and a surround processor with THX or Surround EX processing (see Chapter 6), you should set up the DVD player on two different inputs, assuming you have an extra input to spare. One source button, for example CD, would use the 6-channel

DVD-A/SACD audio signal and the component video input, while the DVD source button would use the digital audio signal with the same component video input.

Some processors with assignable inputs might not allow you to use the same signal for different sources. In this case, use the next best video signal for the high-resolution audio input.

Step 4: Playing movies

Wow. You'd think this would be the easy part. Don't worry, there are only a couple things to check before or when you first start the movie, and then you're done, I swear. Make sure the correct soundtrack will be playing and that the TV, if it has multiple aspect ratio settings, will be in the right setting.

Most movies default to the 5.1 English soundtrack, which should subsequently kick on the Dolby Digital surround processing mode in your receiver. Every now and then a DVD, particularly older Columbia/Tri-Star DVD titles, default to a 2-channel soundtrack, which activates the Dolby Pro Logic processing mode in your receiver or preamp. This is less than ideal and you'll have to select the 5.1 sound-track manually. You can do this before the movie starts if the DVD's menu has an option for setup or audio. Selecting the setup menu item will bring up another screen that will likely show the various sound-track options. Choose 5.1 and start the movie.

If the processor still uses the Pro Logic mode even though you've selected a 5.1 option on the disc, you probably have a connection problem. Make sure the digital audio signal is connected to the surround processor and that the source button you've selected on the surround processor is using the correct digital input. See Step 3, on page 67.

Selecting the aspect ratio might not be as easy to do before the movie starts. You can look at the DVD packaging and if it says "enhanced for wide screen" or "anamorphic" you can choose the 16:9 or "full" aspect ratio setting on your TV. If the DVD package just says wide screen, it's probably anamorphic and uses these same aspect ratio settings, but it might just be a wide-screen image letterboxed into a 4:3 aspect ratio in which case it will use the TV's "zoom" aspect ratio setting. Unfortunately, it's hard to know which setting is correct until the movie is playing. When all else fails, do what I do. Wait until the movie starts, then cycle through the aspect ratio settings on the TV to find one that looks best.

 If the anamorphic or "full" setting on your TV makes DVD images labeled "enhanced for wide screen" look short and fat, then you need to set the image output on the DVD player. See Step 2, on page 68.

Secrets

Easter Eggs

One of the cool features about DVDs is the supplemental material that studios add to the disc. This extra material can include anything from the original movie trailers, behind-the-scenes footage, director commentaries, and more. In additional to this extra material, many DVDs include hidden features referred to as "Easter Eggs" which are sections of the disc that are not easily found through the main menu. You might have to use the remote's left arrow button, when the on-screen display says that the only option is right, or you might have to press a certain sequence of buttons on the remote to unlock the additional material. Below are a couple examples. We found these Easter Eggs and others listed at www.dvdangle.com.

On the second disc of *Pirates of the Caribbean: Curse of the Black Pearl*, for instance, you can find one of many Easter Eggs if you select the "Moonlight Serenade Scene Progression" menu. Press the DVD remote's down arrow until the background skeleton skull's molar is highlighted. Hit enter and you'll get a brief interview with Keith Richards. He's just been asked what he thinks of actor Johnny Depp having based his movie character Jack Sparrow on the Rolling Stone guitarist.

Another example is from the *Star Wars: Episode 1-The Phantom Menace* DVD. Go to the main menu and then go to the option menu and type in "1138" (this number corresponds to George Lucas' first movie, THX-1138). Your remote might get to 11 with a button combination of "10+" then a "1", or "1" and "10+", but then press "3" and "8". After you enter the number, you'll get a 2-minute collection of amusing blooper clips from the film. The same Easter Egg is available on the second install-ment of the series.

Advanced audio installation

DVD-A/SACD players that don't have HDMI or FireWire just have 6-channel analog audio outputs. These players internally decode the Dolby Digital signal and output it through the same analog connec-tion. The 6-channel analog input bypasses advanced surround decoding techniques, like THX or Surround EX in your surround processor. If you want to take advantage of these surround enhance-ments, you need to route the digital optical or coaxial signal from the DVD player to the surround processor separately from the 6-channel DVD-Audio/SACD signal so that the surround processor does the Dolby Digital decoding. Set up two different source inputs, like CD and DVD, on the surround controller for the DVD player. One, the CD input, will be for the DVD-A/SACD player, which will use the 6-channel analog signal and, preferably, the component video input. The second source, the DVD input will use the digital audio (optical or coaxial) signal and, if possible, the same component video input. When you select the CD button on the surround controller, you'll hear fabulous audio directly from the player. When you select the DVD button, you'll hear great surround sound using all the capabilities of the surround processor. Players with HDMI or FireWire connections don't need this second connection, as the players pass all the undecoded digital signals to the processor.

The audio button

In Step 4 on page 68, I described the importance of and ways to select the correct audio soundtrack on the DVD. If you forgot to do this before the movie started, or if for some reason something doesn't sound right once the movie is playing, you can always hit the "audio" button on the DVD remote. Pressing this button will cycle through the DVD's avail-able soundtracks and should have an on-screen indicator to let you stop when you get to the 5.1 soundtrack. Again, check to make sure your surround processor switches to the 5.1 mode.

Test DVDs

Woohoo. Rock the house. Test DVDs might not be the pinnacle of excitement in home entertainment, but if you want a way to get the best performance from your system, check out one of the many test discs available. The two that most reviewers favor (and use for product reviews) are *Digital Video Essentials* by Joe Kane Productions and *Avia* by Ovation Software. Both discs have easy to follow tutorials on how to tweak your home theater system. Definitely take 30 minutes to go through one of the two programs and you'll notice a marked improvement in the audio and video performance of your system. For more details, see Chapter 7, "TV and Video Monitors."

Wide-screen TV

DVD is a wide-screen medium. Many DVDs are recorded in an anamorphic format that preserves substantially more vertical detail in the image than a regular 4:3 DVD image retains. If you're watching DVDs on a regular, 4:3-shaped TV, you're throwing away 25 percent of the resolution on most discs, not to mention potentially adding other image distortions in the process. There's no getting around it. To take advantage of the additional resolution on anamorphic DVDs you have to have a wide-screen TV (or a 4:3 TV with a 16:9 mode).

A 5.1 (or better) audio system

Just as DVD is inherently wide screen, it's also a 5.1 medium. Many DVDs include a 5.1 digital surround soundtrack that is comparable in sound quality and effect to the soundtrack you hear in the best movie theaters. To unleash this potential you need a 5.1 or better sound system and a digital audio connection between the player and the surround receiver. If you're still listening to DVDs on a pair of speakers, or worse, through the speakers in the TV, you haven't even started to hear the potential of your DVD player's performance capabilities.

Videocassette Recorders— Really?

With all due respect to the format that helped make home theater possible, the VCR is dead. Let's face it, you can rent nearly any new movie on DVD and now that we have DVD recorders, there's nothing left for our VCR to do. Well, OK, there are two things it can do. One, it can play back our library of videotapes and since VCRs are dirt cheap nowadays, there's not much reason not to have one. Two, a new type of VCR call D-VHS can record and play back HDTV.

For those of you who have been living on another planet for the last 20 years, there were originally two videotape formats, Victor Company of Japan's (JVC) VHS and Sony's Beta. After an infamous format war, VHS won and became the dominant standard in the industry. Sony finally stopped supporting consumer Beta not too long ago. Both formats record analog audio and video signals onto magnetic tape. VHS Hi Fi has decent stereo analog audio quality, but relatively lousy video performance. It is the lowest-quality video source available, short of streaming video off the Internet through a 56K dial-up modem.

Figure 4.7
D-VHS video cassette recorder (VCR), model HM-DT100, courtesy of JVC

What to Look For

D-VHS

Let's just start with the good stuff. For as great as DVD is, the technology lacks the storage capacity to handle HDTV's larger data stream without massive compression, new read/write techniques, or both.

With manufacturers already competing for the licensing rights on such a new format, true HD on disc might be farther off than some people might suggest. VHS may seem an unlikely alternative, given its somewhat meager analog bandwidth capabilities. It turns out, though, that you can store massive amounts of digital information on that metallicized plastic tape.

A number of manufacturers have created what's called, not surprisingly, Digital VHS (D-VHS), which can take advantage of the old VHS format's digital storage capacity to record off-air digital television signals, including high-definition signals. The tape acts as a bit bucket for the digital signal. What goes in is what comes out, which means you get a perfect recording of the broadcast show, complete with the 5.1 digital audio soundtrack and multicasting, if available. D-VHS decks also act as regular VCRs as well, and can record or play back regular, and sometimes Super-VHS tapes.

You need a FireWire output on your DTV tuner, however, for the digital system to work. Ironically, as of this writing, only one D-VHS recorder includes an internal digital TV tuner. Many popular digital tuners, particularly satellite tuners, lack a FireWire connection, though it should be more prevalent in the future. You'll also want an HD-capable TV. A number of manufacturers produce D-VHS recorders, but only one, JVC, includes D-Theater technology.

D-Theater

JVC and a handful of studios are taking the D-VHS standard one step further. JVC has added an additional layer of copyright protection (D-VHS already contains a system called 5C to protect content from being copied endlessly and redistributed) called D-Theater, and the studios are producing pre-recorded videotapes of major Hollywood blockbusters in HDTV. D-Theater on D-VHS is currently the only way to purchase HDTV movies. The format looks and sounds great. The technical specifications are impeccable.

If you don't have a FireWire link to your TV, you can output the video signal via the analog component video connection. You can route the

5.1 digital audio signal to your receiver through the optical or coaxial digital audio connection.

There are only two drawbacks to D-Theater, besides the fact that video-tape is somewhat clunky and "old school." One, repeated use of the videotape causes wear and tear. Fortunately, the information is digital, so the wear and tear doesn't affect the sound or picture quality until the player is totally unable to read the data. At that point, you'll experience picture dropouts or frozen images. The second problem is the looming arrival of HD on disc. It's fun to play HDTV videotapes for family and friends, but unless you have a lot of discretionary income, and watch a great deal of HDTV, D-Theater and D-VHS might not be worth the investment.

S-VHS

In the world of analog VCRs, you can get substantially better quality from a deck compatible with the Super VHS (S-VHS) format. This format records the luminance (or detail) portion of the image separate from the chrominance (or color) portion of the signal with much greater bandwidth than regular VHS. These two signals are kept apart thanks to the S-Video connector, which consists of a round plug with four pins. The format requires that you only record on S-VHS tapes, though in some cases, certain models can record S-VHS signals onto regular VHS tape, too. S-VHS, like D-VHS, is backwards-compatible with regular VHS, which means the VCR will play back your regular VHS tapes, but may not make regular VHS recordings and S-VHS recordings will not play on VHS machines.

Hi Fi

To get the best sound quality from a regular analog VCR, make sure it can read and record with Hi-Fi sound. Hi Fi means the VCR can read and record audio signals across the full width of the tape. The more space used to record the information, the better the sound . The alternative is linear audio, which is audio recorded in a single band at the edge of the tape.

Getting Started

Step 1: Connect the cable or antenna to the VCR

Connecting a VCR is fairly simple. The first step is to connect the cable or antenna signal to the VCR's RF or antenna input. (See Step 2: RF Distribution in Chapter 3 on page 42). Connecting the cable provides the TV signal to the VCR's internal tuner. You can connect an analog VCR's output to your TV or audio-video system in one of two ways.

The easiest, and most common setup, is to connect the VCR's modulated RF TV output (the threaded, single-pin connector) to the TV's RF or antenna input. The VCR's signal is modulated onto either channel 3 or 4, which is usually determined by a switch on the back of the unit. Tune your TV to the appropriate channel and voila, you get picture and sound. You can route the audio signals to your surround-sound processor separately.

The alternative method of connecting a VCR to your system is mildly more complicated but provides substantially better audio and video quality. Connect the audio and video outputs (the yellow, red, and white colored jacks) from the back of the VCR to your TV or audio-video receiver. Use the best video connection possible. For S-VHS this is the round, 4-pin S-Video connection. In order to watch the signal in this configuration you'll either need to change the TV to the video input, change the receiver to the VCR source, or both.

Step 2: Connecting D-VHS

If your VCR also has D-VHS capability, you need to add a few additional connections, depending on the other equipment in your system. First and most important, connect the VCR via FireWire to a similarly equipped digital TV tuner, if available. FireWire transmits audio, video, and control signals to and from the two components. If the digital tuner is built into the display, you can run a digital audio cable from the TV to your surround receiver, which should transmit audio for both the TV and D-VHS signals.

If you don't have a digital TV with a built-in FireWire-equipped digital TV tuner, connect the digital audio cable from the D-VHS directly to the surround processor. Also connect the analog component video signal, where available, to the TV or to the surround processor and then to the TV.

Secrets

Setting the clock

Everyone, including electronics writers like myself, have had a VCR with a clock that continually blinks "12:00" at some point or another. Even if you take the time to figure out how to set it, Murphy's law says the power will go out the next day, and you'll be back to square one. Many new VCRs automatically set the clock. You simply tell the VCR to look for the time code embedded into local TV channels, usually the local PBS station, and you shouldn't have to set the clock again.

Using your VCR as an audio-video switcher

If you're in a pinch and run out of inputs on your TV or audio-video receiver, you might be able to use the inputs on the back of your VCR. Most VCRs have one or two audio-video inputs. If you connect an extra component into these jacks, set up the VCR's signal to play through the TV, then select the appropriate input on the VCR, the signal should route its way through to the TV.

If your VCR looks for copy protection flags at the input (instead of at the internal recording mechanism) you might not be able to route signals through your VCR. If the auxiliary signal is copy protected, the VCR might block the signal, even though you're not recording it.

Using your VCR as an RF modulator

If you have an older TV, you can utilize your VCR's internal RF modulator to convert a device's audio and video signals into a TV channel. Set up the system as described in the above secret, "Using Your VCR as an Audio-Video Switcher." The signal will route through to the TV via the antenna cable to channel 3 or 4, depending on how the VCR is configured.

5

Choosing Source Components: Music

SACD and DVD-Audio— the Next Step in the Evolution of Music

What high definition does for television, the super audio compact disc (SACD) and DVD-Audio disc do for music. These two competing high-resolution multichannel music formats are the next step in music reproduction. Both take advantage of the additional storage capacity on a DVD and new digital audio compression schemes to record up to six channels of music (left, center, right, surround left, surround right, and a subwoofer channel) with much greater quality and resolution than is currently available on a compact disc. The sound surrounds and envelops you while the exceptional level of detail and dynamic range might make you believe you're listening to a live musical performance.

Fortunately, (or perhaps unfortunately, depending on whether you're a glass "half full" or "half-empty" person) the format war never appeared. Combination players that accommodate both systems are now on the market. So now both formats exist and there's no reason not to try either one. If you love music, you definitely want to hear SACD and DVD-Audio.

Figure 5.1

"Universal" DVD-Audio/super audio compact disc (SACD) player, model DPS-10.5, courtesy of Integra

Software needs

Like with high-definition television, you need a few things to add high-resolution music to your system. First, of course, you'll need software. Check your local stores to see if they carry DVD-A or SACD discs before you get excited about either format. Unfortunately, music studios haven't exactly thrown themselves behind either one. There are only a couple thousand titles available so far (mostly on SACD), and all too often these are not prominently displayed at your favorite music retailer. For SACD titles, you can also check to see what's available online at www.sa-cd.net. Not all high-resolution software is multichannel, either. Some of the discs, particularly SACD are two-channel recordings.

Many titles are compatible with your existing DVD or CD player. A number of DVD-Audio titles, for example, include a Dolby Digital or DTS soundtrack, which isn't high resolution but will play back on your existing DVD player, even if the player is not DVD-A compatible. Likewise, there are hybrid SACD discs, which means the disc also includes a regular CD signal and will play back on regular CD players. Like with Dolby Digital-equipped DVD-A discs, you can start collecting high-resolution music now, and add a player later.

Hardware needs

To accommodate the player, you'll need a surround processor that has a 6-channel analog input or one that can process the high-resolution digital signals that are fed through a FireWire or High Bandwidth Digital Multimedia Interface (HDMI) connection. I'll explain these things in more detail later in this chapter. The important thing to know is that DVD-A and SACD require a special connection to the system. Most new receivers will accommodate the signal.

Since one of the highlights of SACD and DVD-A is the multichannel format, you'll also need a surround sound speaker array to play back the signal. This array includes three front speakers (left, center, and right), two surround speakers (left and right) and a subwoofer. A system set up for Dolby Digital or DTS movie soundtracks available on DVD and DTV works just fine.

DVD-A and SACD offer better performance than Dolby Digital or DTS, though, so if the system can keep up with the signal you'll hear a benefit. The SACD and DVD-A signal offers a wide frequency response, up to 100 kHz, and excellent dynamic range nearing 120 dB. If your system can handle the punch of a good movie soundtrack without distorting or popping, you should be OK. Keep in mind, you can always upgrade later.

What to Look For

Price

Prices for DVD-A/SACD players have come down and are comparable with DVD players, so you can add the feature without dramatically increasing the cost of the player. You'll find higher-quality analog outputs and digital outputs on higher-end players. If you use the analog connections from a high-resolution player, the player's internal digital to analog (D/A) converters will have a significant impact on the sound quality of the signal. It's a good idea to listen to various players to see which one sounds best, as there is a noticeable difference between them. More expensive players use better D/A converters and sound better.

Ironically, higher-end players also offer digital connections. If you use the digital connection to your surround processor, the processor, which contains the digital to analog converters, does most of the work to create the audio signal. The player only transports the digital signal to the surround processor. The surround processor will therefore determine the sound quality of the DVD-A/SACD signal. If you have a good sounding surround processor, there's a good chance you'll get better sound from a less expensive DVD-A/SACD player with a digital connection, than from a more expensive player's analog connection.

Outputs

Fortunately, there are numerous DVD players that accommodate both formats, so you don't have to choose one over the other. You do have to choose between players that decode the high-resolution signals internally and then output the signal through six analog audio outputs, or players that pass the undecoded digital signal to your surround controller. The players that pass digital signals use either an HDMI- or a FireWire-type connection.

What really matters are the capabilities and types of connections you have on your surround processor. Most newer receivers and preamps have at least an analog multichannel input. This input might have as many as eight connections, but you only need six for most players. Sound quality through the analog connection is excellent but will likely bypass most of the features on today's digitally processed surround decoders. In some cases, the processor uses extremely high-quality analog to digital converters to re-digitize the incoming signal so that the processor can manipulate it. Newer, particularly high-end receivers and preamps might have built-in DVD-A and SACD decoding and can accommodate the digital signal straight from the player and allow you to use the processor's other audio functions with the DVD-A/SACD signal.

 The optical and coaxial digital audio connections don't carry the high-resolution music signal.

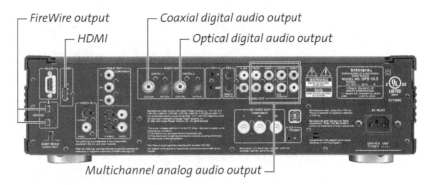

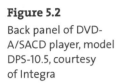

Figure 5.2

Back panel of DVD-A/SACD player, model DPS-10.5, courtesy of Integra

DVD capability

Since the vast majority of DVD-A/SACD players are also DVD players, it's a good idea to make sure the player has all the same capabilities as a good DVD player. See Chapter 4 for more details. Since DVD-A/SACD is considered a high-end feature, players with DVD-A/SACD capability have most of the better DVD features as well.

Bass management

If you use a DVD-A/SACD player with a 6-channel analog output, check if the signal bypasses your surround processor's internal bass management circuitry. In most cases, you can assume it does so you need to make sure the player has some internal bass management capability similar to the speaker output configuration setting in your surround processor. Internal bass management prevents the really low frequencies that are recorded on any channel from going straight to your speakers. At best, the music won't sound good and at the worst, the musical signal could damage your speakers. Most players now let you configure the player's output based on your speaker system's capability. If you have five bookshelf or satellite speakers for your main channels and use a subwoofer for the low bass, you need to configure the DVD-A/SACD player's outputs to direct all the bass from every channel to the subwoofer. Check your surround processors owner's manual for details.

Getting Started

Step 1: Connect the player to the audio system

Since the DVD-A/SACD player is essentially a DVD player with added features, setting up the music player is similar to setting up a DVD player as I described in Chapter 4. Use the diagrams in the Appendix, and choose the system configuration that makes the most sense for your system. Connect the best-quality video signal, usually the HDMI or DVI connection, to either the TV or the A/V processor, depending on your configuration. If your system doesn't accommodate the digital video signal, use the component signal. If you're forced to use the S-Video or composite signals from your DVD player, it's probably time to upgrade your TV or switcher.

Similarly, connect the audio signal to the surround processor. If you use the HDMI connection, then you're done, as the HDMI cable carries digital audio as well as video. If your player offers a FireWire connection, the output transfers the digital audio signal to the surround processor. If the player lacks HDMI or FireWire, you need to use the player's 6-channel analog outputs to send the DVD-A/SACD signal to the processor. The player will also decode the Dolby Digital signal and possibly the DTS signal as well, and will output the signal via the 6-channel connection. If your surround processor has THX, 5.1 EX/ES or other surround enhancements, these enhancements might not be applied to the signals from the 5.1 analog input.

 You usually can't listen to both the DVD-Audio 6-channel signal and the Dolby Digital signal from the same disc at the same time.

Step 2: Configure the player's bass management

Many surround processors route the 6-channel DVD-A/SACD signal directly from the input of the surround processor to the amplifier output. The signal bypasses all the internal circuitry and preserves the purity of the music. The problem is, this signal also bypasses the surround processor's bass management system, as it is described in Chapter 6. Bass management makes sure that low bass frequencies are not sent to small bookshelf speakers that aren't capable of handling the signal. If your surround processor bypasses the bass management, you need to configure the player's bass management, if possible.

The player's setup menu should have an adjustment for the speaker channel outputs. In most cases you assign the outputs of each channel based on the types of speakers in your system. If you want to route the bass to a single subwoofer, for example, you highlight each channel and select the small speaker configuration. If you don't have a subwoofer, but you have full-range left and right speakers and smaller center and surround speakers, you need to configure the speaker outputs accordingly and the player will route the bass away from the small speakers (and the subwoofer) and toward the left and right full-range speakers.

Step 3: Configure the DVD player functions

Check my description on page 66 in Chapter 4 for details on how to access the DVD player's setup menu and access the DVD player functions. From the setup menu you can select the appropriate image output, based on the aspect ratio of your TV. You also need to select the type of audio output. You shouldn't have to select the DVD-A or SACD signals.

In rare cases, you might not be able to send signals to the player's analog and digital outputs at the same time and you will have to choose between them. In this case you should select the 6-channel analog output or the audio output will likely be set to bitstream, which sends the Dolby Digital and DTS signals to the surround processor.

Step 4: Configure the surround processor

Now you need the setup menu for the surround processor. Check your owner's manual for details. As I've mentioned in previous chapters, the inputs on the back of most receivers and preamps no longer directly correspond to the source buttons on the front panel, particularly for digital audio and component video signals. Map or link the surround processor's inputs to the source selector buttons on the front panel using the processor's setup menu. In many cases you select the source from a list, and then select the appropriate video and audio inputs for that source. In some cases you select from separate lists of video and audio inputs, and assign particular sources for each audio and video input. Either way, you need to map the 6-channel or high-resolution digital audio input from the DVD-A/SACD player to the source button that you use for that input.

If you're using the 6-channel analog output and have a surround processor with THX or Surround EX processing (see Chapter 6), also consider configuring a source button for DVD movie playback. This means assigning the regular (coaxial or optical) digital audio output from the DVD player to a separate input other than the one used for the 6-channel analog DVD-A/SACD signal, assuming you have an extra input to spare. One source button, for example CD, would use the 6-channel DVD-A/SACD audio signal, while the DVD source button would use the regular digital audio signal. Usually, both source buttons can share the same video signal. If not, reserve the better-quality signal for the DVD movie playback.

Step 5: Configure the speakers

In a rare move, the music industry finally developed a standard for speaker placement in a 5.1 music system. The standard calls for the listener to sit in front of the center speaker, with the front left and front right speakers placed approximately 30 degrees off the center axis. The left and right surround speakers should be placed 110 degrees to either side of the same listener-center speaker axis. All five speakers should be identical. In most homes, this arrangement might not be practical and it might not sound right for movie soundtrack playback, either, so use the standard as a starting point and experiment.

Digital Music Servers—the CD Changer Replacement

As the DVD-A/SACD player replaces your CD player, the digital music server replaces the CD changer. A digital music server is either a CD player with a built-in hard drive or a computer with musical tendencies. The bottom line is the same in any form of digital music server, music from your CDs are "ripped" or recorded and stored on a hard drive where it can be accessed and replayed or re-recorded whenever you want. You no longer need to keep all your CDs in that cumbersome changer that can only play one or two discs at a time and that changes between discs slowly. You can use your CDs in the car and still have access to the music at home. You can send different outputs to different rooms in the house for a multizone, whole-house audio system and play as many different songs as the unit has audio outputs. Since the server is usually on a network, you can drag and drop files to a portable player or even a car system and can sometimes connect to the server over the Internet from another location. You don't have to worry about losing, breaking, or scratching CDs either since you always have a backup file in the server. Plus you can easily sort songs into play lists by genre, artist, album, date, or whatever criteria you might have. In most cases, the server will find the appropriate CD track from an online database.

Music servers initially became popular with the rise of the MP3 (MPEG 1, audio layer 3), a compression/decompression format, or codec for short. MP3, and other codecs shrink the size of music files by discarding signal information that they perceive as less important. You can transfer the resulting small file over the Internet at reasonable speeds; you can store it onto recordable CDs, or on your computer hard drive. A 650 MB CD-R can store more than 11 hours of music recorded as MP3 files at a 128 kbps data rate. A single-sided DVD-R can store more than 80 hours of music at the same rate.

Figure 5.3
Digital music server, model Tera Pro, courtesy of Audio ReQuest

What to Look For

Price

Music servers aren't necessarily cheap. Better-quality servers tend to cost more than some CD changers and more than a computer (not counting the PC collecting dust in your closet). CD changers tie up all your CDs and are clunky and computers are, well, computers. Accessing your CD collection using a computer can instill fear in the most fearless of people. Dedicated music servers are easier to use and significantly more convenient.

The more expensive the music server, the greater the storage capacity. As always when it comes to hard drive storage, buy as much as you can afford, even if you don't think you'll ever need it. There are a few other things to think about if you can fit them into the budget.

CD player/recorder

Many first-generation music servers didn't include a disc drive. The manufacturers assumed that you would connect the server to your computer network and would transfer the music files from your main computer. This assumption quickly proved pointless, as it is just as easy to connect the digital audio output from your PC to your home theater system. Look for newer CD player/recorder models that include a disc drive that will play CDs, rip them to the hard drive, and possibly even record music from the hard drive to a blank CD-R or CD-RW.

 CD-R is a write-once recordable format that's compatible with most regular CD players. Make a mistake, though, and a CD-R is a shiny, plastic drink coaster or Christmas tree ornament. CD-RW is "Re-Writeable," which means you can record over previously recorded data.

Variable bit rates

Compression schemes use a variable bit rate, which means the amount of discarded signal information varies depending on your storage needs. If you want more music in less space, you can record the music at a lower bit rate. Increasing the bit rate improves sound quality, but requires more space to store the signal. Lossless compression schemes can reconstruct the original file exactly. Lossy codecs throw away data that is irretrievable. Fortunately, hard drive technology has increased storage capacity, which makes it possible to store entire CDs without any compression at all. Still, make sure the server has some variable bit rates available.

 Uncompressed music tracks are listed on a CD as a CDA (CD audio) file. Windows-based PCs store these files in a lossless format called WAV. Mac-based computers can use WAV or AIFF format files.

Multiroom outputs

In addition to the standard analog and coaxials and optical digital audio outputs you connect to your main system, consider buying a music server with multiple outputs that you can use to send signals to other rooms in your house. When connected to a multiroom audio system, you can play *Rush* for the billionth time in the bedroom while your kids listen to *Coldplay* in the family room. For more information on multiroom systems, read the section on multiroom capability in Chapter 6; you should also get information from your local audio-video installation expert, however. Contact CEDIA, the Consumer Electronics Design and Installation Association, at www.cedia.org to find a certified dealer near you.

Network connection

Make sure the server has a computer network connection. The server can connect to an existing PC to download music from the hard drive, which saves you time loading music on the server if you've already started a digital music collection on your PC. A network connection—when connected to the Internet—can download CD track, album, artist, genre, time, and other information from online databases.

A network link also lets you stream audio signals to inexpensive client players in different locations. A client is a device that, when connected to the network, can access the server and provides full control over the server's contents but has no storage capabilities of its own. The lack of storage keeps the cost of the client down, and allows you to enjoy the benefits of the server in multiple rooms without duplicating the server cost in each location. You might even be able to connect a client to a server across the Internet for systems in different homes.

Back up

Some servers use different hard drive configurations to provide some form of back up if the hard drive fails. This back up can range from simple error correction that can overcome portions of a hard drive that might become corrupted, but can't overcome more significant failures to a complete back up that can provide all the information on a drive, even if the entire drive becomes unusable.

Getting Started

Step 1: Connecting the server

Connecting a music server is one of the easier components in your equipment rack to setup. You'll probably have a S/PDIF (coaxial or optical) digital audio connection from the server to the surround processor. If your surround processor doesn't have a digital audio input, it's time to trade in for a new model. Seriously. I'm sure the server has an analog connection but you should use it only for a second room or backup connection, if that.

Step 2: Configure the surround processor

As with all of your A/V components, you have to let the surround processor know where you connected the audio signal from the music server. Find the processor's setup menu and look for the source or input configuration menu. There are a number of ways manufacturers assign the inputs on the back to the source selection buttons on the front. Some manufacturer's processors make you select the source, and then you have to indicate which video and audio inputs to use with it. Other processors list each audio and video input, and you have to assign a source to each one. Consult your owner's manual for details on your surround processor.

Step 3: Load music

The only thing you need to do now is load some music onto the server. Access the music server's settings to determine if it rips CD files into MP3, WAV, or other types of files. Make sure it's the one you want, and that the server's using a bit rate that gives you the best quality sound for the amount of storage it requires. You might want to rip a song or two in various formats to see which codec you like. Then start ripping away.

Secrets

Music CD vs. Data CD

You'll find two different types of recordable CDs available at stores. Some are labeled as a music or audio CD-R, while others are listed as a data CD-R. Music CD-Rs cost a bit more, as they are marketed for recording music and subsequently a portion of the proceeds goes toward the recording industry (for so-called "lost" royalties). This extra charge increases the cost of music CD-Rs compared to data CD-Rs. Music CD-Rs are designed to work with stand-alone music CD recorders, which use low-speed data transfer rates, but they also work on a computer. Stand-alone CD recorders only work with music CD-Rs, however. Data CDs are marketed for storing computer data at higher transfer speeds. Since there's no royalty fee, the discs cost a bit less. Computer CD-R/RWs can record music files, and the discs play back in most CD players. Check your owner's manual to see if your music server can use data CD-Rs.

Digital Satellite Radio

If you want to listen to a random mix of new music, but don't want the static and commercial interruptions of AM or FM radio, try satellite radio. Aimed primarily at the car audio market, satellite radio is slowly encroaching on the home audio front. Just like satellite TV broadcasts, satellite radio provides over 100 different channels and is digitally transmitted nationwide. With satellite radio in your car, you can tune in to a station you like and listen to it as you drive from Los Angeles to New York. The service providers use ground-based repeaters in major markets where various geographical obstacles make satellite reception difficult. Since the signal is digital, you either receive it or you don't but when you do it is crystal clear sound.

 All three digital satellite TV services (DirecTV, Dish Network, and Voom) offer a number of digital music channels. These channels don't include on-air D.J.s or radio news or sports channels. Programming is "limited" to about 20 or 30 channels, though Dish Network recently began carrying all 65 Sirius music channels. Most of the stations are included with each company's basic programming package.

The two U.S. providers of satellite radio programming are Sirius Satellite Radio and XM Satellite Radio. At the time of this writing, Sirius, launched in 2002, offers 65 channels of music and 55 channels of news, NFL game radio broadcasts, talk shows, traffic, weather, and other entertainment programming. XM, launched in late 2001, currently provides nearly 70 music channels, 30 channels of other programming, and 16 channels of traffic and weather for various regions. Neither company currently offers local radio stations through their digital service.

To receive satellite radio, you need an antenna, a receiver, and a subscription to one of the two services. Equipment made to receive Sirius' service won't receive XM's programming and vice versa. Both companies are collaborating on a unified system that should be available in the future. For now, both systems use a small antenna that's about the size of a hockey puck to receive their respective signal. Mount the antenna to your roof or position it on a windowsill that faces toward the midwestern United States. If you live in an area with numerous ground repeaters, you might even be able to get a reliable signal from inside your home, away from a window.

Sirius is partnered with a handful of consumer electronics manufacturers who sell equipment that can receive Sirius programming. Just connect the antenna to the tuner. XM's home receiver is made by Delphi specifically for XM. Like some units from Sirius, XM's home receiver is portable. With a portable receiver and the appropriate docking stations at home and in your car, you can enjoy digital satellite radio in either place. Sirius also offers a multiroom model that sends different signals to different rooms in your home while XM offers its PC version so that you can listen to XM while you work.

The cost for either system is comparable. XM charges about $10 a month and offers better deals if you sign up for multiyear contracts. Sirius costs $12 a month, but drops to $10 if you agree to sign up for a year. If you decide you can't live without satellite radio, Sirius offers a one-time fee of $500, good for the life of the product. Both services charge $7 dollars for each additional receiver.

Figure 5.4

Portable satellite radio receiver, model SkyFi, courtesy of XM Satellite Radio

Figure 5.5

Portable satellite radio receiver, model DT-7000S, courtesy of Sirius Satellite Radio and Kenwood

6

Command Central: Audio and Video Processors

The centerpiece of a good home theater might be a receiver, an integrated amplifier, or even a preamp-processor. Sometimes these devices are erroneously called "amplifiers" or just surround processors, but while amplifying and processing surround signals are necessary functions for your home theater, they aren't quite the right terms for this pivotal device. In fact, all these products provide different functions or groups of functions that are critical to your home theater's performance; they just all go about it in different ways. The best generic name for what will be command central in your home theater is the controller, a title coined by the folks at Lucasfilm's THX division. The controller lets you select one of your source components (DVD player, DTV tuner, VCR, satellite receiver...), control the volume, process the audio and video signals, and send the processed signals to the appropriate places. I'll break down these functions piece by piece for you to understand what all the different names mean and determine which component makes sense for you.

Figure 6.1
Audio/video surround receiver, model STRDA3000ES, courtesy of Sony Electronics

Preamp

The first part of the controller is the preamp. A preamp is basically an audio-video switcher with volume control and possibly tone control (treble and bass adjustment). If you have more than one source component, which you probably do, you need to be able to plug them all into one unit and select which component you want to watch or listen to.

The preamp got its name from the days of turntables when the turntable's output signal was so quiet that it had to be pre-amplified to equal the gain or volume level of a line level signal, such as the signal from a tape deck or CD player before sending the signal on to the main amplifier.

Surround Processor

The most critical component of your home theater is the surround processor. The processor decodes both 2-channel and digital audio bitstream signals. When fed a stereo audio signal from the preamp, like the 2-channel soundtrack from a CD or VCR, the processor uses matrix decoding to derive six or more surround channels. Matrix decoding compares the left and right channels and directs common (in phase) sounds to a center channel speaker and routes opposite (out of phase) sounds to a single surround channel (though the surround channel might be played back through two speakers). With the digital audio bitstream signals on your favorite DVDs and HDTV shows, the processor uses proprietary decoding (see Dolby and DTS surround processing later in this chapter) to derive six or more discrete channels of audio.

A channel is a single audio signal sent to one or more speakers.

In a 5.1 (read "five point one") system, for example, the processor decodes the digital signal into the five main channels (left, center, and right front, and the left and right surround) and the point one, or LFE (low frequency effects) channel.

Figure 6.2

The controller, whether it's a pre-pro, an integrated amp, or a full-fledged receiver will accept the audio and video signals from your source components, decode the surround signals, and output the signal to your speakers.

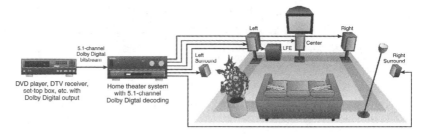

Amplifiers

The analog output of a preamp or surround processor is a line level signal, which has a very low power signal level. The signal level or volume of each audio channel must be increased before the signal has enough power to move the speaker drivers. This is the job of the amplifier. In home theater, you need a single amplifier channel for each separate audio channel, which means you need at least six amplifier channels in a 5.1 system. The six channels can either be included in a receiver, a separate power amplifier, or built into the speakers. Nearly all subwoofers, for example, use a built-in amplifier.

A single amplifier channel can power single or multiple speakers, but using multiple speakers decreases the signal level to the speakers and increases the demands on the amplifier. Low-cost multiroom systems often use a 2-channel amplifier to drive several pairs of speakers throughout the house.

Receivers, Integrated Amps, and Pre-Pros

The preamp, surround processor, and amplifier are individual components and are also the major components of a controller. When you
combine these functions into various configurations, you get different
products. For example, the combination of a preamp and a surround
processor is called a pre-pro and must be accompanied by a multichannel power amp or powered speakers. A pre-pro and an amplifier
are considered separate components, or separates, for short. If a pre-pro
includes a built-in multichannel amplifier it's referred to as an integrated
amp. When an integrated amp also includes an AM/FM radio, it's called
a receiver. I talk about the advantages of separates versus receivers or
integrated amps in the next section. As I talk about what features to
look for, I use some of these terms interchangeably, but only because
what's important to one component is important to another.

Figure 6.3

A receiver includes a
number of functions
in one piece of equip-
ment. These functions
are also available as
separate components.

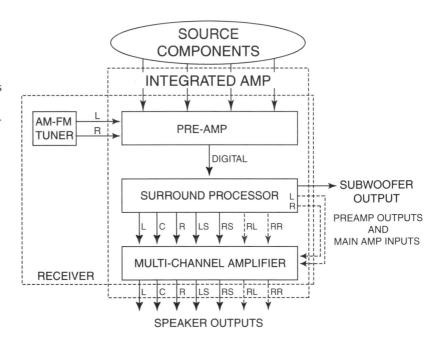

What to Look For

Receivers and integrated amplifiers

The vast majority of home theater users buy a receiver or an integrated amp to control their system. Everything comes in one component, which makes it easy to install and use. More important, receivers are incredibly inexpensive. Receivers benefit from consolidation. All the various functions feed from the same power supply and are housed in the same chassis, which helps reduce manufacturer, and subsequently users costs. You can get a Dolby Digital-equipped surround receiver for less than a few hundred bucks. The only drawback is that everything is in one component. If you want to upgrade a particular function, like the surround decoder, it's often difficult, if not impossible to upgrade without junking the entire unit.

An exception would be a receiver with pre-out jacks. Pre-out jacks are the outputs of the receiver's preamp section. You can connect the pre out jacks to a separate amplifier and increase the power output of your system. Sometimes the receiver uses jumper pins to route these outputs to the receiver's amplifier channel inputs. Remove the jumper pins and route certain channels (like the front three channels) to a better external amplifier, and reroute the surround signals to the more powerful front amps in the receiver.

Figure 6.4

Pre-out jacks let you route signals to a more powerful or better quality external amplifier.

Separates

You might prefer to use separate components, however, for improved performance and upgrade flexibility, even though separate components tend to cost more than a comparably equipped receiver. Amplifiers, for example, draw the most electrical current in a receiver and the amplifiers, surround processor, and preamp all draw from the same power supply. Musical peaks can cause the amplifier to pull more power, which might prevent other components from getting the power they need, and affect their performance. Separate components have separate power supplies and thus avoid this problem. The amplifier and pre-pro functions are housed in separate chassis, too, which prevents electromagnetic interference from the amplifier's power supply from affecting the low level signals in the pre-pro section. Last, but not least, amplifier technology hasn't changed over the last several decades. A 100-watt-per-channel amplifier made 20 years ago, if still functioning properly, is still usable in a modern surround sound system. Old preamps and surround processors, however, become outdated within a couple years. Purchasing separates allows you to maintain a cutting-edge system without throwing away useful components.

Figure 6.5

Preamp surround processor (top), model MC-12, with separate 7-channel power amplifier (bottom), model LX-7, courtesy of Lexicon

Dolby surround processing

Dolby surround processing is the de facto standard in home theater and Dolby Digital is the most popular of the company's technologies. The Dolby Digital format has been used on nearly every major motion picture since the release of *Batman Returns* in 1992. Dolby Digital—available on DVD, HDTV, video games and some satellite and cable TV networks—provides six discrete channels of audio in a 5.1 configuration. You don't really need to look for Dolby Digital processing though, because it is probably included in any new surround processor you purchase.

What you should look for is Dolby Pro Logic II (PLII). The original Pro Logic system decodes a center and mono surround channel from the left and right audio channels on TV shows, video tapes, laser discs, and even CDs. PLII uses directional cues in the left and right tracks to derive stereo surround channels, creating a 5.1-like signal from 2-channel recordings. The resulting signals aren't totally discrete, but the effect is otherwise convincing and can make 2-channel recordings sound great. PLII has two modes: Movie and Music. The Music mode often offers more appropriate surround enhancement for CDs than some of the digital signal processing techniques I'll talk about later.

Dolby continually innovates, though, and with the release of *Star Wars I: The Phantom Menace*—and in conjunction with Lucasfilm's THX division—Dolby announced an upgraded version of Dolby Digital called Dolby Digital Surround EX (THX refers to it as THX Surround EX). The EX channel is essentially a combination of Dolby's existing technologies. A single surround back (or center surround) channel is recorded equally into both the surround left and surround right channels. The decoder pulls the common (in phase) information out and directs it to the surround back speaker. The format is sometimes abbreviated as 6.1, since there are now six main speakers, though 5.1 EX is more accurate. A 5.1 EX soundtrack is completely compatible with a 5.1 system. If a system doesn't have a center surround speaker, the EX channel information is played back equally through the left and right surround speakers. As effective as 5.1 EX is, it's difficult to implement if your couch sits against the back wall of your home theater. (See **Figure 6.6**.) The 5.1 EX works better if you sit away from the back wall, or diagonally across the corner, so you have some space to put the surround back speaker.

Some receivers and pre-pros use additional processing, or just double the surround back channel, to create a 7.1 system (left, center, and right front, left and right side surround, left and right back surround, and a subwoofer channel). Dolby's most recent processing technology, Dolby Pro Logic IIx, combines their Pro Logic II circuitry with the Surround EX processing to create a 7.1 system. The directional cues from the left and right surround signal help create separate left and right surround back signals. PLIIx works with both 2-channel and 5.1 EX signals, so that any soundtrack you play will come out of the 7.1 speaker system. Like 5.1 EX,

PLIIx is a worthwhile technology, more so than Surround EX, if you have the room to utilize it. If you don't have any place to put surround back speakers, though, PLIIx won't be much use to you.

Figure 6.6

A typical Surround EX, ES, or 7.1 home theater speaker layout. Three speakers are positioned across the front, two at the sides, and one or two behind the listener. (Courtesy of Dolby Labs)

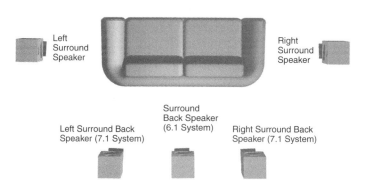

DTS surround processing

In 1993 (a year after Dolby unveiled Dolby Digital), Digital Theater Systems (DTS) released a competing 5.1 technology. Steven Spielberg and Universal studios adopted (and invested in) the technology for use in the movie *Jurassic Park*. Substantially less expensive than Dolby Digital and arguably better sounding, DTS was quickly adopted by theaters and eventually made its way into the home. DTS currently offers three different technologies for use in home theaters.

DTS-Neo is similar to Dolby's Pro Logic II and creates a 5.1-like signal from 2-channel recordings. DTS-ES is similar to Surround EX and matrixes a mono surround back channel into 5.1 digital soundtracks. DTS-ES Discrete adds a sixth, separate surround back channel, instead of the matrixed channel ES and EX techniques use. The ES Discrete decoder reads the sixth channel and outputs a true 6.1 soundtrack. ES decoders ignore the discrete sixth channel and just output the basic 5.1 signal with the matrixed ES channel.

Like Dolby Digital, DTS processing is nearly ubiquitous in surround processors. There's much debate between enthusiasts about the merits and sound quality differences between Dolby and DTS processing techniques. If you're interested in achieving the last ounce of sound quality, you should test the two techniques yourself. In my opinion, both sound great. Fortunately, DVDs that include a DTS soundtrack also include a Dolby soundtrack, so you're not left out if you don't have or aren't able to utilize DTS.

Digital signal processing

Recording studios often use digital signal processing, or DSP, to add ambience to instruments and vocals that are recorded in an otherwise acoustically dead studio space. DSP engineers record the acoustical effect that famous concert halls have on sound, and then use computer processors to create that same effect with recorded music. With the introduction of Dolby Surround, electronics manufacturers added DSP technology to their surround processors. The sounds reflected from the side or rear walls in the concert hall, for example, can now be played back through the surround speakers, with additional reverb and ambience effects added to other channels.

DSP can add great ambience to otherwise flat recordings, but more often than not, the added reverb becomes a hindrance and in some cases sounds downright dreadful (why manufacturers think that Stadium reverb is a good thing is a mystery). Most people experiment with these faux surround settings for the first few weeks then ignore them. Some companies do a better job than others; so if you like the effect, check out processors from Lexicon and Yamaha. Otherwise, stick with simple techniques like Dolby's PLII for Music. (See the section on the previous page on Dolby.)

THX Select and Ultra2

THX is one form of DSP that is worth considering. Rumor has it that when George Lucas originally heard his first Star Wars film in a regular movie theater, he was appalled at the lack of sound quality. The THX division was soon born, not as a surround decoding technique, as is often mistakenly thought, but to establish minimum performance standards for theater sound quality. Thanks to various standards committees, most professional film recording stages already meet certain sound and image performance criteria. Sound and image quality, on the other hand, can range drastically from one commercial movie theater to another. THX-certified theaters guarantee that a film will sound as good as what Lucas, or other directors, heard on the original recording stage.

THX certification migrated to the home environment to continue the goal of reproducing the film director's original intent. The home THX system certifies various components, including speakers, amplifiers, and surround processors. When THX components are used together as a system, the results you hear are as close as you can expect to what the movie director heard. As someone with a complete home THX system, I can attest that the system works well. You can, however, use any THX component in a non-THX system and still benefit from that particular component's THX certification. The products are complementary. Currently there are two THX standards, Select and Ultra2. Select is aimed at products used in smaller rooms (approximately 2,000 square feet), while Ultra2 is for larger rooms. The amplifier specification, for example, requires a certain amount of clean, undistorted power for Select systems and substantially more power for Ultra2 systems.

In THX surround processors, the THX enhancements are added to the Dolby or DTS decoded signal. Both Select and Ultra2 start with an important re-equalization of the front three speaker channels. Soundtracks recorded for large theatrical auditoriums have a noticeable and standardized boost in high frequencies to compensate for the expected loss in the theatrical speaker system. Play these soundtracks at home, where there is no complementary loss in high frequencies and the movie will sound bright or shrill. THX Re-EQ electronically adds that high frequency loss back into the system to create a more neutral response.

THX Select controllers add some DSP to the surround channels, called timbre matching and adaptive de-correlation. Timbre matching helps compensate for the sound quality differences you hear when a sound is played through the front speakers as compared to the surround speakers. Timbre matching helps sounds that pan from front to back maintain the same sonic signature. Adaptive de-correlation uses electronic tricks to create an enveloping surround field that matches the sound heard from the array of surround loudspeakers used in a movie theater.

As I talked about in "Getting Started," in Chapter 5, a different speaker configuration is recommended for use with multichannel music systems than the typical home theater surround system. THX Ultra2 certified processors start with the same enhancements mentioned previously, but add some advanced DSP, called the Advanced Speaker Array (ASA) to the surround signals of a 5.1 soundtrack to accommodate for these differences so that one speaker setup can effectively be used for both multichannel music and movie surround sound. If you use Ultra2's speaker arrangement (see "Surround Speakers," page 158), I definitely recommend the Ultra2 processing.

Bass management

It's unlikely, and for most systems unwise, to use five full-range speakers for your main channels. For one thing, you probably don't want to live in the home theater version of Stonehenge. For another, the optimum position for reproducing bass frequencies is usually not the best place in the room for reproducing midrange and treble frequencies. Subwoofers offer a number of benefits, (see "Subwoofers," page 184), one of which is the ability to use smaller satellite speakers without sacrificing system performance. To make this work, though, you need some form of bass management. A 5.1 digital audio system, including DVD-A/SACD, provides five, full range channels. You don't want the low frequency signals in those channels to reach your small satellite speakers. The speakers can't reproduce those frequencies so you won't hear them, and there's a good chance those low-frequency signals will degrade the sound you do hear. Make sure the controller you buy provides independently adjustable crossovers for each main speaker and the subwoofer so that you can route all the low-frequency sounds to the appropriate speakers.

The system's bass management might not be active with 6-channel analog inputs, though. The 6-channel signals, typically from DVD-A/SACD players, bypass the digital electronics in the controller so that the pure high-resolution signal can pass straight to the amplifiers. If your surround processor's 6-channel input lacks bass management, make sure the DVD-A/SACD player can redirect low frequencies appropriately.

Amplifiers

Next to the surround processor, the most important part of a receiver or separate component combination is the multichannel amplifier. Make sure the amplifier has the same number of channels as the surround processor has output channels and that the amp has enough power to drive your speakers. Subwoofers typically have built-in amplifiers, so you only need to worry about the main channels. If you have a 5.1 system, for example, you need a 5-channel amplifier.

The big question is "How much power do I need?" My generic answer is "as much as you can afford." Power, in this case, is determined by the amplifier's output and is measured in watts (W). How much power you really need depends on a number of factors, including the sensitivity of your speakers, how far away you sit, the size and acoustical makeup of your listening room, and how loud you like to play music. Ideally, you should have the same amount of power output for each channel. At the very least, the surround channels should have no less than half the power available to the front channels.

Music playing at moderate listening levels typically uses 5 or maybe 10 watts of amplifier power. It's the musical peaks, the crescendos, the drum solos, or other dynamic moments that really suck the juice from the amp. If the amp doesn't have enough power to compensate for the sudden increase in level, the sound will distort and crackle, or worse, damage your speaker. An underpowered amplifier is actually more likely to damage a speaker than an overpowered one. The amount of power available for these brief moments is called peak power or head-room. Peak power is measured in dB and an amp should have lots of it (3 dB is good, more is better).

Speaker sensitivity determines how much sound pressure level (SPL) output, in decibels (dB), the speaker generates when fed a 1W signal and measured 1 meter (3.3 feet) from the speaker. The greater the speaker sensitivity, the less power you need to reach a reasonable volume level; 90 dB is a moderate sound pressure level. Movie theaters peak at 105 dB (115 dB for the subwoofer).

Decibels are logarithmic, which means it takes twice as much power to increase the level by 3 dB, which is a noticeable increase in volume, but not twice as loud. A 1 dB difference is subconsciously noticeable (e.g., you hear a difference, but don't attribute it to volume). It takes a 10 dB difference for the music to seem twice as loud. Keep this in mind when a salesperson tries to sell you a more expensive model that has only 10 or 20W of more power.

If your speaker sensitivity is 90 dB with 1W, the output will be 93 dB with 2W, 96 with 4W, and so on. The speaker needs only 35 W to reach a theatrical 105 dB SPL.

Sound Pressure Levels of Common Sources
(Loudness levels, in decibels (dB) of various noises)

Sound Source	dB
Saturn Rocket	194
Prop Airplane	160
Threshold of Pain	140
Heavy Truck	100
Heavy Traffic	80
Conversation	60–70
Avg Living Room (Daytime)	40
Avg Living Room (Night time)	30
Recording Studio	20

The previous example assumes you sit 1 meter away from the speaker, which you probably don't. Sound gets quieter (loses power) as you sit farther away (roughly 4 dB every time you double the distance in an enclosed room), so using the speaker example in the last paragraph, if you sit 13 feet away, you need about 150W of power (70W at 2 meters, 140W at 4 meters). The actual amount of attenuation with distance depends on the acoustics, or reflectiveness of your listening space. If the walls, ceiling, and floor are a hard, solid surface, much of the speakers' energy remains in the room, and you'll need less power to drive them. If the room's surfaces are covered with 10 inches of foam padding, drapes, carpets, and plush furniture, much of the speaker's energy will be absorbed and you'll need even more power.

But all 150W amplifiers are not created equal. Make sure the amplifier specifies the output as RMS power, or root mean squared, which is a continuous power output, as opposed to a peak power output. An amp with only 150W of peak power delivers far less during regular use. Peak power is important, but should be considered separately. You should also make sure the output is specified with a full range signal (20 Hz to 20 Khz), and allows for very little distortion (less than 0.1 percent). It's easy to get higher amplifier specifications if you measure them over a limited frequency range and with higher distortion levels.

The amplifier's output specification should also be measured with a given impedance, usually 8 ohms. Impedance is the speaker's electrical resistance to the signal and is measured in ohms. Even though most speakers are listed as "8 ohms," this rating is an average. The impedance level varies with frequency and your speakers will likely drop to 4 ohms or less, particularly at lower frequencies. Make sure the amplifier can deliver more power to these lower impedance loads, and ideally twice as much power with half the impedance (but this level is hard to achieve). A high-end, 100W amp should deliver 200W into 4 ohms and 400W into 2 ohms. If the amplifier or receiver doesn't list the output into lower impedances, you can safely assume that the amplifier's power output doesn't increase with lower impedances.

And make sure the amplifier sounds good. Good sound is certainly a more subjective impression than output measurements, and if the amplifier fulfills the qualifications listed above, the likelihood that the output will sound good is substantially greater. But you should always check it out with music and movies you're familiar with, preferably with the same speakers you have or plan to use. Some specialty stores even have in-home trial periods. Take advantage of them.

Connections

The main function of your preamp, or the preamp portion of your receiver, is to connect to all of your sources. Therefore, the controller should have enough inputs to accommodate the sources you have now, and ones you might have later. For audio, this includes left and right analog, optical, and coaxial digital and some form of multi-channel audio input. Multichannel audio might be a group of 6, 7, or 8 analog inputs that accept the decoded signals from a DVD-A/SACD player. If the controller has DVD-A/SACD decoding, look for a FireWire or HDMI digital input and make sure that whatever inputs are available on the controller are also available on your multichannel, high-resolution player.

If your amplifier is 20 to 30 feet from your pre-pro, consider finding a controller with professional-style balanced or XLR outputs. These connectors use three pins in a locking mechanism. Balanced signals prevent noise interference in long cable runs, which is critical in a professional music studio environment, but is not necessary for the average home user.

Make sure there are plenty of video inputs. Beyond composite and S-Video signals, look for component, HDMI, and FireWire switching. Less expensive (under $500) receivers won't have component video inputs, or won't have many of them. It's easy to rack up three or even four devices with component outputs so make sure your controller has at least two or three if not more. HDMI is also becoming more popular on controllers, but is currently found only on higher-end products. It's worth having if you can afford it. Make sure the video switching functions can handle the extra bandwidth of HDTV, though. The controller should specify that at least 30 to 40 Mhz of bandwidth is available to pass the video signal, otherwise the image performance suffers.

Advanced control inputs and outputs are also important for automating functions and making complex systems easy to use. These controls come in the form of 12-volt relays and triggers and RS232 connections. Connect the 12-volt relays and triggers to amplifiers, powered sub-woofers, or other components with similar inputs and when you turn on the controller, the other components will also turn on or activate. You can have screens drop from the ceiling, projectors drop from the ceiling, or turn on the popcorn maker at the touch of a button.

An RS232 input looks like a VGA computer monitor connection, but has 9 pins instead of VGA's 15 pins. RS232 is a basic method of directly con-trolling various aspects of a product's features. Automation systems use RS232's two-way communication to tell the controller when to turn on, what input to switch to, what surround mode to select, and so on.

If the controller is already turned on or selected, the RS232 communica-tion prevents sending duplicate commands that might otherwise disable a particular function.

Video transcoding

One handy feature to have is video transcoding. Video transcoding converts various video input signals so that the signal is available from any of the video outputs. For example, a typical receiver only outputs composite video signals for the components connected with composite inputs. The receiver can't output an S-Video signal for these compo-nents. In this case, if you have composite, S-Video, and component signals connected to the receiver, you have to run composite, S-Video, and component signals to three different inputs on the TV. Transcoding, however, converts composite signals into S-Video and component signals, depending on how advanced the transcoding is. A composite input doesn't look any better from the component output, but trans-coding all the video input signals into a single output means you need only one connection to, and one input on the TV, which makes the system easier to set up and use.

 Outboard composite to S-Video converters can eliminate your composite inputs. If you have only one or two composite sources and your preamp doesn't transcode the signals internally, outboard composites to S-Video converters are a good idea. They make the system easier to set up and use. Most video cable companies sell outboard composites to S-Video converters.

Video processing

Some high-end receivers include built-in video upconversion or de-interlacing. This process converts interlaced 480 signals into 480p. (See "Interlaced vs. Progressive," page 22, for more details about interlace and progressive signals and check out the Video Processor section in this chapter for more information about de-interlacing.) Upconversion is another way to convert all the input signals to a single output which offers the same benefits as transcoding, described in the previous paragraph. Whether or not the 480p signal is an improvement depends on the capabilities of your TV and its worthiness is similar to the qualifications for progressive DVD players described in Chapter 4.

PC networking/file sharing

One of the newest trends in audio is to record and play back music from a computer. Never heard of this? Find a teenager. This trend is possible thanks to a compression system called MP3 that reduces the music's file size. You can download MP3 files from various Internet sites or you can create them from CDs you own. If your computer is close to your home theater system, you can connect the PC's digital audio output to the receiver, which only requires an extra input on the receiver. You can then select the music tracks from your computer. An easier way is to connect a receiver or preamp that's equipped with an Ethernet connection to your computer network. Then you can select the music tracks you want from the computer and play back the MP3 files through the home theater system. Your receiver becomes a terminal to your PC.

Multiroom capability

It's one thing to play music in your home theater, it's another thing entirely to be able to play music through speakers in every room of your house or backyard. Some receivers offer a second or multiroom option to route signals to other rooms. The more advanced the feature, the more flexibility provided. In it's simplest form, a multiroom feature is a set of audio and video outputs that sends the same signal you're listening to in the home theater to other rooms in the house. More advanced versions let you play different source components in different rooms at the same time, while controlling the system through wall-mounted keypads that connect to the main receiver. Because you might need other equipment and in-wall wiring to make this work, I suggest talking with a custom installation specialist in your area. Go to www.cedia.org to find a dealer near you.

Equalization

Another new feature making its way into controllers is a built-in parametric equalizer (EQ). Parametric EQs offer an extremely precise level of audio control and is useful in fine-tuning the acoustic response of your system. See my note about parametric EQs in "Subwoofers," page 184.

Ergonomics

As with other devices, it's a good idea to check out how the receiver or pre-pro works when you're in the store. Is the controller easy to set up and use, can you access the setup menu without the manual, and is there an easy to read on-screen menu? If so, you're more likely to get things set up correctly and sounding good. It's also helpful if the receiver comes with a universal remote that will control your other equipment so you only need one remote for the system. You can buy automation remotes separately, (see Chapter 9, "Remote Controls"), but this adds to the system cost.

Also make sure that the surround processor has built-in test tones for each speaker channel, including the subwoofer, to help you calibrate the output level of each speaker. Less expensive processors don't include the subwoofer test tone, which makes it extremely difficult to balance the subwoofer output level to the other speakers. Higher-end processors use automated systems to calibrate the output levels, which is very cool.

Getting Started

Step 1: Connect the source components

Using the guidelines described in previous chapters, connect all your source components to the controller. Although this can seem daunting, remember, you're just making the same types of connections, multiple times. I often start with the component at the top of the rack, and work my way down to the bottom of the rack. If the controller doesn't have specific inputs for particular devices, which is common, I connect that top component to the first digital audio or video slots on the controller, (i.e., Digital 1, Component Video 1), depending on what signals the component needs. The second component in the rack then gets connected to the next available input, and so on. This procedure makes it easier to configure the processor later.

Make sure the preamp or receiver and all the components are turned off before making any connections. Wiring powered components can damage the devices in the chain.

Step 2: Connect the output to the TV (even a portable)

Many receivers use on-screen menus to access the setup menu, and your installation will go quicker if you have the TV hooked up to the receiver. Typically, the on-screen menu only works through the controller's composite or S-Video output. If your TV isn't accessible, use a portable TV. Unless your controller transcodes video signals (see the previous section), you need to connect one of each video signal type used on the controller to the display including composite, S-Video, component or RGB, and DVI or HDMI. You'll most likely need separate inputs on the TV. Most TV inputs don't function correctly if two different signal types are connected to the same input, even when there aren't any signals coming through one of the connections. If you don't have enough inputs on the TV, you might have to be creative. Route signals through the A/V inputs on your VCR, for example, or send common signals (like all your composite video sources) to the receiver, then to the TV.

Step 3: Connect the preamp to the amp

If you have a receiver or integrated amp, you can skip this step.

Make sure you pay attention to which preamp output you're connecting to which amplifier channel input. There are anywhere from five to seven cables to connect, depending on whether or not you have a 5.1,

5.1 EX/ES (6.1), or 7.1 system. Some manufacturers use a single DB 25-pin connector between the two preamps and the amplifier, which eliminates confusion and clutter.

Step 4: Connect the main speakers

Again, there are anywhere from five to seven cables, depending on whether or not you have a 5.1, 5.1 EX/ES (6.1), or 7.1 system. Make sure you pay attention to what amplifier output channel you connect to which speaker. More important, pay close attention to the speaker polarity (see **Figure 6.7**). Each amplifier and speaker terminal has two connectors, one red (positive) and one black (negative). Make sure you connect the amplifier's red, or positive terminal, to the speaker's positive terminal. The two-conductor wires that connect the amp to the speaker will likely have a marking of some kind on one of the two wires, such as a ribbed edge, white stripe, or different colored wire. It doesn't matter which wire you use for the positive or negative connection, so long as you're consistent at both the amplifier and the speaker. I typically connect the marked wire to the red terminal. You can use whatever system you want, just be consistent. If a speaker is wired backwards (positive to negative and negative to positive) the sound will be out of phase with the other speakers. This will cancel out some frequencies, usually the low bass, and make upper frequencies sound disembodied and out of place.

Be extra careful and make sure the bare positive and negative wires do not touch or you'll shut down and possibly damage your amplifier.

Figure 6.7

Make sure the wires connected to the positive and negative terminals on the amplifier are connected to the same terminals on the speaker. (Image courtesy of Sony Electronics.)

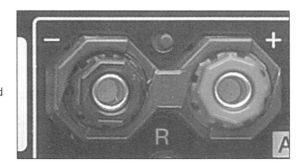

Step 5: Connect the subwoofer

Because the subwoofer has its own amplifier, connect a line level signal from the output on the surround processor labeled "subwoofer" to the amplifier input on the subwoofer itself. For now, set the volume control on the subwoofer's back panel at a low setting and disable the subwoofer's crossover control, if possible. If the subwoofer's crossover doesn't have an "Off" or "Bypass" position, set the crossover frequency at its highest frequency setting.

 Make sure all the components are on before you turn on the amplifier. This will prevent any electrical pops from playing through to the speakers. Similarly, turn the amp off first and let it discharge completely (30 seconds) before turning off the other components.

Step 6: Access the setup menu

With all your hardware connected, you're ready to configure the controller. In many cases, is reasonably simple. In some situations, though, finding the setup menu for the controller is as easy as finding Big Foot. Consult the owner's manual for specifics on this one.

Once you've found the setup menu, assign the audio and video inputs to the various source selection buttons. Inexpensive receivers might have particular inputs on the back that are wired to specific source buttons on the front. Better receivers, though, have assignable inputs (though the analog inputs may or may not be hardwired). In other words, the inputs on the back are just labeled 1 through whatever. You have to tell the receiver that when you press the DVD button on the front, you want it to select the audio that's connected to input 4 (assuming that's where you connected the audio). That "top down" numbering scheme mentioned in Step 1 of "Getting Started" comes in handy now. Do the same procedure for the analog, digital, and multi-channel audio; component and DVI video; and HDMI signals. Make sure that when you select each source button, you get the audio and video signals you want.

Your next step is to enable the appropriate speakers and crossover settings. Again in the setup menu, find the speaker adjustment page that allows you to configure the speakers. I'll set the speaker outputs in a moment. How this menu is presented can vary, but generally you can enable or disable various speakers, and set the bass management controls. If you don't have a center speaker, for example, you can disable the center channel output and automatically re-route the center channel information, which is predominantly dialogue, to the left and right speakers.

Entry-level receivers provide the option of choosing small or large speakers. Select small and the processor routes signals that are below a predetermined crossover frequency from that channel to the subwoofer. Unless you have floor-standing speakers with 10-inch or larger drivers, or don't have a subwoofer, small is your best bet. Higher-end processors allow you to fine-tune the crossover frequency. When available, you can choose a crossover point that is one octave above the low frequency cut-off of your speakers (or the point where low frequency response diminishes by -3dB). The cutoff point should be listed in your speaker's literature.

 An octave is twice or half of a given frequency. A crossover setting of 70 Hz is one octave above a cuttoff frequency of 35 Hz.

If the cutoff point is 50 Hz, you should choose a 100 Hz crossover frequency; 80 Hz is a safe choice and is the preferred crossover frequency in THX systems. Frequencies below 80 Hz are considered nonlocalizable, meaning you won't notice that the sound isn't coming from the speaker it was originally supposed to come from. Frequencies above 80 Hz, when sent to the subwoofer, can become noticeable, which in turn calls attention to the subwoofer, particularly if the sub is placed far from the main speakers. Ultimately, the goal is to create a good blend between the main channels and the subwoofer. Feel free to vary the crossover, if possible, to improve this blend.

Within the speaker configuration menu, you should also be able to input the distance to each speaker. The surround processor uses this information to adjust the time delay settings for each speaker so that the signals all arrive at the listening position at the same time. Measure the distance from your primary listening position to each speaker and input the distance information in this menu.

Now you're ready to adjust the speaker output levels for each channel. The outputs should match so that sounds traveling from one speaker to another are played back at the same volume. Every Dolby surround processor includes a built-in test tone to help set the output levels. From the output level menu, enable the test tone, which will play what's called band-limited pink noise (and sounds like radio static) through each speaker. First, make sure the sound comes from the correct speaker that corresponds to the on-screen indicator. If not, check your wiring connections and amplifier outputs. Once you've confirmed that sound is coming from each speaker in the correct sequence, adjust the output level so that the sound seems the same from each speaker. This task is made immensely easier with a sound pressure level meter available from Radio Shack for about $40 (see **Figure 6.8**). Adjust the output levels so that the meter reads 75 dB for each channel. Move the meter around the room and average the results when adjusting the subwoofer output level, as the level can vary dramatically from one position to another.

When you're finished, play some music and movies. You might need to fine-tune the output levels for your taste, particularly the surround and subwoofer outputs, which most people like to bump up a bit. Make sure you test plenty of material first, though. You don't want to make adjustments based on the results of one recording that might have anemic bass and little surround information and then have another recording blow you out of the room.

Figure 6.8

Sound pressure level meter, model 33-4050, courtesy of Brent Butterworth

Secrets

Re-assign the default surround modes

Your surround processor will likely assign default surround modes for each input. Switch to the DVD input, for example, and the processor will kick on the Dolby Digital mode. If you prefer DTS, though, you can go into the processor's setup menu and change the default surround mode. You can even set up duplicate inputs with different default modes. If you like to watch movies on DVD and your spouse or kids like to watch music videos, set up two different inputs to switch to the DVD signal. Set the default surround mode for one input to Dolby Digital and the other input for a Music Surround mode.

Check phase

Making sure that you've connected the positive and negative speaker terminals correctly is critical to your system's performance. With two terminals per connection (one positive and one negative) and two connections per cable (one at the amp and one at the speaker) there can be as many as 28 connections to make just to hook up a 7.1 channel speaker system (not including the subwoofer). Don't be surprised if you wire something backwards. I've wired up hundreds of systems and have flipped a connection more than a few times. One way to test the connection is to play an identical signal through two speakers at the same time. Pink noise is preferable and is available on test DVDs (see the next section), though vocals or movie dialogue will also work. As you stand an equal distance from both speakers, the sound should appear to come from a point between the speakers. If not, it will sound shallow and disembodied, which means one of the two speakers is wired out of phase. Check all of the main channels. The front three channels are the most critical, though the surround channels should be in phase with each other. I'll talk about checking subwoofer phase in the Subwoofer Secrets section of Chapter 8.

Use test DVDs to fine-tune performance

As I mentioned in the DVD player section, there are a couple DVDs available to help you fine-tune the performance of your system. Joe Kane Productions' *Digital Video Essentials* (available at www.dvdinternational.com) has a number of video tests as well as a simple audio section for confirming that speakers are setup, balanced, and in phase. The 5.1 Audio Toolkit, (available at www.51toolkit.com) has these same tests, and a number of others that are useful for setting equalizers or just testing the performance of your system. Explaining them all would take another book. Download the manual at www.gold-line.com. Combine these tests with the Radio Shack SPL meter (or a more accurate and more expensive SPL meter from Gold Line), and you have the equivalent of test equipment costing thousands of dollars. You'll be amazed at the improvements you can make.

Upgrade your receiver's internal amplifier

If your receiver or integrated amp has pre-out jacks on the back, you can use them to upgrade the internal amplifier with a higher-power or better-quality external model. The pre-out connections tap the signal from the output of the surround processor just prior to the input at the amplifier. You can connect these outputs to a separate amplifier, and bypass the internal amp. This is an easy way to upgrade to a separates system. Later, if you get an external amplifier, you can replace the receiver with a high-quality pre-pro.

In some receivers, there's a jumper pin that connects the pre-out jack to the amplifier input. You can connect the signal to an external amp and you can re-assign the internal amps for alternate duty. Remove the jumper pins and attach the pre-out jacks to the external amp as described above. Then route another signal to the now-empty receiver's amplifier input. Make sure you connect the speaker wires to their newly assigned outputs. You can use the internal amps to power a multiroom system, or increase the power available to surround channels.

Always turn off the amp, preamp, or receiver when making any type of connection. Let it sit for a minute to discharge excess electricity before making any connections.

Program the universal remote

Want to eliminate the clutter on the coffee table and impress your spouse? Program the receiver's universal remote to control your whole system. Universal remotes control a number of different devices made by a number of different manufacturers. They're even pre-programmed with the other remote codes. You just have to tell the remote what other gear you have.

Find the receiver (or the remote) user's manual for specific details. The manual will describe how to place the remote into a learning mode and will have lists of codes for various manufacturers. Find your equipment's manufacturer in the list and type in the corresponding code. There may be more than one, and you might have to try a few of the codes before you find the one that works. Once it works, move on to the next component and find the next code. Within a few minutes, the remote's buttons will activate functions on your other equipment—and your spouse will be impressed.

Video Processing

Video processing is a generic term for line-doublers, scalers, and de-interlacers that enhance or convert images from one format into another. Video processors are a bridge between our old low-resolution, interlaced TV signals and higher-quality formats like DTV and new digital television technologies. In many cases, the most common image you'll watch on an HDTV set is one that's been upconverted from a VCR, cable box, satellite receiver, or even the DVD player. Most, if not all HDTVs have a video processor built in. TVs that use digital technologies, like plasma, LCD, DLP, or LCoS require some form of video processing to make the image fit the TV's native pixel resolution. One way to improve the picture is with an external video processor. If nothing else, an external video processor can act as a video switcher to route all your video signals to the TV with one cable.

All of our existing, non-HDTV formats are based on the old NTSC signal, which consists of a signal with 480 interlaced horizontal lines, measured vertically. Interlaced means that each complete original video frame, or image, is split into two frames, or fields, with odd numbered lines and even numbered lines in different fields. The 240-line fields are shown sequentially and quickly so that your eye will blur the two fields back into one. (For more details, see "Interlaced vs. Progressive" in Chapter 3). While this might have been fine for the 13-inch TV that your parents grew up with, there are a number of problems when NTSC signals are displayed on big screen TVs, let alone on a seven- or eight-foot-wide projected image. And once you're used to the quality of HDTV signals, going back to NTSC seems downright cruel.

You can't eliminate this problem, but you might alleviate it if you de-interlace and possibly scale the lower-resolution images up to something comparable to HDTV. De-interlacing, also referred to as line-doubling, involves storing the odd- and even-lined fields in memory, reassembling them and outputting the image twice as fast to maintain timing. When done correctly, the end result is a 480-line progressive scan image—also known as 480p—that can be indistinguishable from one that was progressive to begin with.

 Technically, line doubling uses interpolation to generate new information between existing lines of information. This technique is used in scalers, mentioned on page 120, and to some extent in de-interlacing, but is rarely used as a primary form of de-interlacing. Most products labeled as line doublers are in fact de-interlacers.

In some cases, a 480p signal is adequate, or even optimum for the best image. Keep in mind, though, that the display must be capable of accepting this higher scanning signal. In other situations, higher line rates than 480p are necessary. Separate CRT projectors, in particular, often have such high resolution that a 480p signal will appear with distinct line structure. A scaler allows you to increase the vertical resolution, which will fill in the CRT projector's line structure.

It's also possible, and sometimes worthwhile, to de-interlace 1,080i HDTV signals, especially if the signal is scaled to a digital TV's native pixel resolution. Fixed pixel displays, like plasma, LCD, DLP, and LCoS, require that the signal match the panel resolution pixel for pixel. These displays have a built-in scaler that will upconvert or downconvert the signal to match the pixel resolution. Starting with a 1080p signal before scaling is the best way to obtain a good picture with HDTV signals. If the internal scaler doesn't de-interlace 1080i HDTV broadcasts into 1080p, talk to your local specialty video retailer and find a good external scaler that does, and that matches the fixed panel's native pixel structure. Since many scalers now offer multiple output resolutions, it's not hard to find a resolution that matches the ideal rate for your display.

Figure 6.9

Video processor, model KD-1080p HD-Leeza, courtesy of Key Digital

What to Look For

2-3 pulldown recognition

Regardless of whether you're dealing with 480i or 1,080i signals, better de-interlacers use a process called 2-3 pulldown detection (often called 3-2 pulldown, or something similar) when handling film-based inter-laced material. Films are recorded at 24 frames per second. Video runs at 30 frames. As described in the Interlace vs. Progressive sidebar (see Chapter 3), each video frame is split into two fields. Each field contains half the resolution of the original frame. When film is converted to video, the first film frame is split into the two video fields, I'll call them field A and B, where A contains the odd-numbered lines and B contains the even-numbered lines. The second film frame is split into two video fields (A and B), but then repeats the first field (A). The third film frame is split into two fields, but field B is shown first (B-A). Frame four has three fields in a B-A-B sequence. Frame five starts the cycle all over again (A-B). If the de-interlacer doesn't acknowledge the additional fields and the subsequent sequence, the processor mixes and matches incorrect fields when it tries to reconstruct the original progressive signal. The resulting image will have jagged diagonal edges, moiré patterns, or other picture anomalies. I call these motion artifacts because they only occur when there's motion in the image. A static image doesn't exhibit any problems. However, if the de-interlacer detects this 2-3 sequence, and ignores the extra frames, it can assemble a better image that is free of the motion-based artifacts.

Not only should the processor detect the 2-3 sequence, but it also should do so on a line-by-line basis. Many satellite program guides and TV station graphics are generated with 30-frame video sequences. When these images are overlayed on or around film-based material, which might be running in a small, on-screen window, the resulting picture will have both 30-frame and 24-frame source material. If the processor applies only 30-frame video processing to the entire image, the film material will have noticeable artifacts, as described on page 118.

Figure 6.10

Film, which is shot in 24 frames per second, is converted to video in a 2 field- 3 field (2-3) sequence. A good video processor must find, and compensate for this 2-3 field rate.

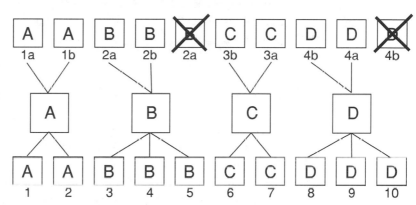

Figure 6.11

If a video processor doesn't compensate for the additional fields in film-based material, the processor will "reassemble" incorrect frames causing noticeable errors in the output, particularly with material that depicts motion.

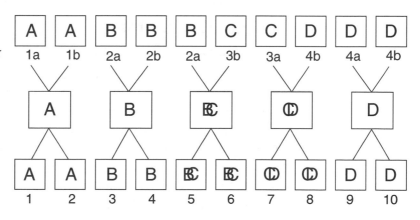

Motion adaptive interpolation

Regrettably, the world of moving images is not neatly divided into 24-frame film and 30-frame video material. There are, on occasion, other nonstandard frame rates, particularly when a program shot on film is edited in video. Slow or fast motion effects applied in the editing stage will alter the original frame rates. In these cases, it would be ideal if a video processor could detect the frame rate and compensate for it. If

it can't, it needs to interpolate the progressive information instead. Ideally, the processor looks at previous and future images and detects where objects in motion come from and where they are going. The video processor then creates interpolated data based on this information to fill in the alternate field's information. This feature is called motion adaptive interpolation.

Scaling

In many cases, accurately de-interlacing a video signal is the hardest part of the video processors job. Scaling the signal to higher resolutions should be a fairly easy task, though it's not always done well. Using test patterns on test discs like *Digital Video Essentials* make it possible to detect when the scaler is adding artifacts, but the differences are subtle, at best, and difficult to see in regular video. Scaling might be useful, though, if your display doesn't accept a 480p signal.

Aspect ratio control

One extremely handy feature found on most scalers is the ability to internally convert all images to fit a 16:9 shaped screen. Movies letterboxed to fit a 4:3 screen and DVDs that are "enhanced for wide screen" (aka anamorphic, or wide screen) have noticeably different signal resolutions. Early scalers required two different output rates to display anamorphic or letterboxed images without compromising one signal for the other. Not using different output rates results in a noticeable difference in line rate resolutions on screen. Now, many scalers manipulate these images internally so that the line rate on the screen is the same with all images. Since all the aspect ratio control is done with the scaler, less effort is needed to calibrate the TV.

Getting Started

Step 1: Install the video processor

Connect the video processor between the outputs of your video sources and the TV or projector. This might be at the output of the receiver or pre-pro, or at the output of the video components, depending on how your system is set up.

Step 2: Configure the video processor

You might need to configure the video processor based on your system. For example, if you connect the processor to a plasma TV with a 1,366-by-768-pixel resolution, select that resolution as the output of the video processor. Also, double-check to make sure the processor is set for the aspect ratio of your TV. This setting should probably be 16:9, unless you're using an older projector or a projector geared more for business presentation use.

7

TV and Video Monitors

Remember when your only TV choice was either a tabletop or console? Now there are an incredible number of technologies to choose from that provide all kinds of options. In this chapter, I separated TVs as direct view, flat panel (though flat panels technically are a form of direct view), rear, and front projection and explain the differences between the technologies so that you'll have a better idea of what's right for you. Once you know what's available, I'll talk about the various features you should look for in a TV, regardless of how it creates the image.

Direct View CRT

The most common television technology is the direct view CRT or cathode ray tube display. This technology has been around longer than *60 Minutes'* Andy Rooney, but is relatively inexpensive and capable of a great picture. CRT's use an electron gun to ignite horizontal lines of phosphors on the screen surface. The result is a very smooth, lifelike picture with good contrast, dark blacks, and vivid colors. If you're picky about picture quality, you want a CRT-based TV. The phosphors fade with use but should last 10 years or more. Keep the contrast and brightness levels down to preserve lifespan. Screen sizes extend up to 40 inches, but the image isn't as bright from larger tubes.

One obvious downside to CRT is the size of the cabinet. A 36-inch TV is nearly 3 feet deep. And the technology's resolution and light output capabilities are also limited. Most tube wide-screen TVs have a horizontal resolution that's about 800 to 1,000 pixels, horizontally. Given the screen size of most tube TVs, this resolution is more than adequate, because you can't see greater detail on a small screen without a magnifying glass. In order for the manufacturer to increase the resolution, they must sacrifice light output for CRTs, and light output isn't that high, relative to new technologies like LCD.

Figure 7.1

Direct view CRT TV, model 30XBR910, courtesy of Sony Electronics

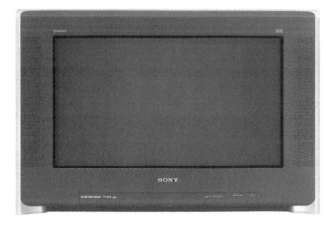

Many tube TVs actually have a flat screen surface. A flat screen is a subtle but important semantic difference from a flat panel display. Older TV screens are somewhat fishbowl-like, but flat screens have a squared-off, flat tube face. The rest of the cabinet, however, is still 3 feet deep. There's no technical advantage to a flat screen surface, especially if the manufacturer just adds extra glass in the corners, and in most cases a flat screen adds additional engineering challenges for the manufacturer to overcome. But, it is more cinematic to look at.

Flat Panel

The hot, new technology is the flat panel, which has a flat screen, but more importantly is incredibly thin. The average flat panel TV is about 4½ inches thick and can hang on a wall (as long as your wall is fairly sturdy). Flat panels come in two varieties: Plasma and LCD. Both technologies use a fixed grid of individual picture elements, or pixels. The more horizontal and vertical pixels there are, the higher the resolution capability of the display. Larger panels tend to use plasma technology while LCD, or liquid crystal display technology is typically used for smaller displays and has been used for computer monitors for quite some time. There are a growing number of ever-larger LCD TVs.

Ranging in size from 15 inches up to 42 inches diagonally, LCDs use a backlight that shines through a grid of image-creating crystal elements. Each crystal becomes either translucent or opaque depending on whether light in that particular portion of the image should pass through (to create a bright pixel) or be blocked (to make a dark pixel). Since the light comes from a bulb, and not charged phosphors, the image can be as bright as the bulb. There is almost no fear of image burn-in as there is with plasma and CRT-based TVs. In rare circumstances, for example when a corporation uses LCD screens to generate a company logo every day of every week for years on end, it is possible for the crystals to discolor. This is an extreme case of abuse, though; video game fans and stock or news channels junkies can use LCDs with no problem. LCD TVs are typically much brighter than plasma or CRT, which is good if your room is bright. But since it's hard for the crystals to completely block the light, LCDs don't have the deep, dark blacks and image depth of better tube displays or plasma TVs. It's a small price to pay for the convenient form factor and durability, though.

If you want a larger screen in that flat panel form factor, look at plasma TVs. They are generally bigger than LCD TVs, with screen sizes from 32 inches up to 60 inches and greater. Plasma TVs energize a grid of colored gas pockets, where each pocket is used to create a pixel of the image and provides a large, flat, full color image. Gas plasma phosphors fade like CRT phosphors. Uneven image wear from channel logos or stock-price tickers are a concern for plasma displays, but less so with CRT-based TVs (and rarely with LCD). Plasma can seem brighter than CRT, but the light output varies with the picture. A peak white image in a bright scene won't be as bright as the same image in a darker scene, the voltage level changes to keep the panel from overheating. Black levels tend to be better on plasma displays than LCDs, but blacks aren't quite as good as on the average CRT. Generally, plasma images do not look as smooth or natural as a CRT-based TV, but higher-end plasma TV images are more than acceptable and for some, the thin cabinet design makes up for the difference.

 If you live in the mountains and want a plasma TV you need a high-altitude capable model. Plasma gas reacts differently at higher altitudes. A plasma TV manufactured for use at sea-level atmospheric pressures will emit a loud buzzing sound when used at high altitudes.

Figure 7.2

Digital plasma TV, model MU-60PZ90V, courtesy of LG Electronics

Image Burn-in and Wear

Phosphor-based displays, like CRT or plasma, energize a material to create light for the image. This process uses up this material over time. Plasma and direct view CRT TVs should last 20,000 to 30,000 hours, when used appropriately. Like everything, though, the phosphors eventually wear out. Light output might drop noticeably at first, but will likely remain stable through most of the TV's life until dropping off significantly in a tube's "twilight years."

You can inadvertently accelerate this process and wear out the display prematurely. If the TV's contrast and brightness adjustments are set too high, more energy is applied to the phosphors, which will wear them out faster. Plasma displays are especially sensitive, as are three-gun front and rear-projection CRT-based TVs. These technologies are driven to the end of their limits to create large, bright screen images. Direct view CRTs are more resilient, but can still be susceptible to wear. LCDs are nearly immune to wear.

You can also overly use the phosphors in just one part of the image. When video material doesn't fill the whole screen (when you watch a 4:3 program on a 16:9 screen) or if a particular portion of the image is consistently brighter than the rest (like the news ticker on the bottom of the screen, or the solid-white network logo in the lower right-hand side of the image), the phosphors in the active or bright area of the screen wear out more than the rest of the picture. After a while, no matter what image you watch, the worn portions of the screen will be darker than the rest of the screen (and likely a different color, as one phosphor color fades faster than others). High contrast and brightness settings make it that much easier for the CNN logo to etch itself into the screen, for example.

If you have, or plan to buy a plasma or CRT-based TV, keep the contrast and brightness settings at modest (50 percent or less) levels to avoid excessive wear and burn-in. (I'll discuss accurate adjustments in the "Getting Started" section later in this chapter.) Also avoid displaying any static images, like stock-quote or news-ticker channels or video games, for too long. And if you really have to watch the Bloomberg channel all day, consider buying an LCD or digital rear-projection TV.

CRT Rear-Projection Television

When you want a big screen and plasma just doesn't seem right (or is too expensive), check out rear-projection or front-projection big-screen technology. The most common big-screen choice is the CRT-based, rear-projection display. This old standby can be somewhat enormous but like its sibling, the direct view TV, it is relatively inexpensive and generally has excellent performance. Separate tubes for each primary color: red, green, and blue are converged on screen to create a single, full-color image. The downsides to CRT technology, besides the requisite cabinet size, are the relatively dim image (compared to newer technologies), the fact that the image will fade with time and that portions of the picture can burn in or excessively wear into that section of the tubes. Over time, the three tubes can become misconverged, as well, creating color fringes around objects and a soft, defocused picture. When properly calibrated, however, rear-projection CRT displays offer the best performance of any single-box TV.

Figure 7.3

Rear-projection CRT TV, model 57S715, courtesy of Hitachi Electronics

Digital Rear-Projection Television

If you want a big image in a thin form factor, and you can't afford or don't want plasma technology, a digital rear-projection television (RPTV) might be what you need. When I say "digital" I'm referring to displays that use a digital technology to create the image. Usually, the term "digital TV" refers to any display technology, analog or digital that creates an image that is compatible with the country's new digital television broadcast standard (see Chapter 3, "Choosing Source Components: TV Programming"). Nearly all the projection TVs based on digital technology are compatible with DTV broadcasts, as well. TVs that use digital technology include projected LCD (liquid crystal display), DLP (digital light processing), and LCoS (liquid crystal on silicon). These technologies all share a number of attributes. For example, each technology uses a grid of pixels, fixed in place, to create the image. A light bulb provides illumination. The fixed-pixel system allows the digital TV to be much thinner than a CRT-based TV (which use a long electron gun to "draw" images on the face of the tube), but the digital TV is usually not quite slim enough to be mounted on a wall like a plasma or direct view LCD TV. One exception is Infocus's new DLP-based rear-projection TV. This TV uses proprietary techniques to make it only 7 inches deep. Infocus and RCA will sell TVs based on this technology later in 2004. Picture quality on TVs using digital technology is notably better than most flat panel TVs, and the digital image is not susceptible to burn-in like plasma and CRT products are. Digital TVs also have better geometry and corner-to-corner focus than tube-based products and remain exceptionally detailed throughout the life of the product. The only maintenance required is an occasional light bulb change.

There are, however, some general differences between the technologies. Projected LCD TVs, for example, might be less expensive than DLP or LCoS sets, but LCDs have a more noticeable pixel structure and a higher black level. Like flat panel LCDs, the projected LCD uses a grid of liquid crystals to create the image. A light bulb shines through the grid, projecting the image through a lens and onto the screen. Each pixel requires a certain amount of space around it for wiring and electronics so that the TV's processor can tell the crystal to be translucent or opaque. This means the pixels are further apart, which makes the dot structure visible and can seem like your watching the picture through a screen door. The opaque pixels also have a tough time blocking all the light, which makes a higher black level that turns deep shadows into a light gray. This can wash out and flatten the picture when viewed in darkened surroundings, but can make darker images more visible if you watch TV in a sunny room or with the lights turned on. Consider your viewing environment carefully when selecting a TV.

DLP technology, on the other hand, has darker blacks than LCD and brighter images than CRT and creates excellent contrast or punch. Texas Instruments (TI) created and licenses the technology to dozens of manufacturers. DLP uses hundreds of thousands of microscopic flipping mirrors to create the image. Each mirror represents a pixel. If the pixel should be bright, the mirror reflects light from the bulb through a color filter and onto the screen. If the pixel should be dark, the light for that pixel is reflected away from the screen. Since the light is not shining through dark pixels, blacks can be much darker than on an LCD. Only in a darkened room will a CRT's blacker blacks offer an advantage. The DLP's mirror pixel structure is also more closely packed together (called fill-factor) than an LCD, rendering it nearly invisible, though better tube TVs might still seem to have a smoother image.

Most consumer DLP TVs use a single DLP chip to create the image. Placing a color filter wheel in the projection path adds color to the image. The filter wheel might leave rainbow-like trails of colors behind moving objects and is visible for a small percentage of viewers. You may or may not be sensitive to it. LCD and LCoS TVs (and three-chip DLP projectors used in digital cinema applications and on newer, high-end consumer front projectors) don't have this issue. Most people will never notice the trails anyway. I don't.

LCoS technology is the most expensive of the digital technologies I've mentioned, mainly because it is the most difficult to manufacture. The technology is similar to LCD in that it uses a grid of liquid crystals that become opaque or translucent, but instead of having a light bulb behind the crystals, the light bulb is in front. A reflective surface behind the pixels reflects the light back to the lens and screen when the pixels are translucent. The electronics needed to drive the liquid crystals can be placed behind each pixel, so the pixels can be placed much closer together, creating higher pixel density than LCD or DLP (DLP still needs space for the arc of the moving mirror). LCoS TVs also deliver the greatest resolution of all three technologies. There are at least two LCoS TVs with a 1,920-by-1,080 (horizontal by vertical) resolution, matching or exceeding the resolution of virtually all high-definition broadcast television shows. LCoS black levels are good, too, though they fall somewhere between LCD and DLP performance. Several manufacturers have had a difficult time actually delivering these products, and often discontinue them before they even reached the sales floor. Product delivery might improve in the future. Computer processor giant Intel, maker of the Pentium series of computer processors, announced in early 2004 that it would begin producing LCoS chips and hopes to deliver where other manufacturers have not been able to.

Figure 7.4

DLP-based rear-projection TV, model Scenium HD61THW263, courtesy of RCA

Front Projection

When you really want a theatrical-style image, or just something larger than what's available from single-box, rear-projection units, you should consider front- or two-piece projection systems. The technology used in front projection is essentially the same as that used for rear projection, so be sure to read my descriptions of CRT and digital rear-projection TVs first. A front-projection TV uses a separate projector, mounted on the ceiling or on a coffee table and requires a separate screen. Though I refer to them as "front" projectors, you can configure any front projector to work in a customized rear-projection installation.

Three-gun CRT projectors offer the best picture quality, bar none. This quality comes at a price, though, and not just a monetary one. For instance, the viewing room must be completely dark and the image should be projected on a matte white screen with limited gain, or reflectivity. Also, the screen size should be within 6 or 7 feet wide to achieve the best quality picture. Larger screens just aren't bright enough. Finally, most CRT projectors require careful alignment by a qualified technician, often on a regular basis, which adds to the already high expense of the unit.

Figure 7.5

CRT-based front projector, model DTV-947, courtesy of Runco International

Single-lens, digital front projectors (LCD, DLP, and LCoS), however, are easier to install, set up, and maintain than three-gun CRT projectors are. They are more like installing a slide projector. Just plug in the power and the signal, focus the lens, and you're watching TV. Single lens projectors, like their rear-projection brethren, are capable of bigger, brighter images and need little or no maintenance compared to three-gun projectors. Differences between LCD, DLP, and LCoS technologies are similar to the differences described for rear-projection models. Gray matte or negative-gain screens are a good choice for these projectors, as they absorb some of the picture's excess light, which improve image contrast and makes the black parts of the picture darker.

Figure 7.6

Digital front projector, model HT500L, courtesy of SIM2

Projection Screens

Big images require big screens and the largest single-piece TV you can buy is 80 inches. If you want a larger picture, or want to create a custom rear-projection system, you need a front projector with a separate screen. There are three things to know about projection screens: mechanics, material, and gain.

On the basic mechanical side, you have a number of options. For one, if you can afford a few luxuries, buy a motorized, retractable screen. Retractable screens lift out of the way when not in use and can often automatically drop down when the projector is powered on. Tension mounting on the screen can help keep its shape over a long period of time. If you don't want to invest that much cash, though, you can save money getting a fixed-frame screen.

The aspect ratio of the projection screen should match the shape of the projector's native output, which is likely to be 16:9. Again, if you have some extra spending money, treat yourself to a screen masking system that drops black panels over unused portions of the screen depending on the aspect ratio of the image.

Most people will use a front-projection screen, but some of you might want to create your own custom rear-projection system. A rear-projection system provides a substantially larger and better image than the typical, one-box RPTVs you find in stores and can be almost completely hidden from view. This system is also much more tolerant of ambient light than a typical front projector. The projector in a rear-projection system can be mounted in a garage, closet, or spare room behind the screen wall, with nothing visible but the flat screen and frame. If you reflect the projector's image off of a mirror, called an image-fold, you can reduce the amount of space needed between the projector and the screen, but you will sacrifice a small percentage of light. Use a first-surface mirror, which has the reflective material on top of the glass, not beneath it, to limit the light loss. Regardless of how you set up the system, you also need a translucent rear-projection screen.

One of the more important decisions you'll have to make will be about screen gain. Gain refers to the amount of light reflected (or transmitted, in the case of rear-projection screens) from a screen material back to the audience. Manufacturers measure screen gain by projecting the same amount of light onto the screen material in question as a reference material and comparing the light output reflected from both. If the screen and reference material both reflect the same amount of light, the screen has a gain of one, which is referred to as unity gain. Unity gain is considered a diffuse screen, which typically reflects light equally in all directions. Higher gain screens, which are typically used in commercially available rear-projection TVs reflect more light than a diffusion screen, but the reflected

continues on next page

Projection Screens *(continued)*

light is more focused on a single spot. You will often see a hot spot in the middle of the image. If you're using a three-gun CRT projector, a high-gain screen also has a color shift based on the different position of the three tubes, relative to any viewer. The hot spot causes the brightness to change as you stand up or sit down while looking at a rear-projection TV. The screen gain might be necessary if you have a large screen, but the hot spot gets more noticeable as you get closer or further off-axis. A gain of 1.3 is typically considered normal.

A new breed of screen, called gray material screens, might help augment the black level performance of digital projectors that use DLP, LCD, or LCoS technology. Normal screens use a white material. Gray material screens reflect less light than the reference material, and are sometimes considered negative-gain screens. Gray screens help lower the projector's black level, which can improve contrast ratio. These screens also come in "Unity" gain and high gain varieties.

With a good screen coupled to a front projector, you will have an excellent two-piece system that will rival the local multiplex.

Figure 7.7
Front-projection screen with tab tension and black masking panel system, model Dual Mask with StudioTek 130, courtesy of Stewart Filmscreen

Screen Size

There are many conflicting criteria you need to determine the optimum TV screen size for your home theater. Screen size is relative to viewing distance, for one. A 30-foot screen viewed from several miles away can look minuscule compared to a 27-inch TV that's sitting right next to you. However, sitting too close to a large screen also makes the quality of the picture readily apparent. You want to sit close to feel like you're watching a large picture, but not so close that the picture elements become noticeable. After looking at the criteria, I came up with an approximate reference.

First determine the screen size based on the signal quality. The interlaced line structure in 480i NTSC signals, for example, can be horribly apparent if you sit too close to a large screen. Early studies by the Society of Motion Picture and Television Engineers (SMPTE) determined that sitting approximately three or more times the diagonal measurement of a 4:3-shaped TV makes the line structure not noticeable. So, if you sit 9 feet (108 inches) from the screen, a 4:3 TV should be no larger than 36 inches (See Screen Size vs. Seating Distance on page 136). Simple algebra says that if you're watching 480i material on a wide-screen (16:9) TV, you should sit about 2.5 times the diagonal from the screen. With a 9-foot seating distance, the picture on a 42-inch plasma or a 43-inch DLP rear-projection TV will look good.

No similar study has been done with HDTV signals, but personal observations and similar sentiments by other writers agree that you should sit 1.5 times the diagonal measurement from a 16:9-shaped HDTV to yield good results. You can sit closer to HDTV than you would with NTSC signals because there's more resolution in the HDTV image. So, using the above example, you will be happy with a 70-inch screen if you're 9 feet away.

Fortunately, a 70-inch screen meets the second set of criteria. A SMPTE study for movie theaters found that the movie screen needed to fill approximately 30 degrees of your horizontal field of view to be perceived as large. The movie screen only needs to fill 15 degrees of your vertical field of view. This equates, roughly, to a 16:9 screen size placed about 1.5 times the diagonal from your seating position and corresponds nicely with HDTV (As far as I know, this is a coincidence), but you'd be sitting far too close to watch NTSC signals.

So, while you can't sit too close to an NTSC image without noticing the inherently low signal quality, you can optimize HDTV. Unfortunately there isn't enough HDTV material being broadcast to watch it exclusively, so unless you put your couch or TV on a sliding rail that can move back and forth as you change from analog to digital TV signals, you'll need to compromise. If you plan to have HDTV soon, it makes sense to set up your system around HDTV and accept the less than optimum

NTSC image quality. If you don't see yourself having HDTV anytime soon, then you're better off optimizing the NTSC signal and realizing that HDTV signals, when you eventually get them, will still look great, but may seem relatively small.

Screen Size vs. Seating Distance

Distance to Screen (ft.)	Distance to Screen (in.)	Optimum Screen Size* NTSC image – 4:3 screen (in.)	Optimum Screen Size* NTSC image – 16:9 screen (in.)	Optimum Screen Size* HDTV image (in.)
1	12	4.0	4.8	8
2	24	8.0	9.6	16
3	36	12.0	14.4	24
4	48	16.0	19.2	32
5	60	20.0	24	40
6	72	24.0	28.8	48
7	84	28.0	33.6	56
8	96	32.0	38.4	64
9	108	36.0	43.2	72
10	120	40.0	48	80
11	132	44.0	52.8	88
12	144	48.0	57.6	96
13	156	52.0	62.4	104
14	168	56.0	67.2	112
15	180	60.0	72	120
16	192	64.0	76.8	128
17	204	68.0	81.6	136
18	216	72.0	86.4	144
19	228	76.0	91.2	152
20	240	80.0	96	160

*Measured diagonally

This chart shows you how far you should sit from the TV to perceive the best picture for various sources (NTSC to HDTV) and screen sizes.

What to Look For

SD, ED, and HDTVs

Your old TV is analog and receives analog format signals, which are referred to as standard definition, or SDTV. Your new TV might use analog or digital components to create the picture, but will ideally be compatible with the new digital television format, DTV (see Chapter 3, "Choosing Source Components: TV Programming"), which offers improved picture and sound quality. In this chapter on TVs, I'm referring to certain TV products as digital TVs because of the way the signal is received, not how the picture is created. Regular analog format, NTSC-only TVs are cheap, but they'll be obsolete long before they wear out. I suggest you go for DTV compatibility.

The real question is which type of DTV you should buy. DTVs are subdivided into two groups: extended definition (EDTV) and high definition (HDTV) and there's no clear winner. EDTVs have better vertical resolution than regular TVs (480 progressive lines, instead of 480 interlaced lines), but you won't see the additional image detail in an HDTV broadcast as you will with an HDTV, which scan as high as 720p or 1,080i. Many LCD and plasma TVs and a handful of entry-level LCD and DLP front projectors have EDTV resolutions and are almost always less expensive than HDTVs. Keep in mind, though that on anything smaller than a 40-inch screen, measured diagonally, you might not notice the difference. Plus, if you're only going to watch DVDs and standard definition satellite or cable, get an EDTV. With screens larger than 40 inches, and in areas where HD programming is or will soon be available, you should buy an HDTV.

Digital-ready vs. integrated DTVs

Until recently, the majority of digital TVs were sold without a digital tuner and won't, by themselves, receive the new digital TV channels. Without a separate tuner to get the DTV signals to the TV, you're watching regular TV, albeit on a high-resolution display. Manufacturers invented all kinds of terms, from "digital-upgradeable" to "digital-compatible" to describe TVs without digital tuners. "DTV-monitor" or "digital-ready" are the most common terms. A TV that includes the digital tuner is considered an integrated DTV or HDTV. In 2003, the Federal Communications Commission (FCC) mandated that all TVs include a digital tuner by July 1, 2007. Larger sets are required to have tuners at first, and as the deadline approaches, smaller screen sizes are added to the list. (See the table below.)

Unless you have or plan to have digital cable (see "Digital Cable-Ready" below), you're better off buying a digital-ready TV. If you have or plan to get a satellite system, most HD satellite tuners actually come with built-in digital terrestrial tuners. Also, prices drop and advances in tuner technology (like the addition of digital video recorders) are more rapid than with display technology. In other words, you might want to replace the tuner before you need to replace the display. You can always bypass the internal tuner, but why pay for it if you're not going to use it?

FCC DTV Tuner Adoption Schedule

Screen Size	50% of All Units	100% of All Units
36" and above	July 1, 2004	July 1, 2005
25" to 35"	July 1, 2005	July 1, 2006
13" to 24"	July 1, 2006	July 1, 2007
TV interface devices*	N/A	July 1, 2007

*TV interface devices refer to products that include TV tuners but don't have a display, like a VCR or DVR.

The FCC mandates that manufacturers begin to incorporate digital TV tuners into televisions according to the following schedule. *TV interface devices refer to products that include TV tuners but don't have a display, like a VCR or DVR.

Digital cable-ready

If you can get digital cable, you might want to take exception with what I said before and buy an integrated HDTV. Most new TVs are digital cable-ready. Digital cable-ready means the TV will receive over the air signals and will connect to any CableCard cable system—which larger cable companies put in place July 1, 2004—to receive basic and premium HDTV channels without a cable box. This system requires a credit-card-sized security access smart card from the local cable company (see **Figure 7.8** and note the small slot in the lower-left corner). If you move, you simply return the card and get a new one from your new cable company. The integrated tuner allows you to watch digital cable programming with the TV's remote control. But, you might still need a separate box, provided by the cable company, to view pay-per-view, video-on-demand (VOD) channels, or to get an interactive electronic program guide (EPG).

There's little incentive for the cable company to provide the CableCard, even though federal mandate requires larger cable companies (with 750 Mhz or greater systems) to offer them. Why? Because they can make more money providing two-way services like video on demand and electronic program guides that still require an external cable box. At the time of this writing, the CableCard system had just begun rolling out, but in theory, unscrupulous cable companies could suggest to consumers that they don't have any cards available. Smaller cable companies are not required to use the CableCard system.

Resolution

When a TV set is labeled as HD-ready, or HD-compatible, or whatever (See "Digital-ready vs. integrated DTVs," page 137), you know that the vertical scan frequency of the display will be equal to or greater than the resolution needed for high-definition signal formats. Horizontal resolutions vary, however. All things being equal, a display with greater horizontal resolution creates a sharper picture when displaying high-resolution images. But all things are not equal. Various picture quality elements, like black level, color fidelity, or brightness, can dwarf the differences between resolutions.

TV manufacturers used to "bend" the rules when describing their products' capabilities. Most analog TVs list horizontal resolution across the full screen width. Since a typical 4:3 screen is 1.33 times wider than it is tall, this means the horizontal resolution specification is 30 percent greater than it should be. Therefore, if a TV lists 500 lines of horizontal resolution, but doesn't specify that this is measured "per picture height," you should assume that the real resolution is closer to 375 lines, which might be adequate for videotape and broadcast TV, but you won't see everything a DVD has to offer.

Screen shape (aspect ratio)

Normal TVs are four units wide for every three units tall (also referred to as 1.33:1), and appear nearly square. HDTVs are wider, with sixteen units of width for every nine units of height (referred to as 1.78:1). HDTV programs are recorded and broadcast in the 16:9 format. The HDTV screen shape is also fairly forgiving to wide-screen theatrical movies (filmed with even wider aspect ratios of 1.85:1 or 2.35:1). (See "Anamorphic Explained—Or Why Wide-Screen Movies Need Black Bars," page 57.) You might see only a little black space above and below the movie image to make it fit the screen shape. A 16:9 TV can also take advantage of anamorphic DVDs, which have more detail than nonanamorphic discs, but require a wide-screen TV or 16:9 mode to keep the geometry correct.

The future of TVs is heading toward wide screen and 4:3 TVs are becoming scarce. If you watch mostly 4:3 shows (i.e., no HDTV), sports, and few movies, consider buying a 4:3 TV or the shows you watch won't fill the screen, leaving blank space on the sides, or the image will be stretched. A 4:3 set with a 16:9 mode option can accurately display 16:9 HD programs and DVDs with black bars above and below the image as well. If you like watching movies, particularly on DVD, and plan to get HDTV soon, a 16:9 TV is the way to go.

Connections

To get the best picture, run the video signals to your A/V receiver or preamp, and from the preamp to the TV. In some cases, where the video bandwidth of the receiver is limited and degrades the video signal quality, you might get a better picture by running the video signal directly to your TV. In either case, you should buy a TV with more connectors than you have components. What type of connections you need depends on what components you have or plan to have. You need at least one of each type, if not more, including composite (single-pin, yellow connector), which is used on most gear, and S-Video (four micro-pins an a round casing), found on better NTSC equipment.

DVD players and HDTV tuners use a connection that's a step above S-Video called component or YPrPb (three separate cables, similar to composite, but carrying different parts of the video signal) and sometimes RGB (red, green, and blue, with additional cables for horizontal and vertical sync). Some TVs use a single input for both YPrPb and RGB signals, which is fine, but make sure there's more than one. Also, some YPrPb inputs can only accept 480i, or regular DVD signals. Wideband component inputs are preferable, as they can handle 480i, 480p, and HDTV signals.

Digital-ready and integrated DTVs might include DVI (digital visual interface) or HDMI (high definition multimedia interface), which is the best way to connect to more advanced satellite and cable tuners. Both connectors carry the same video signal. HDMI also carries audio signals and some control communication. Integrated HDTV sets should definitely have at least one FireWire (IEEE-1394) connector, which allows them to send the digital audio and video signals to digital recording devices, like a D-VHS machine or HD-DVR.

Figure 7.8

Digital cable–ready TV back panel with CableCard slot, courtesy of Mitsubishi Electronics

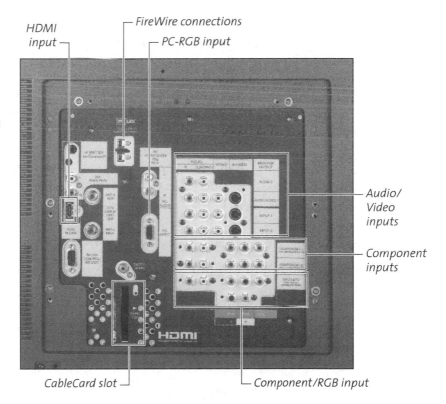

HDMI input

FireWire connections

PC-RGB input

Audio/ Video inputs

Component inputs

CableCard slot

Component/RGB input

Don't overlook your audio connections when you buy your TV. Make sure there are enough for all your components. Some HDTVs offer digital audio inputs that are routed to a digital audio output along with the integrated HDTV tuner's Dolby Digital output, which is handy. Other TVs decode the 5.1 signal internally, which is fine too, but I recommend letting the surround processor do the decoding. If you want an entry-level system, a TV with internal amplifiers and speaker level outputs gives you the opportunity to connect better quality speakers as you upgrade your system. Variable audio outputs go a step further and let you connect your TV to an external power amplifier and external speakers, for even better sound. You can use these audio options until you buy a surround system.

Light output and contrast ratio

TVs with digital components (LCD, DLP, LCoS, and plasma) typically list their light output and contrast ratio measurements. Higher numbers would be better, if I thought they were accurate, which I don't. Use these measurements as a rough guide, but nothing more. Like resolution, other parameters can make the light output relatively unimportant. Just trust your eyes.

Video processing

At this point, most high-end digital-ready TVs come with some form of built-in video processor that converts low-resolution 480i signals to match the scan rate of higher-resolutions images like 480p or HDTV. When done correctly, this conversion can make low-resolution images look good (though not as good as true high-definition images). When done poorly, images can appear worse than their original 480i format. The key feature is called 3:2 pulldown recognition, though different manufacturers call it different things. 3:2 pulldown recognition helps correctly convert material that originated on film and was converted to video. Film has a different frame rate than video-based material. Extra frames are added in a 3-frame, 2-frame sequence to maintain timing. If the video processor doesn't account for the extra frames, the image will break up or look jagged. For more details, see the section on video processors in Chapter 6.

Performance

There are two ways to judge the performance of a TV. One way is to buy a TV that accurately reproduces the video signal as the program producer intended. Finding a TV that does so requires some effort, but can be worth it in the long run. The other way is to just pick a TV that looks appealing. What looks good to one person might not look good to another, however.

An accurate display, or one that reproduces the signal as the program producer intended will look better with a wider range of programs than a display enhanced for certain images. So, if you want to get an accurate picture, do your homework, first. Audio/video magazines like *Digital TV* measure various performance parameters that consumers can't analyze without test equipment. These tests are more absolute measurements, like checking the TVs overall color accuracy and light output, for example, to make sure it meets industry standards.

A good magazine review will also help you find a TV that doesn't add unnecessary features, or at least a TV that lets you disable the extra features. These extra features are particularly prevalent on CRT-based models. For example, be sure the TV keeps the black level consistent, regardless of the brightness of the rest of the picture. Many tube-based TVs have a feature called black level enhancement, which uses the overall picture level to influence the black level. If a scene gets brighter, shadow images might disappear. Likewise, as a scene gets darker, shadows and black images might brighten. I call this an unstable black level, though most engineers refer to it as poor DC restoration. Manufacturers enhance the brightness intentionally to make the image more dynamic. Unfortunately, the image is no longer accurate. Test DVDs described in the "Secrets" section on page 114 make it easy to spot this feature. Look for a TV that has a black level enhancement menu setting that will disable the feature.

A similar function is called scan velocity modulation, or SVM. This enhancement burns CRT phosphors brighter in white areas, at the expense of definition in dark areas. The resulting image appears sharper, because midlevel details are slightly brighter, but upon close inspection you'll realize that fine details are lost. SVM also introduces severe ringing or ghosting around the edges, which is particularly noticeable with black lines against a gray background. If you want better detail, you'll need to disable this function. Most TVs use the sharpness control's lowest setting to disable the SVM. Some TVs disable SVM in the more accurate picture modes like Movie, or Theater. To learn more, check with the manufacturer, your TV's manual, or a good magazine review.

A feature common to both analog and digital TV technologies exaggerates certain colors. Sometimes called Flesh Tone or something equally as obnoxious, the feature boosts reds to make skin tones appear pink or boosts greens to create vibrant green grass. Since we often use these images, seen in nearly every program or sports game, to evaluate TVs, manufacturers want them to look "correct," even though the rest of the picture might be tinted blue (see "Adjust the picture," on page 147). Correct the rest of the image and the skin tones appear excessively pink or sunburned. If the TV can't disable this feature, you have to turn down the color control, which de-saturates other colors and make the image less vibrant.

It's a good idea to read a few digital magazine articles to learn about displays and their manufacturers. Once you've narrowed your search to a few models, though, check them out for yourself.

First read the "Getting Started" section in this chapter on display calibration. To legitimately compare various TVs, make sure the TVs are equally set up to create as accurate an image as possible. Turn off any "enhancement" settings the TV might have as your eye will be drawn to the brightest, most exaggerated picture. I've read too many buyer's guide articles that advise you to set the picture controls to the manufacturer's reset setting. Though this advice is well intended, it doesn't achieve its intended result. Manufacturers don't use a standard for these settings and the reset position is often not accurate. You are better off tweaking the controls yourself using a test DVD or movie as a reference. Or, you might want to find an ISF certified dealer at the Imaging Science Foundation website, www.imagingscience.com. The ISF trains dealers to calibrate TVs to get the most accurate image. There's a good chance the ISF-certified dealers have calibrated their displays so that you don't have to (see my description in the "Getting

Started" section). Don't be afraid to bring your own test DVDs and tweak the TVs controls yourself. The store can always hit the Reset button when you're finished, though the picture will probably look better if they don't. Mass-market retailers like Best Buy and Circuit City, however, don't always have a DVD player connected to each TV.

You should also compare TVs with as many different types of sources as you have at home. Don't let a store only show you pristine HDTV or DVD footage. Ask the dealer to put on a non-HD sports game or a "Seinfeld" rerun at some point. If you watch the History channel most of the time, see if they can tune in that channel. And feel free to bring DVDs from home (or consider buying some, if you don't have any). Using your own DVD is a great way to have a common reference point, particularly if you visit several stores.

What should you look for? Look for a TV that's bright, but doesn't lose detail in white areas of the picture. Clouds and shirt collars should not be big white blurs. Also make sure the TV can produce deep, dark blacks, which helps give the image a sense of depth and dimension. If the black parts of the picture are really gray, the image will look flat and washed out. The picture should have vivid colors, too, but not too much to appear unnatural. European flesh tones (to be politically correct) should not be too pasty or overly sunburned but will have some yellow in the flesh tone. You want a picture with good resolution, as well, which will make fine details appear sharp. And the picture shouldn't have any distracting elements, like video noise (snow, graininess, or speckles) or ghost images.

Ergonomics

Since your TV will likely be the main interface between you and the rest of your home theater equipment, make sure it's easy to use and that it has a few extra convenience features. For instance, it's handy to be able to adjust the picture separately for each input. It's also a good idea to have a backlit remote. And if you're planning to buy a flat panel or thin rear-projection TV, make sure you have space for your center channel speaker, because it probably won't be able to sit on top of the TV anymore.

Getting Started

Step 1: Connect the source components

How you connect your source components depends on how you've decided to set up your system. Other than connecting your cable signal or antenna to the RF input, you have numerous options that I've described in the Appendix. No matter what method you choose, you should follow a couple simple tips. For one, use a single input for each video signal type or source. For example, use one input for composite, one for S-Video, and so on. Don't try to connect two signals to the same input figuring you'll have one component powered off while you use the other because most video connections won't work like this, though there are exceptions.

Second, for performance, connect the best signal type for each source to the TV. For a VCR, that's composite video, satellite benefits from S-video but for a DVD or an HDTV tuner, use component or, when available, DVI or HDMI. If you route these signals through a separate receiver that lacks transcoding functions (see Chapter 6 on page 106), make sure you route all the receiver's various output signals to different inputs on the TV. In other words, if you have composite and component sources connected to the receiver, you'll probably need to connect composite and component outputs from the receiver to the TV.

It might not be easy to use a system configured as I've described, with multiple sources connected to the receiver, and multiple video outputs connected from the receiver to the TV. You'll have to switch the audio input on the receiver and then switch the video input on the TV. Many people use the signal type that's common to all the sources, which in most cases is composite video, to make things easier. If you only use composite video connections, you sacrifice picture quality with better sources (and won't get HDTV), but you only have to use one input on the TV. It's also possible to run multiple connections to the receiver. For example, you can run both composite and component signals from the DVD player to the receiver. This allows you to watch everything on the composite input for day-to-day operation, and switch to the component input to get a better signal when you want.

Step 2: Run a channel scan

With your new TV connected to the cable or antenna signal, run a channel scan. You'll find the channel scan function in the user menu under something like "Setup" or "Installation." The channel scan searches the TV signal for existing TV channels and adds them to your channel list. Use the delete channel function to get rid of channels you don't want.

Step 3: Adjust the picture

The most important step to get the best performance from your television is to calibrate the picture to match the NTSC or HDTV standards as closely as possible. To do this, you need some test signals for each signal type and often for every input. Use a DVD player and a test disc like Joe Kane Productions' *Digital Video Essentials* (*DVE*) or Ovation Software's *Avia* or *Avia Pro*. *DVE* has the advantage of being available in HDTV on D-VHS videotape. Both *DVE* and *Avia* contain tutorials on how to set up the display. The goal, after you've disabled any enhanced settings as described in "Performance" on page 143, is to adjust the six main picture controls: brightness, contrast, color, tint, sharpness, and color temperature.

Brightness, as the programs point out, is best used to adjust the black level in the picture. Raise the control too much and dark shadows turn gray, which makes the image appear flat and washed out. Lower the brightness setting too far, and you'll lose detail in those dark shadows. You need to raise the black level of the display to the point below where the darkest parts of the picture start to turn gray but above the point where you lose shadow detail. Test patterns on the disc make this adjustment setting easy to find.

Contrast, also called picture or white level, adjusts the peak light output of the TV. As white objects get brighter, the differences between light and dark increases, thus increasing contrast, or dynamic range. Contrast adds more punch to the image and gives it a three-dimensional sense of depth. When contrast is pushed too far, though, various distortions appear. CRT phosphors bloom, for example, which makes the picture lose detail, the phosphors burn up prematurely, geometry distort, and the picture sometimes change color. Nice, eh? Digital displays like plasma, LCD, DLP, and LCoS only get as bright as the internal bulb (or plasma phosphor, which reacts the same as a bulb). But as the contrast is pushed past the bulb's peak output, the rest of the image still gets brighter, which will "crush" whites, or make nearly-white images too bright, and totally indistinguishable from peak white images. Raise the contrast as high as you can without making the image distort and without losing detail in the peak white areas. Brightness and contrast are inherently interactive; more so on some sets. Go back and forth between the two controls until they're both correct, and then move along to the color.

Rarely, if ever on a consumer set (more often on professional monitors), will you find the color control called saturation, chroma, or chroma gain. Regardless, this control adjusts the color's intensity level for composite, S-Video, and component video signals, relative to each signal's black and white elements. RGB signals don't need color controls. Set the color level too low and you're watching a black-and-white picture. Raise the level too high and everything will look like a cartoon. Color is difficult to adjust without a reference. If you don't know what the picture is supposed to look like, you're flying blind. Color bars are the most recognizable test pattern and used to come on late at night when stations went off the air. You don't see color bars as much now that we have 24-hour TV, but the test pattern is available on test discs.

Tint also uses the color bar test pattern and is equally difficult to set without a reference. Also called phase or hue, the tint control adjusts the color balance or phase of composite and S-Video signals, which only have a single color channel in the signal. The tint control ensures that the picture's color is neutral, or does not favor magenta or cyan as it's decoded from this single color channel. There should be no tint adjustment with component, RGB, or DVI inputs, which have multiple color elements. Like contrast and brightness, color and tint are interactive. Go back and forth between the two controls to make sure the levels are set correctly.

It's possible to use the test discs to calibrate your TV and still find that the picture doesn't look that good. As I mentioned, many sets tweak the color decoder to push red and make skin tones on an accurately calibrated TV look sunburned. If you can't disable this color "enhancement," you'll have to compromise and lower the color control to a less exaggerated level.

Of all the controls at your disposal, sharpness, or sometimes called the detail control, has the least useful purpose and sometimes the greatest detrimental affect on the picture. On older TVs, when source material was processed by the TV's primitive electronics, what little fine detail that existed was lost. The sharpness control helped make up for that lost detail by artificially sharpening the edges of high-frequency signals or fine details. Most modern consumer displays, however, use more advanced filters that don't sacrifice detail. The sharpness control is now unnecessary and typically adds more problems than it solves.

Increasing the sharpness control too much distorts the image by adding white edges around objects, creating ghosts of images, or making noise and compression artifacts more noticeable. While the sharpness control rarely lowers the detail level to a point that actually softens the picture, it can occur on occasion. Usually, the lowest point of the on-screen scale is the accurate sharpness setting. Ideally, this setting eliminates any edge enhancement without softening the picture.

Many new TVs have an additional control called color temperature, sometimes more appropriately described as color balance. To create an accurate image, the system uses the correct amount of red, green, and blue. White, or various shades of gray in a video system are made of equal parts red, green, and blue. So, to measure the system's color accuracy, you can look at a white or gray image. The image should be a neutral white referred to as D6500 Kelvin, or roughly equivalent to the color of daylight. If the image has color, you know the TV is not putting out accurate levels of red, green, or blue. Most viewers see a blue white as brighter than a red white, so manufacturers tend to push the image toward blue. The color temperature setting lets you to pick a more neutral-looking image that will usually be the low, or warm setting. You can hire an ISF technician to calibrate the color temperature to make sure it's accurate if you'd like. See the "Secrets" section below.

I refer to the color of the white image as a "temperature" because the color of white is compared to the color of a particular object that's been heated to a particular temperature. As the object heats up to about 3,000 Kelvin (a scientific measurement of temperature) it turns a reddish-white, around 6,500 K it turns a neutral white, and above 9,000 K it starts to turn blue. Ironically, the highest temperature, which is closest to blue, is referred to as being cool, as in a "cool blue." Red images are considered warmer, visually.

That's all there is to adjusting your TV. The two test discs have more thorough instructions and specific tests patterns for each adjustment. Remember, you've been living with grossly misadjusted pictures for most, if not all your life. It will take a couple weeks to get used to the new settings. Ideally, your TV has a stable black level, an accurate color decoder, can disable various "enhancements" like scan velocity modulation, and, at the flip of a switch, go back and forth between factory and your carefully adjusted, correct settings. Now you can watch an accurate picture when you want to, and the grossly distorted one when you need to.

Secrets

Hiring an ISF technician

It might not be much of a secret that I recommend hiring an ISF-trained technician to calibrate your new TV. The Imaging Science Foundation trains dealers to tweak televisions and projectors so that a display will reproduce the most accurate picture possible. You can go to www.imagingscience.com to find a dealer in your area. Good technicians use expensive test equipment to help measure the actual color balance of a TV. They then access factory-level service adjustments that aren't available to consumers to make specialized changes to the image. This process includes adjusting the picture controls (brightness, contrast, color, tint, sharpness, and color temperature) as well. Prices for this service range from a couple hundred dollars for tweaking direct view and flat panel TVs, several hundred for rear projection, and up to a thousand dollars or more for calibrating front projectors. It can be worth it, though, to know your TV is performing as well and as accurately as it can.

Room environment

The room environment has a profound effect on your perception of an image. If the room is hot pink, an otherwise neutral gray image will seem the opposite of hot pink, and most likely appear a bit bluish-green. To obtain the most accurate image you can, the room, or at least the area in view around the TV should be a neutral color. You might not have to go to the extreme of painting the room gray, but you should definitely avoid extremely rich or vibrant colors. Lighting should also be controlled. Any light placed in front of the TV causes a glare on the front of the screen and washes out black levels and make it difficult to view the image. With front-projection television any light that falls on the screen limits the system's contrast capability. You should turn off any lighting in front of the screen to get the best picture. The room should not be completely dark, though.

Bias light

There's a simple trick you can use to make the picture look better and make the TV easier to watch; use a bias light. Once again, a SMPTE study looked at the effects on viewers of watching television in bright and dark rooms. Watching television in a totally dark room for any length of time was found to cause significant eyestrain. The relatively small picture is bright and causes the eye to dilate rapidly with changing content. SMPTE found that having at least some light in the room, particularly a diffuse, low-level light surrounding the area behind the TV biases the eye, which keeps it from rapidly dilating, eases the eyestrain, and improves your perception of the picture quality.

SMPTE was mostly interested in the effect of viewing on television engineers. In dark rooms, the engineers would have to take frequent breaks to ease the eyestrain. With bias lights in place, engineers could work long hours with little or no problem.

Placing the light behind the TV prevents glare on the front of the screen. It also helps our perception of contrast. Various articles by video expert Charles Poynton suggest that dark images set against an even darker background appear grayer than the same images set against a lighter background. So while the room should be kept mostly black, the area around the screen should be lit a dark gray. The color of the light should also match the color temperature of the image. Otherwise, the difference in color will affect your perception of the picture. If your TV is accurately calibrated, the color of the light should be close to 6,500 K, or daylight.

You can easily build a bias light for about $20. Find a small (6- to 18-inch, depending on the size of your TV) fluorescent light fixture at any hardware store. Then buy a daylight colored replacement bulb from a specialty lighting supply store. Finally, you need a theatrical lighting reseller that sells neutral density lighting filter. The filters look like sheets of dark-tinted, stiff plastic wrap and are available from filter companies like Lee (www.leefilters.com) and Rosco (www.rosco-ca.com). Cover or wrap the daylight bulb with enough filter material to dim the light output so that its output is no more than 30 percent of the brightest image from the TV. Place the bulb in the fixture and place the fixture behind the TV. Sit back and enjoy.

If you don't feel like building a bias light, or don't have lighting or theatrical supply stores nearby, you can purchase pre-assembled bias lights from Ideal-Lume at www.ideal-lume.com.

Figure 7.9

Bias light, model Standard, courtesy of Ideal-Lume (www.ideal-lume.com)

External de-interlacer or progressive scan DVD player?

Nearly all digital or digital-ready TVs upconvert 480i NTSC signals to 480p or higher. Playing back all signals at 480p or higher scan rates makes it easier to design the TV and, when done correctly, helps make NTSC images look better when compared to superior HDTV pictures. Unfortunately, not many TVs can upconvert the 480i signal very well, and the result is often a 480p image that looks worse than if it were displayed at 480i. If your TV doesn't convert the signals well, or if your DTV doesn't upconvert interlaced signals at all but it can handle the higher scan resolution of a progressive signal, using an external de-interlacer or scaler that upconverts NTSC sources will make a noticeable improvement in picture quality. At the very least, using a progressive scan DVD player improves DVD images on the DTV. For more information on de-interlacing, see my section on video processors in Chapter 6 (page 116) or the section on progressive scan in Chapter 4 (page 62).

8

Speakers

Your speaker system is the defining point of your audio equipment.
If your speakers don't sound good, nothing sounds good. You can
certainly degrade the sound coming from good speakers by driving
the speakers with poor electronics, and you can make the most of a
bad set of speakers with good electronics, but your system will never
get any better than the speakers allow. I'll talk about the various
popular speaker types, materials, cabinet configurations, and so forth,
but in the end the only thing that matters is sound quality. For the
most part, in this chapter, I'm referring to the front main speakers,
though most of the information applies to surround speakers and in
some cases even subwoofers. Look for the sidebar on surround
speakers and the separate section on subwoofers for more specific
information about these speakers.

A speaker consists of two active components, the crossover and the drivers, housed in a cabinet. The crossover divides the incoming signal into various frequencies. The crossover in a two-way speaker, for example, divides the signal into high and low frequencies. A three-way speaker's crossover splits the sound into three parts: high, middle, and low frequencies. This division of signals sends a particular frequency range to the speaker driver that is most adept at reproducing that range. Small speaker drivers, or tweeters, reproduce high frequencies while lower frequencies require larger drivers, called woofers. A speaker manufacturer can substitute multiple small drivers for one larger driver to handle low frequencies. In a three-way system a midsized midrange driver handles middle frequencies. Neither the two-way nor the three-way (nor the four-way nor the five-way) design is necessarily best. These are just different techniques that different speaker designers use to achieve the sound they want.

Figure 8.1

Speakers, model System 6, courtesy of Paradigm

The audible range of frequencies extends from 20 Hz on the low end to as high as 20,000 Hz (or 20 kHz) on the high end. Think of the range as the keys of a piano, the bass or low frequencies are on the left, the treble or high frequencies are on the right, and midrange frequencies are, well, in the middle.

LCR or main speakers

LCR stands for left, center, and right and refers to the three front speakers used in a home theater system. Unlike a typical music system, which relies on left and right speakers for the majority of sound, the center channel is the most important home theater speaker because the dialogue and major special effects are anchored to the on-screen action. The left and right speakers are used for additional sound effects that travel left and right and for the film score. Regardless of your focus—movies or music—try to get three matched, or identical front speakers whenever possible. For a home theater, the front soundstage, or the sounds that stretch out in front of you from left to right should be as seamless as possible. You want the sounds that travel from one speaker to the next to be consistent. If it's not possible to get three identical speakers, at least try to get a center speaker from the same manufacturer's family of speakers as your left and right speakers. Since the center speaker usually rests atop a TV, manufacturers often make them with the same components as their left and right speakers, but in a horizontal configuration. If you already have a pair of speakers and can't add a matching third, consider using your existing left and right speakers as the surround channel or in another room and buy three new speakers for the front channels.

Figure 8.2

A generic speaker layout, courtesy of Dolby Laboratories

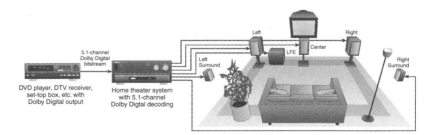

Surround Speakers

How many surround speakers you need depends on the processing capability of your surround processor and the physical layout of your room. If you don't have an EX/ES audio system or a form of 6.1/7.1 processing, you probably don't need more than two surround speakers unless you have a really large theater room (greater than 3,000 cubic feet). Likewise, if your couch is pushed up against the back wall, it's extremely difficult to add the EX or ES surround back channel without using in-wall speakers, and even with in-wall speakers there's a good chance your head will be too close to the speakers for the effect to work properly. At the very least, you need two surround speakers for a 5.1 system. If you have space and 6.1 or 7.1 processing, add a third or fourth speaker as appropriate. Just like with the front speakers, it's a good idea to match the four rear speakers. The surround speakers don't necessarily need to match the front speakers, but it's certainly a bonus. You also don't need full range surround speakers, which means you can use smaller speakers for the surround channel.

Figure 8.3

A 5.1 system has a pair of surround speakers to the sides or slightly behind the listener. A 6.1 or 7.1 system uses a pair of speakers to the sides of the listener and either one or two speakers directly behind the listener. (Courtesy of Dolby Laboratories.)

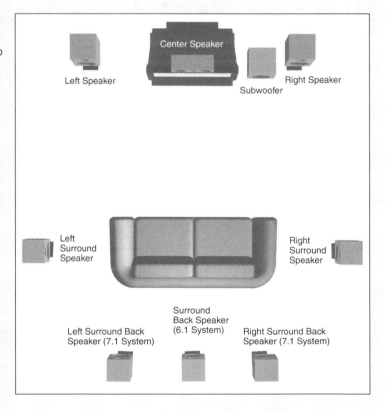

Surround Speakers *(continued)*

Next you'll have to choose between using regular, monopole bookshelf speakers. See **Figure 8.4** for the surround channels or for more diffuse designs see the section on "Radiation Patterns," page 160.) Some enthusiasts recommend monopole speakers because they can pinpoint directional surround effects, like the sounds of planes, cars, or missiles traveling from the front to the back speakers. The THX group, on the other hand, originally recommended using diffuse surround speakers so that you can create the same effect you get from a movie theater's array of surround speakers. The diffuse speakers also keep you from hearing where the surround speakers are placed. THX has changed this stance somewhat with the introduction of its Ultra2 specification, which uses two diffuse speakers to the sides of the listener and two monopoles behind the listener. THX claims that this arrangement, combined with added surround processing creates the best compromise between the two options. Some manufacturers have created hybrids of monopoles, dipoles, and bipole speakers (See "Radiation Patterns") with switches that let you change the radiation pattern of the speaker so you can enjoy some form of compromise between hearing distinct or ambient surround effects. I haven't extensively tested THX's Ultra2 system layout, but I performed several basic tests between monopoles and dipoles and found that I prefer the diffuse nature of dipoles and was distracted by my ability to localize monopole speakers. No one in the test group agreed with me, though. There's ultimately no right or wrong answer. Find the solution that works best for you.

Figure 8.4

THX recommends placing dipole surround speakers to the sides of the listener to create a diffuse and enveloping surround soundfield.

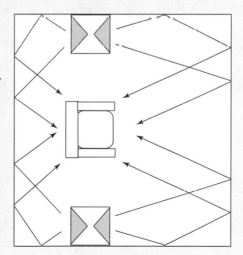

What to Look For

Radiation patterns

Most speakers are monopole, or direct radiating, which means they radiate sound in just one direction. Bipole speakers, on the other hand, radiate sound in two directions, usually front and back. Dipole speaker's radiation patterns are similar to bipole speakers except that the front and back halves are out of phase. This means that the two halves are exact opposites of each other. If you sit to the side of a dipole speaker, there's an area where the positive and negative sound waves meet and cancel. Speakers that use ribbon and electrostatic technology to create sound (see "Driver technology," page 165) are inherently dipole in nature.

Figure 8.5

A monopole speaker sends sound predominantly in one direction, bipole speakers project sound in two directions. Dipole speakers also project sound in two directions, but the two wave fronts are out of phase, and cancel, or create a null at the sides of the speaker. An omnipole speaker sends sound in multiple directions.

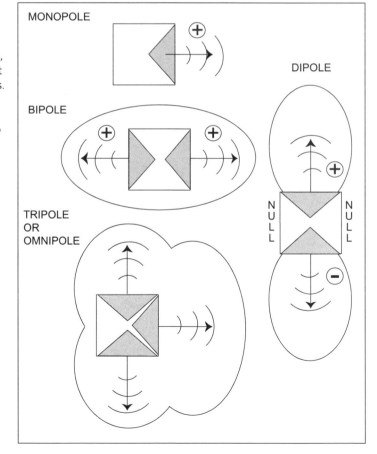

Typically, the front three speakers use monopole designs while surround speakers use either monopole, dipole, or a combination (see the sidebar on surround speakers, page 158). A number of manufacturers sell bipole and dipole front speaker designs to help create a more spacious sound-stage from the front speakers. Because bipole and dipole speakers rely on reflections of sound from the wall behind the speaker, if you have large, heavy drapes behind your speakers, these diffuse designs might not work as planned. Even if you have a flat surface behind your speakers, it's impossible to say whether bipole or dipole radiation patterns are good or bad. Direct radiating speakers will likely create a more precise soundstage, which is generally good for home theater, especially since the surround speakers add ambience to the sound. Ultimately, though, the only thing that matters is that you like the way the speakers sound and that they work for you.

Speaker types—satellite, bookshelf, and towers

The Dolby Digital, DTS, DVD-A, and SACD encoding schemes provide at least five full-range main channels and one low frequency channel. You might think that you need five full-range speakers to reproduce the signal but full-range speakers work well in large theatrical auditoriums because low frequency signals have time to propagate and the large space needs more bass energy. Low frequencies, however, can't be localized and are best handled by a dedicated subwoofer, which means you can use smaller speakers that have more limited low frequency, or bass response with a single, well-placed subwoofer to get good sound. That said, the front speakers should have decent low frequency capa-bilities, better than the other speakers in the system, so that they can blend easily with the subwoofer and have decent output (volume).

Your three main types of speaker are large towers, midsized bookshelf speakers, and small satellite with subwoofer speaker systems (often called sub-sat systems). Tower speakers come in large cabinets and have multiple drivers that generally reproduce the full range of audible sounds at loud levels. Some tower speakers add a built-in powered subwoofer and might save space and seem economical, but they prevent you from placing the subwoofer in a different position from the midrange and high frequency drivers, which can often be desirable for the best performance. Otherwise, tower speakers work well in a large home theater.

Figure 8.6

Tower speaker, the Salon, courtesy of Revel

Bookshelf speakers are smaller than tower speakers, with less deep bass in exchange for the lower cost and decreased size. THX refers to large bookshelf speakers as "satellite" speakers, mainly because the company suggests that the user add a separate subwoofer to augment the low frequency response. While I think THX's terminology is strange, I agree with its recommendation. Bookshelf speakers are an excellent choice for most home theater systems.

Figure 8.7

Bookshelf speaker, model XdS, courtesy of NHT

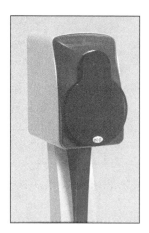

Bookshelf speakers are at least 8 to 10 inches tall and 6 to 10 inches deep so not everyone can or is willing to fit a bookshelf speaker in their room. Sub-sat speaker systems, on the other hand, are minuscule in comparison. The satellite speakers are typically inconspicuous 4-inch cubes or spheres connected to a separate bass module that is about the size of a desktop computer. The bass module is usually referred to as a subwoofer. This is a misnomer. The bass module is usually passively driven (it doesn't have its own amplifier) and replaces the bass portion of a large bookshelf or small tower speaker and will rarely have the output capability or depth of a separate, powered subwoofer. Sub-sat systems work surprisingly well despite their size, particularly in smaller rooms. In a larger room, the sub-sat system can strain to reproduce realistic volume levels and you'll notice its limited bass response.

Figure 8.8

Sub-sat speaker system, model SCS300.7, courtesy of JBL

A real subwoofer is a separate speaker, using one or more large drivers. It almost always includes a dedicated amplifier that's either built-in to the cabinet or connected externally. The surround processor's crossover restricts the signals going to the subwoofer to the bottom two or three octaves of the audible range (20 Hz to 80 Hz). The separate amplifier provides much-needed energy to these power-hungry frequencies, increasing their output. In comparison, full-range speaker systems must share a single amplifier's output across the entire range of audio signals. Since low frequencies are much less directional than midrange or treble frequencies, you can often place the subwoofer to the side so that only smaller bookshelf or satellite speakers are visible in the room.

Figure 8.9

Subwoofer, model DD-18, courtesy of Velodyne

In-wall/in-ceiling speakers

For the space and aesthetically minded, you will find solace knowing that flush-mounted or in-wall speaker technology (including in-ceiling speakers) has advanced significantly in the last few years. It's quite possible to find an in-wall speaker that provides excellent sound quality while at the same time preserves your room's décor.

Most in-wall speakers mount speaker drivers in a box-less baffle that mounts directly in a cutout in your home's plaster or gypsum board wall. The speaker uses the space behind the gypsum board and between the studs as the speaker cabinet. Unfortunately, the gypsum board is too flexible and re-radiates much of the drivers' rearward sound wave back into the room, which in turn muddies much of the system's low frequency response. Better designs hide a rigid "backbox" or speaker cabinet in the wall behind the speaker drivers. In this case, the speaker is like any tower or bookshelf model, except that the cabinet is made to fit in a 3 1/2-inch space (the average wall depth).

Figure 8.10

In-wall speaker, model 3.1, courtesy of Infinity

Driver technology

Speaker manufacturers use a number of driver technologies to create the sound they want. While none of the technologies are inherently perfect, they all have unique properties. Most speakers use cone and dome drivers. Cones are made in all sizes, from materials like paper, plastic, metal, and even ceramic. They are typically used for reproducing midrange and bass frequencies, with much smaller domes used for higher frequencies. An electromagnetic coil, called a voice coil changes polarity with the musical signal, which forces it to react against the magnet that's attached to the recessed center of the driver. This pushes and pulls the cone material back and forth to create sound. Domes are similar, except that the magnet rings the outer edge of the material, which is also inverted. Broad frequency response, reasonably high output capability, and great musicality are the main reasons for the popularity of cones and domes. They're an excellent choice for home theater.

The only driver technology that's more dynamic than a cone is a horn speaker. Horns, as the name implies, use a megaphone-like cavity in front of a driver to project more of the driver's output toward the audience. Horns are incredibly efficient and can play extremely loud with very little power. They are used predominantly in movie theaters and large-venue concerts, though a handful of companies (like JBL and Klipsch) make horn-loaded speakers for the home market. Horn-based speakers can sometimes sound less musical than cone-type speakers but horn-based speakers more than make up for the sound with dynamics, which is an important part of the home theater experience.

At the opposite end of the spectrum from horns are planar, or panel speakers. Generally, planar refers to ribbon-based speakers, though electrostatic speakers also qualify as a panel speaker and have much of the same qualities as ribbons. Ribbon drivers use a strip of metal placed between two magnets. The metal strip is charged with the positive and negative polarities of the signal. As the polarity changes, the ribbon is pushed and pulled between the two magnets. Electrostatic speakers are similar, except that instead of a ribbon, the drive element is an electro-statically charged Mylar material sandwiched between electrically charged grids. The signal is applied to the grids, which react electro-statically (instead of electromagnetically) with the Mylar material.

The sound from ribbon and electrostatic speakers is musically enticing. Due to the incredibly light and thin nature of a panel speaker's driving material (otherwise known as the diaphragm), the speaker reproduces musical transients extremely well. And since there's no speaker cabinet-ribbon and electrostatic speakers are mounted in an open panel, you don't have any interaction with the wood of the cabinet and the sound plays freely, both from the front and back of the driver, creating incred-ible spaciousness. Finally, the panel's large surface area restricts the radiation pattern so that, other than the sound coming from the back of the panel, the sound is directed almost straight at the listener, with less interaction from the listening room. (For more details on the importance of the listening room on sound, see Chapter 12.) Listening to music through panel speakers is a unique experience.

Unfortunately, panel speakers have their drawbacks, as well. Because of the delicate nature and limited excursion of the drive element, panel speakers are inefficient, which means they demand a tremendous amount of amplifier power and current to create reasonable volume levels. Even at a reasonable volume level, the speakers aren't capable of the dynamic range needed for bombastic movies. Since they're dipolar, panel speakers also lack significant bass response and must be paired with a subwoofer. Many are built as hybrid speakers, using cone woofers and panel-based midrange and high-frequency drivers. Panel speakers also require careful placement in the room to sound their best. And a panel speaker's extremely directional radiation pattern also creates a precise sweet spot for one or two listeners. While the system might sound great for that one person, it's not the best for the communal aspect of home theater. Even still, it's an awesome experience that's worth listening to.

Active vs. passive vs. powered

Active speaker systems, dominant in the professional music and movie industry, are rarely used in the consumer market with the exception of powered subwoofers. Presumably the added cost of the active components and amplifiers is prohibitive to the average consumer. The location of a speaker's crossover determines if the system is active or passive. A passive speaker places the crossover after the amplifier and uses the energy coming from the amplifier to drive the signal through the crossover network. The single amplifier reproduces the full frequency range of the signal, which lowers the cost of the system, but also makes it somewhat inefficient and less dynamic.

In an active system, the crossover comes before the amplifiers. In a two-way speaker, for example, the crossover splits the signal in two parts. Separate amplifiers are used for the high- and low-frequency signals that are then sent to the tweeter and woofer. This way, each amplifier can be designed to match the needs of the particular signal and speaker. The result is an incredibly dynamic system, but one that uses more amplifiers and places the amplifiers within the speakers themselves. If you use active speakers, you need to send the single wire line level signal from the pre-pro to the speakers directly instead of using the typical speaker wire connection. There are a growing number of active speakers available in the home theater market so if you're willing to deal with unorthodox connection schemes, active speakers are worth exploring.

While all active speakers are powered, not all powered speakers are necessarily active. Computer speakers, for example, are powered, but unless the amplifiers come after the crossover, there's no significant benefit to the system. The amplifier channel was likely just moved to the speaker, which may house passive crossover components.

THX certification

THX, as described in greater detail in Chapter 6, was started to create performance standards for theatrical sound systems and eventually migrated to home theater. The goal of a THX system is to faithfully reproduce the sound a film's director heard on the dubbing stage while making the film. THX certifies speakers in two categories: Select and Ultra 2. The main difference between these two categories is that Select speakers are made for listening rooms that are approximately 2,000 cubic feet while Ultra 2 speakers are designated for larger rooms. THX certification ensures that the main speakers offer a smooth frequency response, both on- and off-axis, and can play at theatrical playback levels (i.e., loud) without distortion. THX Select offers either direct radiating or dipole surround speakers. Ultra 2 uses two dipole surround speakers placed to the sides of the listener while two direct radiating speakers are placed close to each other at a point behind the listener. Ultra 2 surround processing uses various DSP techniques to make the two surround speakers sound more spacious than their placement might suggest.

Boundary compensation

As you place a speaker near a room boundary, you'll get a 3 dB boost, or a noticeable increase in volume of the low or bass frequencies. This boost can be used to your advantage and can be a hindrance, as well. If you need more low-end fullness or bass from a speaker, position it closer to a wall. If you need the speaker to sound clearer and less boomy, or bass-heavy, place it out into the room. However, if you don't have many options for your speaker placement and know that the speaker will be placed against the wall, you should either buy a speaker made to be used in that position, or find a speaker with a boundary compensation switch. The switch will cut or boost the bass depending on where you place the speaker.

Performance

The only speaker parameter that really matters, besides the way it looks, is the way it sounds. After all, the job of the speaker is to make sound, right? Assemble a collection of CDs and DVDs that you can take with you from store to store. These should range in characteristics from low key male or female vocal recordings, to dynamic rock or orchestral music. And don't forget the obligatory bombastic movie demo. If you play the same DVDs and CDs on several different systems, you'll get a good idea of how well the different systems perform. Here are a few things to listen for:

- You want a speaker that sounds natural, which is admittedly tough to qualify if you don't know how a recording is supposed to sound, but if you try a variety of music, you should be able to get a good idea of the speaker's effect.

- A sound system that covers a full frequency range, from the deepest low bass to the brightest high treble will be more appealing than one that's limited in range. You don't want to feel like you're stuck in an elevator listening to Muzak.

- The system should sound clean and clear, too, not soft or muddy. Dialogue intelligibility is extremely important when you watch movies. You don't want to strain to hear what the actors are saying. By the same token, you don't want it to sound harsh and fatiguing. And pay particular attention to low frequencies. It's difficult to have both deep bass and good definition at low frequencies.

- The left and right front speakers should create a good soundstage, or an impression that the music is occurring between and beyond them, both left to right and front to back. With movie soundtracks, this same characteristic helps sounds that are supposed to travel around the viewer smoothly transition from one speaker to another.

- The speakers should also *image*, which means that specific instruments or voices are clearly discernable at particular points between the speakers. Again with movies, this helps define sound effects that occur between speaker locations.

- Good music and movies demand excellent dynamic range. This means the speakers need to be able to play the softest parts of the soundtrack with finesse, yet still drive the loudest portions of the score without compressing or constraining the sound. All at the same volume level.

- The performance characteristics I mentioned also apply to surround speakers. In addition, the side and back speakers should create a sense of ambience and spaciousness. They shouldn't be glaring or call attention to themselves.

Specifications

Speakers are often quantified by certain specifications that can help you match a speaker system with your electronics. For example, speaker sensitivity tells you how much sound pressure level (volume) output you'll hear when you're one meter (just over 3 feet) away from a speaker driven with 1 watt of power. The greater the sensitivity, the less amplifier power you need to drive the speaker to theatrical sound pressure levels. See the section on amplifier power in Chapter 6 on page 102.

Sensitivity, measured in dB is more useful to know than a speaker's power handling capability. Power handling describes the amount of amplifier power a speaker can handle for continuous periods and is rated in watts (W). While power handling is important to know, it's not nearly as important as most people think. There is nothing inherently better about a speaker with 100W power handling capability than one that can handle 200W except that the latter speaker, in theory, can be driven with more amplifier power. If the 100W speaker has 3 dB greater sensitivity, though, it needs half as much power to achieve the same volume level as the 200W model. And if that isn't enough, there's no real industry standard for measuring a speaker's power handling capability.

Another useful specification, called frequency response, measures the speaker's ability to reproduce all audible frequencies at equal levels. Ultimately you want to confirm the manufacturer's claims with your own listening tests, but the spec is a good guide. Presented graphically, frequency is represented on the horizontal or X-axis with the sound pressure level output noted on the Y-axis. If the speaker's output level is equal at every frequency, the graph will have a flat line across the middle. This consistent output versus frequency is referred to as a "flat" response and will drop or roll off at some upper and lower limit.

Speakers rarely have a perfectly flat response, though. Variation is measured in dB from a baseline or average level. A response that's notated with a variation of plus or minus 3 dB is common and means the frequency response can vary as much as 6 dB from one extreme to another. If the response deviates from the baseline over only a narrow range of frequencies, it will be less noticeable than the same amount of deviation over a wider range of frequencies. Overall, though, less variation is better.

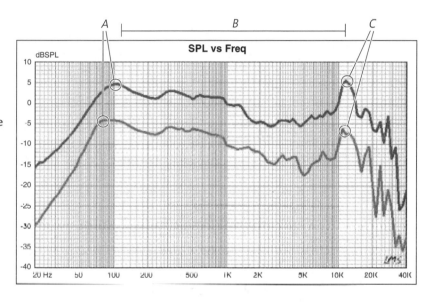

Figure 8.11

The graph shows the actual frequency response of home theater speakers. The top trace is the response of the left and right speakers. The lower trace (lowered for visual clarity) is for the center speaker. The peak at A (100 Hz), will likely give the system a bit more punch at low frequencies. The gradual decline in amplitute through section B, from 100 Hz up to 10 kHz, will probably make the system seem warm, or bass heavy, though the peak at C just above 10 kHz will give the sound some high frequency sizzle.

The frequency response specification also defines the upper and lower frequency limits of the speaker's response. Low-frequency extension is more difficult to achieve and determines how deep the speaker will play. This lower limit is listed as the cutoff frequency and is usually taken at the point the response rolls off or decreases 3 dB from the average or baseline level. The lower the cutoff frequency, the more deep bass the speakers will have. The slope of the cutoff is also important. A speaker with a gradually sloping bass roll off (like from what's called an acoustic suspension or sealed speaker) is still reproducing audible low frequencies below the cutoff point. These lower frequencies just aren't as loud as ones above the cutoff frequency. A speaker with a gradual low-frequency roll off can seem to have better low-frequency extension than a speaker that has a lower cutoff frequency, but has a steeper roll off (like what's called a ported, or bass-reflex speaker, or one with a passive radiator).

Frequency response is typically measured on-axis, which means the measurement is taken directly in front of the speaker. Off-axis measurements are also important, but are rarely noted by the manufacturer. Better audio/video magazines will report a speaker's off-axis response. The response will not be flat off-axis; it will gradually decrease at higher frequencies. The response should be smooth, though, meaning there are no significant deviations from the baseline level—other than a gradual high frequency roll-off—as compared to the on-axis response.

Getting Started

Step 1: Speaker placement

Setting up speakers is like solving a Rubik's cube. It's a great deal of trial and error to get to the final answer, but when it's right, it's right. The problem is that what's right to someone else might not be right for you. Keep fiddling around until you get the sound you want. To start, place the three front speakers around the screen, with the center channel on or near the TV. This anchors on-screen action with their accompanying sound effects. In a music system, the left and right speakers are often placed as far from each other as each speaker is from the listener. In other words, if you sit 10 feet from each speaker, then start with the speakers 10 feet from each other. You can bring the left and right speakers forward so that each of the three speakers is an equal distance from the central listener. Play some two-channel music and leave the center speaker turned off. You should hear a good, wide soundstage between the left and right speakers. If there seems to be a "hole" in the sound-stage, or a gap between sounds coming from the left and sounds coming from the right, move the speakers closer together. In a home theater system, unless you have a really large screen, this advice might still place the speakers too far from the edge of the picture. Bring the speakers closer so that on-screen action matches the location of the sound effects. If the system will perform double duty for music and movies, you need to find a speaker position that is a good compromise.

All three speakers should ideally be placed at the same height. The THX group advises that, if necessary, the center speaker should be no more than two feet higher or lower than the left and right speakers so a sound that travels from one side of the screen to the other doesn't seem like it's rising up or dropping down as the sound passes through the middle. In most cases, it's better to have all three speakers a little high than low near the ground.

Figure 8.12

Front speaker placement

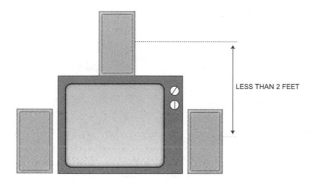

LESS THAN 2 FEET

The surround speakers in a 5.1 system can go any place to the sides, above, or behind the listeners that will create an enveloping sound field, or field of sound that surrounds the audience. Start with the speakers at the sides and slightly back from the listening position. Position them a couple feet above the heads of the seated listeners if you can. If you use monopole speakers, angle them across the room, not directly at the listener, so you're less likely to call attention to the sound coming from the speakers. If you want the sound to be more distinct, angle the speakers more toward the listeners. Test different surround speaker angles to see what you prefer. If the surround speakers are diffuse (dipole, bipole, or some other multidirectional radiator) position the speaker null, or direction with little or no sound toward the listening area.

In an EX/ES, 6.1, or 7.1 system, the side surround speakers will preferably go directly to the sides of the audience with the surround speakers placed behind the listening position. If you have an Ultra2 system, the two surround back speakers should be near each other. In anything other than an Ultra2 system, the speakers should be placed the same distance apart as they are from the central listener.

If the listening position is against the back wall, you can also position monopole speakers face up on the floor between the couch and the back wall. Place dipole surround speakers in the corners of the room, with the null firing slightly forward of the listener, or on the ceiling above the couch (firing forward and backward). If there's an L-shaped couch in the corner, place side surround speakers at either end of the couch, with a mono surround back or Ultra2 configuration in the back corner. There are any number of variations you can try. Again, there's no perfect answer. Be creative.

Figure 8.13

Surround speaker placement gets more challenging when the couch sits against the back wall. In the image on the left, dipole surround speakers are on the ceiling, with the null firing down. In the image on the right, the surround speakers are in the back corners of the room, with the null firing towards the center of the room.

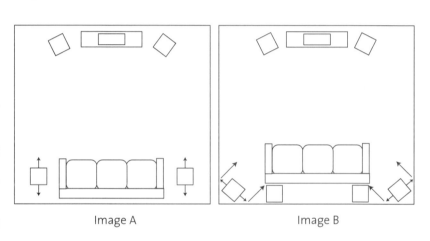

Image A   Image B

The subwoofer is omni-directional and can go in any position that achieves good bass response. This might be in a corner or along a side-wall. There are a few tricks to finding a good spot that I'll discuss in depth in "Secrets," page 176.

Step 2: Connect the speakers

Connect the speakers to the appropriate amplifier outputs. You'll notice the speaker wire has two conductors and that one of the two conductors is marked in some fashion. Use the marking to make sure you connect the positive terminal on the amplifier to the positive terminal on the speaker for every speaker. Do the same for the negative terminal. Always keep the amplifier turned off when you're making connections. I mentioned in "Check phase" in Chapter 6 that when you set up a 7.1 surround sound system you will make as many as 28 different connections between the speakers and the amplifier. That's a lot of connections. Don't be surprised if you wire a couple speakers backwards. Double-check your setup when you finish.

Step 3: Configure the surround processor

You're ready to set up your surround processor, which is probably the most difficult task in this whole procedure. You have to find out how the processor enables or disables particular speaker outputs, configures the system's bass management and adjusts the speaker output levels. This process might be as easy as pressing the "setup" or "menu" button, or it might be more cryptic. Check your surround processor's owner's manual for details. For more details on what adjustments to make and how to make them, see "Access the setup menu" in Chapter 6.

Secrets

Speaker and listener placement

Where you place your speakers and where you place the listener in the room will likely have as much or more impact on the system's performance as the quality of the speakers themselves. For one thing, as I talk about in "Boundary compensation," page 168, the closer a speaker or listener is to a room boundary, the more bass you'll hear from the system, which makes male vocals and other sounds seem congested and "chesty." If you or a particular speaker is near multiple room boundaries, like in a corner, you'll hear an even greater bass boost from that speaker. It's usually best, though not always practical, to place the listener away from a wall. But, if you have very small cube-like satellite speakers that lack significant bass response of their own, they will benefit from being placed near the wall. Larger speakers may or may not need the bass boost. If they don't need it, place them further out in the room. Placing a subwoofer near the wall or in a corner adds significant low-frequency energy while using less power to drive the sub, while at the same time you excite more room resonance. It's a matter of trial and error to find the right blend of bass boost.

Speaker placement and resonant frequencies

How your speakers interact with your room's resonant frequencies is another factor in the quality of sound coming from your speakers. At some point, half the wavelength of a particular frequency will fit into one of the three room dimensions of your listening space. These frequencies, called the room's resonant frequencies (room modes or standing waves), will build into peaks, or areas of excessive sound pressure level and cancel out into nulls, or areas of little sound pressure level, in various spots in the room. If your speaker is in one corner of the room and you sit in the opposite corner, all these peaks and nulls will stand out against the otherwise flat frequency response of your speaker. Different speaker and listening positions in the room energize certain resonances, but not others. Ideally the three room dimensions (height, width, and length) will vary, and won't be multiples of each other so that the room modes for each dimension won't be identical (see "Room Acoustics," in Chapter 12 for more details). No matter how good your room dimensions are, you will always have room resonances. You should place the speakers and the listener in a position that avoids or takes advantage of these resonances.

Room resonances can be calculated by dividing the speed of sound in half (1,130 feet per second, which divided by 2 equals 565), then divide 565 by a particular room dimension. In a room that's 19 feet long, the first resonance is roughly 30 Hz (565/19 = 30, rounding up). Subsequent resonances for this length occur at multiples of the first resonance (60 Hz, 90 Hz, 120 Hz ...). Resonances below roughly 150–300 Hz are the most important. The quality of the room construction can shift the resonances slightly, so it's always good to test the math results with a DVD like *The 5.1 Audio Tool Kit* and an SPL meter. Play the test signals on the disc and walk around the room with the SPL meter.

Resonances for any given room dimension occur at the outer boundaries of that dimension, near the wall. The null for the first resonance frequency occurs halfway between the two opposing walls for that room dimension. In other words, you'll probably hear a dip at about 30 Hz if you sit dead center between the front and back walls in a 19-foot-long room. There will be a peak in the center of the room at the second harmonic of this resonance (in my example, this will be 60 Hz). This frequency will have nulls a quarter of the way from the walls. The center spot will have another dip (90 Hz), for the third resonance, which has nulls one-third away from the walls, and a peak (120 Hz) for the fourth resonance, and so on.

Figure 8.14
This chart maps out room resonance peaks and nulls. Various positions in the room have sound pressure peaks at some frequencies and dips or nulls at other frequencies that depend on the room dimensions.

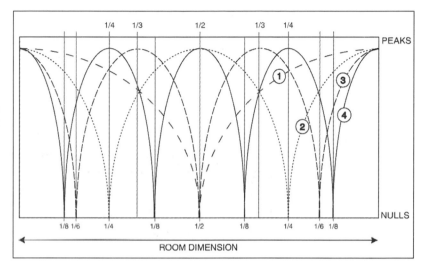

If, however, you energize the dimension's resonant frequency from the null of that frequency (the center of the room), the response at the peak of that frequency (the wall) should smooth out and equal the output of other frequencies. You have effectively eliminated that peak. Unfortunately, the speaker will now be at the peak of the second harmonic, which means that in my example, when I play something at 60 Hz the response at the resonant peak for that frequency will be even louder. Placing the speakers becomes a balancing act between one resonance and another.

The best speaker/listening position is where there are few, if any peaks or nulls. For a dedicated home theater, you might choose not to have a center seat at all, because of the number of peaks and nulls at that location. After all, the center speaker anchors sounds that correspond with the center of the screen anyway, allowing off-center listeners to still hear a good soundstage. **Figure 8.14** maps out the peaks and nulls for the first few resonances of a given dimension. As you can see, positions at thirds or fifths of the room's dimensions provide the least peaks and dips and seem to offer an equal amount of sound pressure for the majority of resonances and is certainly a good place to start.

When placing the listener at either the one-third or two-thirds length position, though, there is still a peak for the third resonance of the length. In my example, this peak would be at 90 Hz. So, I would place the speakers at the null for this resonance. The null would be at a position about one-sixth of the room's width away from the wall. (Nulls for a listener placed at one-fifth of the room's dimension will be about one-tenth away from the wall.)

Note that I've only talked about finding the resonant frequency for one room dimension. Once you determine a potentially good spot along one axis, you need to calculate a good position for another axis. The third axis, the height, gets tricky since there's often little we can do about how far our head is from the floor. You might have to adjust the speaker or listener position along the room's width and length to compensate. The bottom line is simple, in many cases just changing the speaker or listener position six inches in any direction can make a huge difference. Don't be afraid to experiment.

Adjusting speaker and listener positions based on room resonant frequency peaks and nulls applies to both the subwoofer and the main or satellite speakers. In fact, you should position the main left, center, and right speakers for the best possible full-range sound. Even though the low frequencies from these speakers will likely roll off—as the bass is usually directed to the subwoofer—the frequencies below the crossover's cutoff point will still be present to some extent from the main speakers. If the main speaker position interacts with a resonant peak in this rolled-off range, it can boost the rolled-off response to an audible level.

Improve your room's acoustics

I mentioned that below about 150–300 Hz, resonant peaks and nulls dominate the room's impact on the speakers' sound quality. Above this frequency, room reverberation and reflections become an issue. As sound emanates from a speaker, it travels in all different directions. Direct sounds travel in a straight line from the speaker to your ear. Reflected sounds bounce off nearby walls, floors, ceilings, tables, etc., and reach your ear a few moments later. Reflections heard 30 ms or more after the initial sound are detected as separate sonic events and add to the room's reverberation, but can obscure the initial sound.

Adding acoustic material to reduce, but not totally eliminate the room's reverberation level, will help preserve the clarity of the sound without making the room sound too dead.

Figure 8.15

Direct sounds reach the listener straight from the speakers. Reflected sounds bounce off room surfaces and reach the listener shortly after the direct sound.

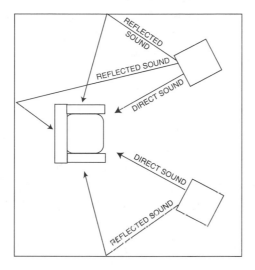

There are three types of acoustic materials you can use: materials that absorb, reflect, or diffuse sound. Soft, fuzzy, and/or porous materials absorb sound and transform it into heat through friction of the fibers or trap it in the porous cavities. Hard, flat surfaces reflect sound in a different direction. Diffuse materials are reflective, but redirect the sound in multiple directions at the same time. Many materials, however, can be both reflective and absorptive at the same time. A single layer of regular drywall mounted on 2-by-4 inch studs placed 16 inches on-center, for example, will absorb sound below 250 Hz, but will reflect frequencies above that point. One-inch-thick fiberglass will absorb sound evenly down to 1 kHz but less sound between 250 Hz and 500 Hz and almost nothing below that point.

Figure 8.16

Soft and fuzzy materials absorb sounds. Flat, hard surfaces reflect sounds while varied surfaces diffuse sound.

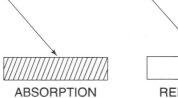 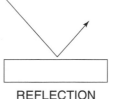 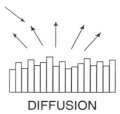

ABSORPTION   REFLECTION   DIFFUSION

Lining the walls with 1-inch-thick pressed fiberglass boards wrapped in acoustically transparent fabric is an attractive, common, and somewhat flawed approach. The absorption characteristic of a material is based largely on its thickness. The thickness determines the wavelength of the frequencies being absorbed. (See **Figure 8.17**.) An entire room filled with 1-inch-thick fiberglass will absorb a substantial amount of your sound system's high frequency energy (above 1 kHz) but has little or no effect on mid- to lower-frequencies (below 500 Hz) and makes the system sound dead at high frequencies, but thick and boomy at midrange and low frequencies. You want to control reverberation across a full range of frequencies, not just high frequencies. Thicker absorption materials (2 to 4 inches or more), thin materials spaced out a few inches from the wall, or specially designed low-frequency absorbers can help absorb sound over a broad frequency range. See the section on acoustic treatment in Chapter 12 for more details.

Figure 8.17

The absorption characteristics at various frequencies of Owens Corning 703 pressed fiberglass insulation

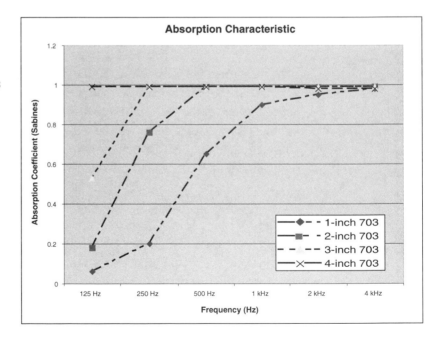

When you don't need more absorption (say, if you have thick carpet and a number of 2-inch or thicker absorption panels around the room), use diffusers. Any non-flat surface is a diffuser. Typically, diffusers are

made of collections of long slats or small blocks placed at mathematically determined but varied heights. A diffuser can also be just a curved or cylindrical surface. If designed correctly, slat or cylindrical diffusers reflect sound equally in a horizontal plane, while the small block diffusers re-direct sound both horizontally and vertically. A flat, hard surface (like drywall) tends to reflect sound as well, but reflects the majority of the sound's energy away from the surface at an angle equal to the angle that it hit the surface. By diffusing the sound in multiple directions, less energy is traveling in any one direction. The fact that there's less energy reflected in any one direction helps alleviate first order reflections (see "Eliminate early or first-order reflections," below) yet you retain most of the sound's energy level throughout the room, which is ideal. A stacked bookshelf creates a similar effect but only if the books are placed at varied depths.

To reduce reverberation, acoustic materials should be placed evenly around the room so that every wall has an equal amount of treated area. Alternate absorptive and diffusive materials so that absorptive material is across the room from diffuse or reflective material. Don't add too much absorptive material, though, or the room will sound overly dry and dead. See Chapter 12 on how much acoustical material to use. Eliminating early reflections, discussed in the next section, might dictate that some of the material be placed in more specific places.

Evenly placed and alternating acoustic material will also help eliminate slap echo, a zinging effect that occurs when sound bounces repeatedly between two parallel, flat, hard surfaces.

Eliminate early or first-order reflections

If reflected sounds arrive within 20 to 30 ms of the direct sound (called early reflections) and are not at least 10 dB lower in level than the direct sound, our brain blends the direct and reflected sounds together. When this happens, the brain can no longer distinguish the location of the source and attributes the sound to both the speaker and a virtual source determined by the point the sound was reflected from. This causes the sonic image to widen and become somewhat indistinct in addition to other problems. You can preserve the clarity of the direct sound with some carefully placed acoustic treatment.

First-order reflections are the early reflections that only bounce off one surface before reaching the listener. These are the easiest and most destructive reflections to find and to deal with. The most severe of these reflections come from the floor and the ceiling. If you absorb or diffuse sound at these reflection points, you'll help preserve the clarity of your speaker system.

The fancy way to determine what reflections will reach the listeners within 20 to 30 ms is with a CAD (computer aided design) program. Draw lines from the speaker to the walls then to the listening area, making sure the program keeps the angle of incidence to the wall equal to the angle of reflection from the wall. If you don't have this handy, multi-thousand-dollar computer program, grab a friend and a mirror.

As you sit in the listening position, have your friend slide the mirror along the walls, floor, and ceiling. At any location that you see a reflection of one of the front three speakers in the mirror, mark the point on the wall. These marks are the location of your first-order reflections and are where you want to add absorption or diffusion material. Intermix absorptive and diffusive material around the room. Add more diffusers to the back of the room to help the surround speakers create a more ambient soundfield. Alternate the materials as needed, though, to evenly reduce reverberation and to eliminate slap echoes.

Angle the speaker toward the listener

One simple, popular trick to fine-tune the sound of your speaker system is to angle or "toe-in" the left and right speakers right or left, respectively, toward the central listener. This will help tighten the soundstage image, or the impression that certain sounds are actually happening at a point between the speakers, and direct the most neutral, on-axis sound toward the listening area. If the sound gets too bright (has too much high-frequency sound), or becomes less spacious (the sound doesn't seem to extend beyond the outside edges of the speakers at all), reposition the speaker angle so that it's directed more to the outside of the listener.

Figure 8.18

Angle, or "Toe in" the speaker towards the center listening seat to create a more distinct soundfield.

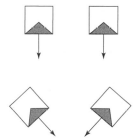

You can also angle all three front speakers up or down. The arrangement of drivers in many speakers often causes the best axis of sound coming from the speaker to aim slightly downward. Placing the speaker's tweeter at ear level, as many magazine articles and books recommend, directs the optimum sound axis into the floor. Having the speaker at ear level is good—it keeps the sonic image at the same height as the audience—but if you can't tilt the speaker up, try to move the speaker so that the listening position is in line with the speaker's optimum sound axis.

 If you have stand-mounted mini-monitors, you can flip them upside down so that the tweeter's on the bottom and the optimum sound axis is angled upward toward the listener.

Figure 8.19

Position or tilt the speakers so that the listener is getting the optimum sound. This may require the speaker to be tilted back or placed higher up.

IF OPTIMUM AXIS IS DOWNWARD

OPTION 2 - RAISE SPEAKER

OPTION 1 - TILT SPEAKER

OPTION 3 - INVERT SPEAKER

Full-frequency pink noise is a test signal found on test DVDs like *The 5.1 Audio Tool Kit* (not the band-limited pink noise generated by your surround processor, which lacks significant low and high frequencies) and is helpful when you want to find the best angle for your speakers. Play the pink noise through the speakers and have a friend change the angle (or move around the room) so you can listen to the speaker from different angles. Find the angle that sounds best and direct it toward the listening area.

Cabinets

It's common to hide speakers in a bookshelf or to build a cabinet around them. Think of how the sound of your voice changes, though, when you cup your hands around your mouth to yell. The cabinet has this same effect. To avoid degrading the sound of your carefully selected speakers, make sure the space behind the speaker is ventilated (not for transferring hot air, but to minimize cabinet resonances) and stuff the cavity with acoustically absorptive material like foam or fiberglass. If the speakers are hidden behind acoustically transparent cloth cabinet doors, and important sound design elements aren't integrated into the speaker grills (like foam blocks or a plastic wave guide for the speakers), you should remove the grills from the speaker.

Subwoofers

Subwoofers are so cool, they get their own section. Subwoofers add all the super-low-frequency oomph to a movie's soundtrack. They make music and vocals sound full and rich. They reproduce the deep, groaning roar of a spaceship engine, the ominous tones of a horror movie soundtrack, or even the thumping impact of a slammed door. Without subwoofers, movies lose their dynamics. You don't necessarily have to have a subwoofer, but you don't have to have a home theater either. Lest you think "oh, but I live in an apartment and I can't turn up the bass that loud," know that as the system volume gets more quiet, bass gets even more difficult to hear. It becomes that much more important to have a subwoofer to fill in those low-frequency ranges. If you want to have some fun, here are a few things to look for.

Figure 8.20

Subwoofer, model DD-18, courtesy of Velodyne

What to Look For

Price

Decent subwoofers will likely cost anywhere from $500 to $3,000 or more. Below $500, the subwoofer will be small and might not add any more low-frequency extension to your system than what you already get from your main speakers. As the price increases, so does the size of the woofer and the power output of the internal amplifier. Cabinet construction also improves with greater cost—the more solid the cabinet, the better sounding the subwoofer, usually. Performance-wise, more expensive subwoofers should have deeper low-frequency extension and greater output with less distortion. They might also add some room mode compensation or equalization.

Size

You used to be able to judge a subwoofer by its size. Creating deep, loud low frequencies requires moving lots of air, which also means needing large drivers, large amplifiers, or large cabinets. Designers have realized, though, that you can trade one of these characteristics for another. It's entirely possible to decrease the size of the cabinet (and the woofer), for example, if you increase the amplifier power.

A smaller woofer needs to have greater excursion and power handling capabilities to move the same amount of air as a larger speaker, but for the most part it works.

Parametric EQ

Given the unavoidable interaction between the resonant frequencies of the listening room and the low-frequency response of the speaker system, many installers and manufacturers are realizing the benefits of equalization. In short, equalizers alter the frequency response of the signal at the input of the amplifier to compensate for the room's effect on the output of the system as heard at the listening position. Particularly at low frequencies, equalizers can be beneficial, but typical fixed-frequency band equalizers have a limited capability to deal with low-frequency sound. Among other things, the peak resonant frequency varies from one room to another and the range of frequencies that are affected will also vary. One room might have a narrow resonant peak while another might have a much broader resonant peak. Even if the equalizer offers a level control at the exact frequency that needs adjustment, it's unlikely that the control will cover the full range of effected frequencies.

Enter the parametric EQ. A parametric EQ has three controls for each frequency band that it affects. One control adjusts the output level at a given frequency. Another control adjusts the frequency that is affected. This adjustment means you can dial in exactly the frequency you need to change. Last but not least, the parametric EQ offers a bandwidth control, which increases or decreases the range of frequencies that are affected by the output level control. This combination of adjustments gives you the ability to deal with the most troublesome of resonant frequencies.

A number of the better subwoofers on the market include at least one and in some cases as many as three bands of parametric equalization to help tame unwieldy room resonance peaks. These subwoofers typically include some sort of CD with test signals and an SPL meter specifically calibrated for those test signals. It doesn't take much for an enthusiastic and patient user (or well-compensated dealer) to get the system up and running and sounding great.

You can lower the level of a room's resonant peaks and can increase dips in the subwoofer's own response. You can't increase the level of a room-induced null. The null is a point in space where sound cancels itself out. Adding additional energy will just increase the amount of sound that's cancelled. You are better off moving the speaker to a point where there are few, if any nulls, and deal with the peaks using an EQ.

Getting Started

Step 1: Position the subwoofer

The tricks discussed in the "Secrets" section of Chapter 7 apply equally to subwoofers. Low-frequency sounds are omni-directional, which means you can't really tell where they are coming from. Omni-directional sound allows much greater placement flexibility than with your main or satellite speakers. Placing the subwoofer close to the room's boundaries boosts the speaker's output, but also accentuates certain room resonant frequencies. Use the steps described in the speaker section to smooth out these resonant peaks and nulls. It sometimes takes lots of trial and error before you find the perfect spot for your subwoofer. Don't forget to adjust the subwoofer output level every time you move the subwoofer.

Step 2: Connect and configure the surround processor

At this point, you should be an expert at setting up your surround processor and there's a good chance you've already configured the speaker settings for the subwoofer. If you're not sure if you have configured the settings, double-check. In most cases, the main speakers should be set to small or should have a crossover setting of about 80 Hz. Check to make sure the subwoofer output is also enabled. Connect the subwoofer to the surround processor with a line level cable and connect the subwoofer to an electrical outlet.

Step 3: Adjust the subwoofer level

The trickiest part of setting up a subwoofer is adjusting the output level. It's helpful if the surround processor has a test tone signal that cycles through the various speakers, including the subwoofer. If so, measure the subwoofer's output level by ear or with a sound pressure level meter and adjust it to be at the same level as the other speakers for now. You'll likely find that this level sounds good for music, but might be too low for movie soundtracks. Play a few selections from your favorite DVDs (modern day action scenes typically have plenty of deep bass) and fine-tune the output level.

Use the controls on the surround processor to adjust the subwoofer's output level. Leave the sub's output level control at a midpoint or 12 o'clock position on its dial. If the subwoofer has an input labeled THX, a switch for THX/normal, or a setting on its volume knob for THX output level, use the THX option. If you run out of range on the surround processor output control, there's a good chance something is not functioning properly. If everything checks out OK, re-adjust the subwoofer's control to increase or decrease the output as needed.

If your surround processor doesn't run the internal test signal through the subwoofer output you can use the test signals found on DVDs like *The 5.1 Audio Tool Kit, Avia,* or *Digital Video Essentials* instead. Otherwise, your only choice is to play a few movies and adjust the level by ear.

Secrets

Measure your subwoofer's frequency response

You can easily measure the frequency response of your subwoofer's output with a test CD (*Stereophile* magazine sells a number of them) and a sound pressure level meter. Play the test tones from the disc and measure the output level with the SPL meter. Write down the frequency being played from the disc and the level (in decibels) indicated on the meter. Just play the subwoofer at a reasonable level, it doesn't really matter what specific reading you get on the meter. What matters is how the level at one frequency compares with the levels at other frequencies. Once you have the results at every frequency from 20 Hz to 120 Hz, plot it out on graph paper, using the horizontal (X) axis for frequency, and the vertical (Y) axis for level.

If you're using a Radio Shack meter, be sure to use the C weighted response and know that the meter is less accurate at lower frequencies.

SPL meters sold by Gold Line and others are more accurate at lower frequencies. Using a CD and an SPL meter isn't an exact measurement, but it costs less than fifty bucks (or even a couple hundred bucks with a Gold Line meter) and can give you a close approximation to what might otherwise cost several thousand dollars for a more precise measurement. The information you get tells you a great deal about the strengths and weaknesses of your listening room, which will help you make quantitative changes. Note that if you move to a different position, you might get a dramatically different frequency response measurement, but at least you'll be able to "see" what the differences are.

Multiple subs

If you have a large room, or want to get a smoother bass response from your system, you can add a second subwoofer. An additional subwoofer increases your bass output by 3 dB, which would otherwise require twice as much amplifier power. If you can't get a single subwoofer to provide a reasonably flat frequency response, you can use the second sub to cancel out or fill in some of the peaks and nulls created by the first subwoofer. Getting a smooth response takes a fair amount of trial and error or measurement equipment. Find a dealer that can help you.

If you really want to go nuts, research directed by Dr. Floyd Toole, VP of Engineering and conducted by Todd Welti at Harman International (manufacturer of the JBL, Infinity, and Revel loudspeaker brands) determined that you can achieve a nearly flat low-frequency response using four strategically placed subwoofers. Each subwoofer is placed at a midpoint of each sidewall, which tends to cancel most, if not all standing waves. You can find Mr. Welti's research paper at www.harman.com under "white papers."

Adjust crossover settings

The line level input to a subwoofer usually offers an adjustable low-pass filter to eliminate unwanted high frequencies from the signal. Most surround processors however, have already filtered out the high-frequency sounds before sending the signal to the subwoofer. Duplicating the low-pass filter in the subwoofer, called cascading filters, can increase the roll-off slope at the upper end of the subwoofer frequency response, which will lower the output at those frequencies and can prevent the subwoofer from properly blending with the satellite speakers. Most good subwoofers have a direct or bypass input, or a switch that disables the internal crossover, so that the subwoofer doesn't add the additional filter in the signal path.

If there's a large peak in your system's low-frequency response near the crossover frequency, try different crossover points on the surround processor. You might even enable the subwoofer's crossover to cascade the filters and create steeper slopes. Adjust the two crossovers (in the surround processor and the subwoofer) to create a slight dip in response between the subwoofer and satellite speakers that the peak can fill in.

Check phase

Many subwoofers offer a phase control that can make subtle improvements to the system's response if the subwoofer and the main speaker are not equal distances from the listener. (It's also entirely possible that either your main amp or your subwoofer amp inverts the phase of the signal.) Play a test signal from one of the CDs or DVDs that I've mentioned that matches your surround processor's crossover setting. Measure the output of both the subwoofer and the satellite speakers at that frequency. Adjust the phase control to the point that provides the loudest response at that frequency.

9

Remote
Controls

By far the most important component in your home theater is the remote control, also known as the user interface. No matter how technically advanced your home theater is, if you can't use it, you've wasted a great deal of money. Remotes might not be as sexy nor as exciting as a big-screen TV, surround sound, or a stack of subwoofers, but the remote can improve your system's performance just by selecting the appropriate surround processing mode or video input. You should be prepared to spend anywhere from $300 to $10,000 and up, depending on the cost and complexity of your system, for a remote control system that will make your home theater simple to use.

Since different remotes require different installation techniques, some of which are proprietary to a particular manufacturer and will more than likely require a custom installation professional, this chapter doesn't include a "Getting Started" section. I'll cover a few remote basics in the "What to Look For" section, and I'll cover a few "Secrets" later in the chapter.

What to Look For

Price

Like so many things, increasing the amount of money you spend on a remote generally gets you more functionality and simpler operation. You might already have a universal remote. Most TV, VCR, and surround processor remotes are preprogrammed to control other functions. If your system consists of only a few components and everything is connected to the TV, your remote or one like it ($20 to $100, depending on the number of devices the remote will control) may be all you need to eliminate some coffee-table clutter. Hopefully this remote has some global commands to make your life easy.

Figure 9.1

Programmable remote control, model C9800i, courtesy of Philips

If your system includes multiple components and you need to switch video inputs on the TV and audio inputs on the surround processor, then get a universal remote with macro functions. Universal remotes can cost anywhere from $200 to $500. More expensive units are usually programmed using a computer, which can make the process much easier. I'll describe macro functions in greater detail later in this chapter, but macro functions are an important step toward automating your system.

If you spend between $500 and $2,000, you can replace the standard handheld remote with a more elegant and programmable touch-panel remote. Touchpanels are touch-sensitive LCD screens that use customized "soft" buttons or a combination of soft and hard buttons (see "Programmable touchpanels," on page 197) to access various functions. These buttons offer far greater flexibility in designing a system that's both functional and easy to use.

From about $1,500 up, you enter the realm of computer-based automation systems, which are like universal remotes on steroids. The remote itself, likely a touch panel, sends signals to a computer, which is connected to and controls the various components in the system, as well as other functions like lighting, drop-down motorized screens, projector lifts, drapes, heating, ventilation and air-conditioning (HVAC), and more. A computer-based automation system can control everything connected to an electrical outlet. If the concept behind movies like *The Matrix* or *Terminator* scare you, you might not want an automation system.

IR vs. RF

There are two forms of remote control communication, IR (infrared) and RF (radio frequency). Most remotes use IR signals, which are inexpensive and easy to implement. When you press a button, the remote sends a beam of infrared light that transmits the button's command to an IR receiver on the component. IR signals must have an unobstructed line of sight between the remote and the receiver. If anything blocks the light path, or if the remote is facing the wrong direction, the IR signal will not reach the IR receiver.

Radio frequency signals, on the other hand, travel through almost any object to deliver the signal. RF signals require an antenna on the component to receive the signal. As enticing as an RF remote might be, it's nearly impossible to teach a centralized remote RF commands. IR commands are much easier to work with. Better systems use proprietary RF communication between a custom-designed touchpanel and a control box. When you select a function on the touchpanel, the command is sent to the panel's control box via RF signals. The control box then sends IR commands to your equipment.

IR accessories

As restrictive as IR signals might seem, there are a number of accessories that make IR-based remotes more flexible. The biggest addition to your IR remote should be a combination of IR receivers and IR flashers to transmit IR signals around barriers. An IR receiver the size of a pushpin sits on top of your equipment cabinet and captures IR commands from your remote. These signals are then sent to one or more IR flashers that sit in front of your equipment behind cabinet doors or in another room altogether, and relay the commands.

You can even use RF injectors to insert the IR signals captured through an IR receiver, into an RF TV cable. An IR-RF splitter at the opposite end of the cable can separate the IR signal from the TV signal and send the IR signal to the necessary component via the IR flasher.

Universal remotes

The least expensive control system uses a simple universal remote, which controls multiple items, and is often included with better surround processors and digital televisions. A universal remote uses a switch or has a number of buttons on the remote that change the button's functions to control different devices. For example, when you select the remote's TV mode (either by pressing the "TV" button or sliding a switch to the TV slot), the remote will change TV channels, inputs, or menu settings. Switch the remote to the VCR mode and the same buttons will control functions on the VCR. With this simple switch you can eliminate the many remotes that litter your coffee table.

Global commands

A typical drawback to simple universal remotes is that you often want to control different devices at the same time. You might want to change channels on the TV, for example, but control the volume through the surround receiver. Having to switch back and forth between modes on the remote can be as cumbersome as using two different remotes in the first place. Better universal remotes offer global buttons. You can assign global buttons to certain functions that won't change, regardless of the mode. With this feature you can assign the volume up and down buttons to the surround processor volume up and down function, for example, even if the remote is in the TV or VCR mode. If the remote lacks global commands, but has learning functions, you might be able to program the remote to do the same thing, as I discuss in the next section.

Preprogrammed vs. learning remotes

The VCR, TV, and universal remote don't have to be from the same manufacturer for a universal remote to work. The remote can either call up the functions from a preprogrammed database of IR codes or you can teach it manually. Most universal remotes have a preprogrammed database. You can look up your components by make and model type in an index provided by the remote manufacturer. The index gives you a code that you enter into the universal remote. The remote uses its internal memory to call up the remote functions it needs to control your device. IR codes are small and manufacturers often repeat codes from one device to another. A good universal remote can therefore store codes for hundreds of devices. In some cases you might have to try different codes to find the right set for your equipment, but there's usually something that works.

 Check the index of preprogrammed remote codes in a universal remote before you buy. The more mainstream your existing components are, the more likely they'll appear in the list. Esoteric high-end or generic-brand gear might not be listed.

More advanced remotes combine the preprogrammed codes with a learning function. Learning remotes include an IR receiver that reads incoming IR codes and stores them within the remote's memory. Press a button on your component's remote and then press the corresponding button on the universal remote to "learn" the command. Learning remotes cost a bit more because of the additional IR receiver, but can control components manufactured after the remote's preprogrammed database has been stored into its memory.

 Use the learn function to create global commands. Assign the universal remote's volume up and down buttons, for example, to control the volume of the surround processor for every component mode on the remote.

Macro functions

The most important feature on a higher-end universal remote or automation system is the macro function. In any home theater system, you often need to change a number of components to activate a certain function. Making these changes with a regular universal remote can be just as cumbersome as using the separate remotes for each device. A macro is a single button press that activates a string of commands that can include all of the actions necessary to enable a particular function. To play a DVD, for example, a macro button can turn on the TV and change the input to Video 3; turn on the surround processor and select the DVD input, then turn on the DVD player, and play the movie. It can even include commands like selecting the anamorphic aspect ratio and Dolby Digital with THX enhancement surround processing as defaults.

In order for the macro to work on an IR-based remote, however, two things must occur. First, you must point the remote at the equipment the entire time the macro string is being transmitted. If you press the macro button, then wave the remote around the room like a light saber, the line of sight connection to the equipment will be disrupted. Some commands won't reach their intended component, and you'll activate some functions but not others. A remote that uses RF signals to transmit the command string to the remote's main control box, which then resends the appropriate IR commands to the equipment, can avoid this problem.

Secondly, the macro must either know (or be able to guess) the initial state of the components, or must transmit discrete commands that won't disturb the component's current state. For example, some components only have toggle controls for certain functions. A toggle is a single command that performs different functions, like power on/off, depending on the state of the component. If a TV is off, for example, a single power button toggle turns it on. If the TV is already on, the same button turns it off.

If you program a toggle command into a macro that's intended to turn on the TV, the TV must be off for the macro to work. In the previous example, the disrupted macro can cause some components to turn on and others to turn off. If any of these devices use toggle power controls, the system will be "out of sync." Since you could have now turned on the TV but not turned on the receiver, repeating the macro command will turn the TV off and the receiver on. Any discrete "on" commands, not toggles, will be ignored by components that are already on. Preferably, all your components will have discrete commands (e.g., separate commands for on and off, as well as for each available input, aspect ratio, picture mode, or other function). If your components don't have discrete commands, make sure the system is in a consistent state before engaging the macro.

Figure 9.2

Programmable remote with macro functions, model 688, courtesy of Harmony Remotes

Programmable touchpanels

The buttons on the face of a universal remote limit the remote's ease of use. By the time you have enough buttons to control all the functions for all your components, you might have 20 or more buttons on the unit. Even then, you probably won't have enough buttons to control every function available on a component's standard remote. And if there are enough buttons, the likelihood that those buttons will have discernable names is minimal. You need a programmable touchpanel.

A programmable touchpanel allows you (or your installer) to use a computer program to create and design the look of the remote's soft buttons. Soft buttons are drawn on the touchpanel screen and react when pressed. You can design and access different screens with different arrangements of buttons of different sizes for each component. (Each screen is called a page.) You can put the common functions your family needs on the main menu page and place the more advanced controls you want to access in deeper, less accessible pages.

Better touchpanels also have hard buttons, which are like the buttons on any remote, and are fixed in placed. Hard buttons provide great tactile feel for controls like channel up and down and volume up and down that you want to access without looking at the remote or without activating the touchpanel's backlight.

Figure 9.3a

Computer-based automation system control box, model ST-CP, courtesy of Crestron Electronics

Figure 9.3b

Computer-based automation system touchpanel, model ST-1550C, courtesy of Crestron Electronics

RS-232

Advanced control systems use a communication protocol called RS-232 to communicate between the equipment and the controller. RS-232 uses a 9-pin computerlike connection to link to the component. The RS-232 controls often provide more discrete component functions not found on the remote. It can also give feedback to the control system about the state of the component so that the remote control will know exactly what commands to send to the component.

Figure 9.4

RS-232 connection, courtesy of Mitsubishi Electronics

Secrets

Programming macros with toggle controls

In some cases, even though a device uses toggle controls for certain functions, you can still program a macro that will work, regardless of the state of the component. For example, some DVD players automatically turn on if you press Play. And if the DVD player is already on, it won't turn off. You can use a macro to turn on the unit, even if the unit doesn't have discrete on and off commands. Also, if a TV remote uses a single input button to cycle through the TV's various video inputs, it can be difficult to create a macro that will get you to the DVD input every time you want to play a DVD. You can program the macro to enter the input command two times, for example, to cycle through to the second input, but this macro assumes you're on the TV tuner to begin with. If someone had been watching another video source earlier, and the TV is on Video 3, your two input commands will cycle the TV input to the wrong input. Many TVs, however, automatically go to the TV tuner when you press the Channel Up or Down button. If you add a channel up or down command to your macro string before sending the input command, you'll know that the TV will start from the TV tuner each time.

You also need to know how a component that doesn't have discrete on and off commands reacts when the power is disconnected. If a component doesn't need constant power, you can use a number of tricks to switch off the components power when you shut down the system so you'll at least know the system is off. Some components remain off even when the power is reapplied. When you power on this type of component, you'll know you need to send the power toggle command to activate the unit.

One way to disable the power to a component is to connect it to the switched electrical outlets on an audio/video receiver. Switched outlets lose power when the primary device is turned off. Power conditioners also have switched outlets. You can often connect the power conditioner's control cable to a 12-volt trigger output on your surround processor (or a switched outlet on the receiver). When you turn on the surround processor or receiver, the trigger activates the power conditioner, which in turn applies power to all the components connected to the conditioner's switched outlets.

VCRs need constant power to keep the clock and timer running. Other components, like some satellite tuners, might return to the default installation settings every time the power is disconnected (which can occur through a switched power outlet on a receiver or power conditioner). My CD changer, for example, runs through a 5-minute reinitialization every time I turn on the system. It is annoying and disconnecting the power isn't a good idea. Check each component before setting the system to disconnect that component's power.

Sensors

Another way to deal with toggle commands is to use a remote system that accepts feedback from external sensors. Some systems can, through the use of optional accessories, determine if a component is turned on or off. A voltage sensor, for example, can determine if a component is drawing power to activate lights, the front panel information screens, or other internal components. The remote can use this information to determine if it should send a power on/off command or not. Since most video components output some kind of image, even if it's just a blue screen, you can use a video sensor to determine if the image is present, which would also indicate to the remote that the device is already powered on.

Why some remote commands just won't work

You might find that you can't get your universal remote to learn the functions of a particular device's standard remote. Some standard remotes use IR codes of odd lengths or alternating code frequencies. If the codes are odd lengths, you might be able to press the standard remote's button either very briefly or for a longer period of time and get the universal remote to learn the appropriate code length. In some cases, particularly when a standard remote alternates its IR code frequencies, there's no way for the universal remote to duplicate the code. The component just won't respond to the universal remote. Sell the component on eBay and buy something else, or use its standard remote, reserving the universal remote for the rest of your system.

10

Audio and Video Wire

There's probably no other component of a home theater that's more confusing and controversial than audio and video wiring. There are legions of enthusiasts who argue that certain brands of speaker cable and line level audio and video wire can improve the sound and visual quality of your system. Similarly numerous factions adamantly insist that there's no scientific reason or proof that wire makes any sonic or visual difference beyond preserving the signal that's already there and spending any money beyond the free wire that comes with most equipment is a waste.

I'm not here to end the debate, or argue either side. Each manufacturer can argue the merits of their particular brand. This chapter is meant to give you an idea of what the different cables look like, what kind of connections they have, and what they are used for. In rare cases, like speaker wire, TV cable, and high-definition video cables, I will make a few qualitative suggestions because I think better quality wire can make a performance difference, and I definitely don't recommend using the flimsy cables that come free with most equipment, but I also think there's a substantial amount of wire that costs far more than it should. I learned early on while selling consumer electronics at retail, though, that what might be a subtle or even imperceptible difference to one person might be a monumental chasm to another. The bottom line is, look or listen for yourself. Trust your eyes and ears and purchase cables that makes sense to you.

Figure 10.1

Speaker wire, courtesy of Ultralink

Here are a few audio and video wire terms that I'll use frequently in this chapter that you should know about:

- *Conductor:* One or more wires wrapped as one unit within a plastic outer jacket. One conductor can carry a single audio or video signal stream. Various cable types use one or more conductors to transfer the signals.

- *Dielectric:* The space between the conductors and the outer shield or outer cable jacket that's filled with nonconductive material.

- *Shield:* Conductive material around the outside of the dielectric, usually an aluminum-foil-like wrapping or gridlike mesh of wiring that's connected to the cable's grounding point and acts as a shield against unwanted airborne electrical interference.

Speaker Wire

Speaker wire is a two-conductor cable that carries the positive high-level audio signals from the amplifier output to the input at the speaker and the negative signal back from the speaker to the amplifier.

This wire is housed in either a clear or opaque jacket. One of the two conductors is usually marked in some manner, be it with a red or white stripe, ribbed edge, or silver color conductor instead of the copper color you normally see. This marking helps you identify (and remember) which conductor you connected to the amplifier or speaker's positive terminal so that you can be consistent with both connections. The cable might also use a manufacturing product label, printed every foot of cable on one conductor. The wire can be used with bare, stripped ends or can have a number of the terminations listed below.

Figure 10.2
Speaker wire with clear jacket, no terminations (bare wire only), courtesy of Ultralink

Wire gauge

The birth of high-performance wire started when enthusiasts realized that larger speaker wire allows more acoustical energy to travel from the amplifier to the speakers. Larger wire is defined as having a lower gauge (abbreviated as awg for American wire gauge). A 16 awg wire is larger than an 18 awg wire; a 12 awg wire is larger than a 16 awg wire.

How thick your speaker wire needs to be depends on how far the speaker is from the amplifier. Resistance to the electrical signal as it travels down the wire increases as the wire gets smaller and the length gets longer. As the resistance increases, two things occur. One, the signal loses power, which means the speaker won't play as loud as a similar speaker connected with a short, thick wire to the same amplifier. See the section on amplifier power in Chapter 6 for more details on the importance of amplifier power. Two, the effect of the speaker's impedance on the frequency response increases with wire resistance. Peaks or dips in the impedance at particular frequencies begin to cause comparable increases or decreases in frequency response. These effects are more pronounced when the speaker's nominal impedance is less than 8 ohms.

Even though most speakers are rated at 8 ohms, their impedance at different frequencies will vary dramatically, sometimes dropping to as low as 2 or 3 ohms at low frequencies.

As a general rule, use at least 16 awg wire when running speakers up to 20 feet away from the amp, and use larger gauges (14 to 12 awg) for longer lengths. Use larger gauge wire to connect the surround speakers, since these speakers are usually further from the amplifier. The improvement in audio quality to a speaker that plays mostly ambience, however, might not be dramatic enough to warrant the increased cost of the wire. If you want good sound from distant speakers in a whole-house audio system, though, use larger speaker wire.

 Measure the resistance of your existing speaker wires using nothing more than a simple ohm meter (available at Radio Shack for a few bucks). Disconnect the speaker wire from both the amplifier and the speaker. With nothing connected to the length of wire, short (or connect together) the positive and negative conductors on one end of the wire. Place the positive and negative leads from the ohm meter to the ends of the conductors on the other end of the wire, thus measuring up one conductor, across the short and down the other conductor back to the meter. This provides the total loop resistance of the wire. A good rule of thumb is to keep the total loop resistance for any speaker cable less than .1 ohm.

Figure 10.3

Wire gauge chart for recommended speaker wire length vs. gauge

No more than 0.2 dB difference

	Impedence		
AWG	8	4	2
22	5	3	1.5
20	9	4.5	2
18	15	7	3.5
16	22	11	5.5
14	37	18	9
12	60	30	15
10	95	47	23
8	150	75	37

No more than 1 dB difference

	Impedence		
AWG	8	4	2
22	32	16	8
20	48	24	12
18	80	40	20
16	120	60	30
14	200	100	50
12	300	150	75
10	480	240	120
8	800	400	195

Terminations

You can use any of four basic terminations for your speaker wires. Which one you choose depends on your preference and the speaker wire terminals on your speaker and amplifier. Banana plugs are a quarter to half-inch-long post that plugs directly into the center hole of a decent speaker wire connector. Though easy to use, banana plugs are becoming scarce because the two posts on the speaker terminal are the same distance apart as a European electrical outlet. Apparently, too many Europeans plug their hair dryers into their speakers.

Figure 10.4

Speaker wire with banana plugs, courtesy of Ultralink

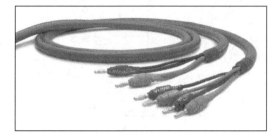

Spade lugs are flat, half-moon shaped connectors that fit around the connector post. Spade lugs come in a few different shapes to match the different thicknesses of the speaker binding posts, but when spade lugs fit they make a great, solid connection.

Figure 10.5

Speaker wire with spade lugs, courtesy of Ultralink

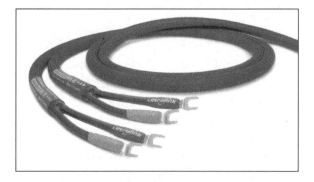

Pin connectors have a thin and sometimes angled post and look like skinny banana plugs. It is best to use pin connectors with spring clip-type speaker terminals. Otherwise, it's just as easy to tin, or solidify the bare end of your speaker wire with hot solder to make a solid pin-like termination that won't fray.

Figure 10.6

Speaker wire with pin connectors, courtesy of Ultralink

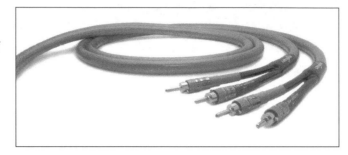

Bare wire is the most common speaker wire termination. After all, it's cheap and easy to make. Just strip a quarter inch of the wire's plastic jacket back to expose the bare wire, twist the wire along its natural winding to tighten the wire strands together, and insert it into or wrap it around the speaker terminal.

Figure 10.7

Speaker wire without termination, courtesy of Ultralink

Connections

Better speakers and amplifiers use speaker wire connectors called 5-way binding posts. The post (see **Figure 10.8**) uses two hex-screw terminals around a hollow center post. The post has one hole at the top and one on the side, near the base. The connector can accept a banana plug in the top opening, either bare wire or a spade lug around the base of the post, and bare wire or pin connectors through the side hole, near the base. It can often be extremely difficult to fit large gauge wire into the small holes provided on the side of the post. Larger holes just weaken the post's strength. At least with the spade lug and the bare wire you can tighten the hex nut for a good contact.

Figure 10.8
5-way binding post

Other connections include the various individual elements of the 5-way binding post. You can have a post, or even a recessed hole that accepts only banana plugs, or there can be two hex nuts that accept spade lugs or possibly bare wire (some older or commercial equipment might even use screw terminals). By far the least expensive speaker wire connection is the spring clip. Spring clips should only be used with bare or tinned wire and pin connectors.

 Save money and buy your speaker cable and terminations in bulk. It often will cost less to buy a few crimping tools and terminate your own cables than it will to buy separate, pre-terminated cables. Plus, you can cut the wires to the exact length you want.

Analog Line-Level Audio Cables
Unbalanced or single-ended cables

The audio wires that transfer analog audio signals from one component to another use a cable with a single conductor surrounded by dielectric and shield. The connectors on audio/video equipment for the left and right audio signals are colored with white for left and red for right. Sometimes cable manufacturers use blue for left. Surround systems often use green for center and various colors for the surround channels. This cable configuration is referred to as an unbalanced, or single-ended coaxial cable. (Coaxial cables are in fact used for a number of different types of cables and signals.) The analog audio cable is typically terminated with what's called either an RCA or phono-type connector that uses a center pin and an outer shield and carries a single audio signal. Though not typically used for audio, a coaxial cable can also be terminated with BNC or F-type connectors that are usually used with video equipment.

Better quality coaxial audio cables often have two conductors. When terminated with an RCA connector, the second conductor is usually connected to the outer shield. The same cable can be outfitted with a 1/8-inch stereo mini or 1/4-inch ring-tip-sleeve connector to provide two separate signals within the same wire. Both connectors use a single tip with three separated sections—the ring, the tip, and the sleeve. Two sections carry the left and right audio signals, while the third section carries the ground signal. Stereo mini connectors are often used with computer audio cards and headphones, which lack the space for full-sized RCA connectors. It's easy to convert a mini connector signal to a quarter-inch connector or to dual RCA connectors with a simple adapter.

You can use up to six analog cables for connecting SACD/DVD-A players to surround processors and separate preamps/surround processors to multichannel amplifiers. That's a lot of cables. Fortunately, the industry agreed upon a standardized configuration to use a DB-25 pin computer connector to transfer up to eight channels of analog audio in a single wire. Because of the decreased size of the conductors within the wire, I don't recommend using DB-25 for long lengths (beyond 10 feet or so), but it can certainly reduce the amount of wiring needed in your system.

Balanced cables

Some high-end consumer audio equipment, and nearly all professional audio products use balanced audio outputs. This signal wire will most often use what's called an XLR connector—a circular connector with three separate prongs—though the wire can also use quarter-inch, ring-tip-sleeve connectors. A balanced cable has at least two conductors for the main signal and a shield or third conductor as ground. The conductors and shield are terminated to the separate prongs on the XLR connector. A single cable carries a single audio signal. The two conductors transmit the same signal, but the signals are 180 degrees out of phase, or opposite of each other. As the signal is received on the other end of the cable, the two signals are compared. Any difference between the two signals, which could only be caused by interference induced along the cable line, is rejected. Balanced signals effectively preserve signal purity over long lengths, which is why they are used extensively in professional recording studios. Using short balanced cables in a home system offers little benefit.

Figure 10.10

Balanced analog audio cables with XLR connectors, courtesy of Ultralink

Digital Audio Cables

Digital audio cables come in many forms, but all perform a single purpose: to transfer the digital audio signal from the source component to the surround processor. In some cases, the digital signal is carried all the way to the speakers. The four main types of digital cables all carry SPDIF signals (Sony Philips Digital Interface Format), which work with PCM, Dolby Digital, and DTS digital signals. DVD-Audio and SACD signals will not transmit through any SPDIF connector. High-resolution, multichannel audio signals require more advanced connectors like HDMI or FireWire.

Coaxial digital cable

Coaxial digital audio cables, as the name suggests, use a single conductor cable with a shield for ground. The cable uses a normal RCA connector and plugs into the orange-colored jack on the back of your equipment. The cable is also terminated with BNC connectors. The one difference between a coaxial analog audio cable and the coaxial digital audio cable is that a digital cable must have a 75 ohm impedance. If you don't have a digital coaxial cable available, use a video cable, which shares the same impedance characteristic; don't use an analog audio cable. Enthusiasts suggest that a coaxial digital audio cable is the best way to transfer digital audio signals.

Figure 10.11

Coaxial digital audio cable with RCA connector, courtesy of Ultralink

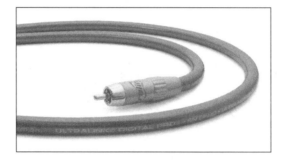

Optical digital audio cable

An optical digital audio cable, commonly known as a Toslink connection, is a nonelectrical alternative to the coaxial digital audio cable. Toslink is the trademarked term of the Toshiba Electronics Corp. Using a plastic fiber-optic cable—really a solid plastic tube—with a square, black connector, the optical connection sends the digital signal from one component to another as a series of light pulses. Since there's no electrical connection, an optical digital cable doesn't radiate any RF interference to other cables or components and doesn't create a ground loop between components. Aficionados, however, argue that Toslink cables introduce a number of errors into the digital signal that degrade performance.

Figure 10.12

Optical digital audio cable with connector, courtesy of Ultralink

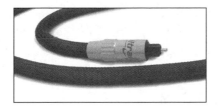

Glass fiber digital cable

Though it's rarely used anymore, the AT&T glass fiber optical digital audio cable is a higher-quality alternative to the plastic fiber optical Toslink connection. At one point it was used on high-end audio equipment. Like with Toslink cables, the signal is transmitted as a series of light pulses but uses a slimmer, locking bayonet-type connection. Improvements in Toslink and coaxial digital audio interfaces, and the adoption of the AES/EBU interface have made glass fiber obsolete.

AES/EBU interface

The AES/EBU (Audio Engineering Society/European Broadcast Union) digital interface is a professional version of an SPDIF connection. Using a balanced XLR connector, the cable transfers two identical, but out-of-phase electrical digital audio signals and a ground signal. The XLR connection is used on professional equipment and high-end consumer audio products.

Digital cables for DVD-A/SACD

Most DVD-A and SACD players decode the digital signal internally and output the signal through six analog, line-level audio cables to the surround processor. Newer players, however, offer digital connections. Early in the development of a digital connection standard for DVD-Audio and SACD (see Chapter 5), manufacturers like Denon and Meridian used a proprietary FireWire connection between their respective DVD-A/SACD players and surround processors to transfer the digital signal. Pioneer then introduced a nonproprietary FireWire connection that passed the digital audio signal. The cable and connector are similar to regular FireWire, except that the player currently doesn't output the digital video signal.

If you want to get both digital audio and video from the disc to the surround processor (so you can route the video to the processor's output), then look for a player with an HDMI connection. HDMI is described in greater detail in "Digital Audio/Video Cables" on page 219.

Figure 10.13

HDMI cable with connector, courtesy of Ultralink

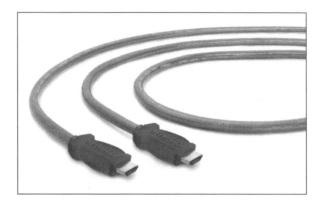

Analog Video Cables

Which type of video cable you need depends on the component you are connecting and the capabilities of your system. Ideally, use the best cable available for each component, assuming, however, that you have similar connections on your surround processor or TV. To understand the benefit of each signal type, I'll discuss briefly how to get from one signal to the next.

The camera at a production studio records images with three separate signals for red, green, and blue information. If the video signal originated on film, the signal is transferred to video with a device called a telecine that essentially records the film image in the same three separate red, green, and blue signals. This RGB signal is too large (or has too much bandwidth) to travel long distances (more than 25 to 50 feet), particularly at higher resolutions, so the signal is quickly converted to component YPrPb as either a digital or an analog signal.

To convert the RGB signal, a portion of each color channel is combined to create a single black and white, or luminance channel. This is the

Y channel of the YPrPb signal and contains most of the signal's resolution. The difference between the amount of red signal in the Y channel and what's left of the red channel in the original RGB signal is proportionately reduced and used to create the Pr signal. The same technique is used for the Pb signal.

The Pr and Pb signals are also labeled as Cr and Cb or R-Y and B-Y. In the professional world, the different nomenclature for component signals indicates different signal formats. In the consumer world, manufacturers use these terms interchangeably. A consumer DVD player with a YCrCb or Y, R-Y, B-Y output will connect to a consumer TV with a YPrPb input. Just connect Cr or R-Y output to the Pr input and the Cb or B-Y to Pb.

From the YPrPb signal, the TV can then re-create the RGB signal with almost no loss in picture quality. YPrPb signals are more robust, though, and can travel longer distances.

If you don't have test patterns to adjust your HDTV or DVD signals, you can disconnect the Pr and Pb channels to create a true black-and-white image. Using this image, you can adjust the contrast and brightness and color temperature controls to get as neutral an image as possible.

But YPrPb signals still have three separate video channels. Combining and further reducing the Pr and Pb channels into a single chrominance or color channel creates what's known as the Y/C or S-Video signal. Color quality and color detail is greatly reduced in a Y/C signal, but it's still a heck of a lot better than composite video.

To go from Y/C to composite requires that the combined color channel be modulated into the video signal at around 3.58 MHz. The TV must use a comb filter to separate the color information from the luminance, or resolution information. Depending on the quality of the comb filter, the image will have rainbows and moiré patterns in areas of fine detail (see the top of the skyscrapers in the movie *Armageddon* in Chapter 2), and might have zipperlike artifacts along horizontal and vertical color borders. A good comb filter can lessen these artifacts but can never truly get rid of them. The majority of resolution in the combined color signal has also been lost for good. As if that wasn't bad enough, the entire video signal is further reduced when it's combined with analog audio and modulated into TV channels.

Figure 10.14

The RGB signal recorded in the production studio gets converted almost immediately to YPrPb and recorded onto formats like DVD. The signal is further compressed into composite signals for recording onto videotape or broadcasting over TV airwaves. Tapping into the signal before it's converted to a composite video signal bypasses the conversion of RGB to composite sequence and preserves more of the signal's image quality.

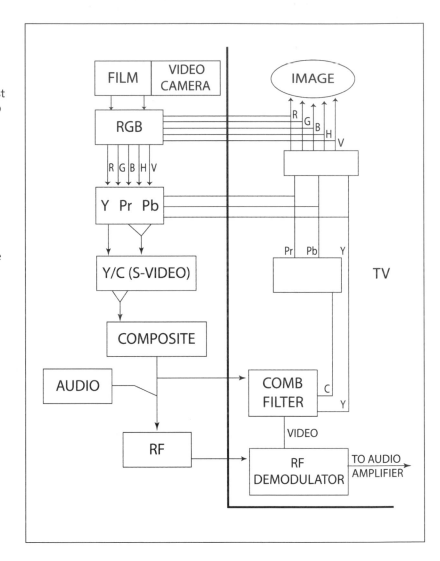

Ideally, use the best signal that's available from a particular device. I've listed various signal types and cables below, in ascending order from lowest quality (and most common) to highest quality.

TV cables

The most basic form of analog video cables is the TV cable, also referred to as an RF cable (because the cable carries an RF signal), or as a coax cable (because, not surprisingly, it uses a coaxial construction). The cable consists of a threaded hex-nut connector with a center pin and has a 75-ohm impedance. The connector, called an F-type connector, is attached to the cable's outer shield. The dielectric prevents it from contacting the center pin, which is an exposed portion of the cable's center conductor wire. A TV cable carries radio frequency-modulated audio and video signals or digital signals from an antenna, satellite, or cable system to a TV, VCR, cable box, digital TV tuner, or satellite tuner.

There are several types of TV cables that are classified as RG-59, RG-6, and RG-11. RG-59 cables have a smaller guage than RG-6; RG-11 is larger than RG-6. The different types designate signal loss over a certain distance (usually specified at 100 feet). RG-59 is best used to connect one component to another. It's more flexible than RG-6, but loses more signal over long distances. RG-6 is large enough to connect your antenna or satellite dish to the receiver, or to send TV signals to another room in the house. In extreme cases, where the antenna or satellite dish is more than a couple hundred feet from the receiver, and there's no way to bring the two closer, consider RG-11. The cable is about as thick as your thumb and is as easy to bend as a coat hanger, but it has low loss over long distances. In most cases, you're probably better off with a signal amplifier. See "RF distribution," in Chapter 3 for more details.

With good crimping tools, TV cables are easy to make. Like speaker wire, you can get TV cable and connectors in bulk and cut them to the length you need. Make sure you have connectors that match the wire, though. It's impossible to cram an RG-59 connector onto an RG-6 wire, or vice versa, without destroying the end of the wire in the process.

Figure 10.15

RF-type TV cable with F-type connector

Composite video cable

Cramming as much signal data as is used in a TV channel into a single, RF-modulated wire makes significant sacrifices in signal quality. The next best video connection is composite video. The composite video output on audio/video equipment is yellow. Composite video cables are similar in construction to analog audio cables except that the video signal uses a 75-ohm impedance. Analog cable, terrestrial TV, VCRs, and laser disc players use composite video signals. If one of these components has an S-Video output, it's because the component has an internal comb filter that divides the Y/C signals. This filter may or may not do a better job than the one in your TV.

If you connect video signals with cables that aren't 75 ohms, you introduce slight ringing or ghosting in the image. The greater the impedance mismatch, the more pronounced the ringing. You might not see anything at all if you replace a 3-foot video cable with a 3- foot analog audio cable.

Composite video cables can also use BNC connectors, which consist of a center pin surrounded by a round, twist-lock mechanism. Where RCA connectors have a 50-ohm impedance, certain BNC connectors have a 75-ohm impedance. BNC connectors with a visible white dielectric have a 50-ohm impedance.

Figure 10.16

Composite video cable with RCA connectors

Y/C or S-Video cables

With the introduction of Super VHS videocassette recorders came the S-Video or Y/C cable. The S in S-Video probably stands for Super VHS, though it should stand for "separated" and technically is known as a Y/C cable. Where a composite video cable contains the entire video signal, the Y/C cable keeps the chrominance and luminance (the color and resolution) portions of the signal separate and bypasses the TV's comb filter, which prevents the composite video artifacts described previously. S-Video cables use flimsy round plastic connectors with four small pins and have a black plastic post to help make sure the connector is inserted correctly. It's still easy to push the connector in the wrong way and break the pins, so be careful. The cable uses four conductors and a shield. Two pin and conductor combinations carry the chrominance or luminance signals, while the other two pins and conductors carry signal grounds.

 NOTE Though S-Video signals provide better quality than composite video signals, neither signal type has enough bandwidth for HDTV signals.

Figure 10.17
S-Video cable, courtesy of Monster Cable

S-Video signals have a 75-ohm impedance and can easily travel a couple hundred feet through good-quality cables with heavy gauge conductors. Initially, S-Video cables used thin conductors that wouldn't carry the signal long distances. Better S-Video cables use two regular-sized coaxial video cables strapped together in the same cable jacket. A simple breakout cable separates the chrominance and luminance signals so that they can be carried on two separate coaxial, composite-type video cables with no loss in quality.

Component video (YPrPb)

YPrPb cables consist of three separate coaxial video cables with either RCA or BNC connectors. You can substitute the component cable for three separate composite video cables, if need be. The cables and their connections are often colored red for Pr, blue for Pb, and green or black for Y. In rare cases, component signals are terminated with a D Sub-15 connector. D Sub-15 is a 15-pin connector used for computer monitors and typically carries RGB signals (See the RGBHV section for details). A simple, inexpensive breakout cable can separate the three component signals from the D-Sub 15-pin connector. Converting YPrPb to RGB, though relatively simple, requires an active component that costs a few hundred dollars.

While "component signal" could equally apply to either RGB or YPrPb signals, in the consumer world the component signals typically refer to YPrPb signals. When discussing your needs with dealers say "component YPrPb" specifically so that there's no confusion.

Component signals provide the best picture quality from sources like DVD and DTV tuners. DBS and digital cable are component sources, but most channels are supplied to the digital service provider's front end as a composite video signal. Once the signal has been converted to composite, the associated artifacts are embedded in the signal for good. Only certain channels, like pay-per-view or HDTV channels, are recorded and broadcast as true component signals. The receiver sometimes generates the menu guides as component signals, as well. Use component signals for these sources, particularly if you have HDTV, but you might still notice composite artifacts from time to time on some channels.

Figure 10.18
Component video cable with RCA connectors, courtesy of Ultralink

RGBHV

RGBHV, or five-wire RGB, stands for red, green, and blue with separate signals (and separate wires) used for horizontal and vertical sync. Without horizontal and vertical sync, the picture would roll side to side or up and down. The sync signals are sometimes combined into a composite sync, which is designated as RGBS (four wire), or the composite sync is included in the green channel (sync on green) and described as RGsB (three-wire).

Like other video signals, each RGBHV wire is a coaxial 75-ohm cable and uses RCA or BNC connectors, though BNC is more prevalent. RGB signals are also output on D-Sub 15-pin, also called HD-15 connectors. The HD-15 connector is a single trapezoid housing with three rows of five pins and is found on nearly all Windows-based PC monitors. You can buy HD-15 to five-wire BNC breakout cables at your local electronics store for a few bucks. Converting RGB to YPrPb is more difficult and requires an active component or converter box that costs several hundred bucks.

When you use five-wire RGB cables, it's tempting to use thinner conductors to reduce the size of the bundle. Wide bandwidth signals, like HDTV, or NTSC signals upconverted to resolutions higher than 480p, lose far more signal strength with distance (say, more than 20 feet) than composite or even YPrPb signals. It's important to use better-quality cables with thick conductors. I've too often seen "mini" RGB cables used in the wrong situation even though the cables are competently constructed and fine for use in short cable runs. On a long cable run, the high-bandwidth signal loses too much power on the way to the TV or projector and creates a dark or streaked image, assuming it creates any image at all.

Figure 10.19

Breakout cable with VGA-type D-Sub 15-pin connector on one end (right) and five-wire RGB with true 75-ohm BNC connectors on the other end (left). Cables with similar connectors on both ends are also available. Image courtesy of Ultralink.

Digital Audio/Video Cables

Regrettably, like everything else in consumer electronics, there's no one way to connect the digital output from your DVD player or high-definition TV tuner to your digital TV. Movie studios wanted the TV industry to adopt a digital video interface so that the studios could protect their content. Analog video signals were too easy for users to record and redistribute. Though all professional broadcast studios use a serial digital video interface (see Serial digital interface on page 224), the signal lacks copy protection. The consumer electronics industry looked to the computer industry for an option and found two, FireWire and DVI, though DVI eventually developed into HDMI.

FireWire

Officially known as IEEE-1394, for the International Electrical Engineering organization that adopted the standard, FireWire goes by many names, including iLink and DTVLink. The term FireWire, the most popular term for the connector, was originally developed for the Macintosh computer and was adopted and adapted (and licensed) to fit the needs of consumer digital audio and video. The cable has a small square metal shield that includes embedded strips or contacts for each conductor and comes in two varieties, 4-pin and 6-pin. The 6-pin variety adds phantom power, which may or may not be active and is backwards-compatible with the 4-pin version. Neither version has the bandwidth to carry an uncompressed high-definition signal. FireWire can carry the already-compressed MPEG-2 digital video signal, along with any 5.1 digital audio signal from any digital audio/video device to the display or surround processor.

To keep Hollywood happy, the FireWire cable uses a form of copy protection called 5C (for the five companies that developed the system: Hitachi, Intel, Matsushita, Sony, and Toshiba), also known as DTCP (Digital Transport Copy Protection). The copy protection flags in the software dictate whether you can record the content freely (like public broadcast programs), once (most regular programs), or never (e.g., pay-per-view programs). You can still legitimately record copy-enabled signals on D-VHS or DVR units. The TV routes the video signal to an internal MPEG decoder and the audio signal to an internal or external surround processor. Requiring an MPEG decoder in the TV may add slightly to the TV's cost, but the decoder will be required in all digital cable ready TVs and this arrangement could ultimately reduce the cost of source components (DVD players, DTV tuners, etc.) that no longer need the MPEG decoder.

Figure 10.20

FireWire cable with 4-pin (left) and 6-pin (right) connectors, courtesy of Randy Cordero

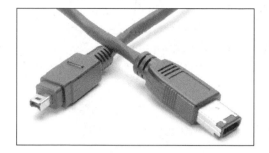

Another major advantage to FireWire, in addition to carrying both audio and video in one cable, its recording capability, and the fact that FireWire might reduce source component cost, is its communication and network capability. In a FireWire-based system, you don't need to route all the FireWire cables to the TV or the surround processor. You can make a daisy chain of the signal through up to three or four components. There are two different FireWire standards, 1394a and 1394b. 1394a is used for single room systems, meaning you can run the signal short distances between components; 1394b is used to transfer signals longer distances, or between rooms. A bridge component connects 1394a to 1394b, which will send signals from one room to the next.

The consumer electronics implementation of FireWire, identified by a DTVLink label, incorporates the AVC or audio-video control protocol, which standardizes basic control and communication between components. Plug a new DVD player into this network and the surround processor and TV will automatically recognize it. The DVD player will configure itself to the capabilities of the TV and surround processor, and the TV will add an icon for the DVD player on the TV's on-screen menu. Select the icon and press Play to watch a movie and the TV and surround processors will switch to the appropriate input, aspect ratio, and surround sound processing mode, as determined by the movie. You don't have to do a thing.

Sounds like a dream come true, no? Well, all is not perfect in FireWire land. Since the cable transfers only the compressed audio and video signal, it can't insert the interactive menu guide from satellite and digital cable tuners without decompressing and recompressing the signal, which would be an ugly proposition. Also, not every FireWire-equipped component is AVC-enabled, which means your TV might not recognize the FireWire signal from your camcorder or DVD-A/SACD player.

Digital visual interface

The digital visual interface, or DVI, looks like a wide, multipin computer connector and carries a digital RGB video signal from the digital audio/video component to the display. The connector won't fit in anything less than a 1.5-inch conduit, or larger, so if you want to pull a DVI cable through your wall, make sure you have plenty of room. You're probably better off pulling HDMI, even if your components lack HDMI capability (see "High definition multimedia interface," on page 222).

Like FireWire, the DVI cable was born in the computer industry to reduce cost in digital flat panel monitors. Since the computer video card output uses digital-to-analog converters (D/A), and the input to a flat panel monitor uses analog-to-digital converters (A/D), a digital connection eliminates the analog signal in between and in turn eliminates the need for D/A and A/D converters in both the video card and monitor. In consumer digital televisions, DVI eliminates the need for an A/D and an MPEG decoder. Satellite and digital cable tuner manufactures also flocked to DVI because it allows them to insert their interactive program guide into the signal without recompressing the signal. Many current HD-ready monitors use DVI connectors.

One drawback to DVI is that it only carries the video signal. HDMI adds audio, though, and is backwards compatible with DVI (see page 223). Like analog RGB signals, lesser-quality cable construction reduces the effective usable distance the DVI signal can travel. DVI maxes out at roughly 16 feet with regular cables, and can travel about 75 feet with better-quality cables. The DVI specification for computers doesn't have copy protection. Some consumer equipment use this connection, which means that if the equipment receives DTV signals that are encrypted, the TV might not play them through the DVI port or will convert them to the nearest computer resolution (likely 640-by-480 pixels). DVI with

HDCP (High Definition Copy Protection) was developed for consumer electronics equipment to keep content "safe." HDCP achieves the same result as 5C (see "FireWire," on page 220). If you output a "copy never" signal from the DTV tuner, a TV without HDCP won't be able to play the signal. Look for DVI connectors with HDCP.

NOTE   Ironically, DVI doesn't need copy protection since the uncompressed HDTV signal has far too much bandwidth to fit on any known consumer recording equipment. It would take a half-million-dollar professional digital videotape to even attempt to record the DVI signal.

Figure 10.21
DVI cable with connector, courtesy of Ultralink

High definition multimedia interface

High definition multimedia interface (HDMI) is an updated version of DVI that adds digital audio, control, and HDCP to the signal. HDMI, like DVI, is still limited in cable length. And even with copy-enabled programs, you can't record HDMI's uncompressed signals on any practical device (See "Digital visual interface," on page 222). The HDMI connector is somewhat flat and wide with several contacts and, with a simple cable adapter, is backwards compatible with DVI. If you have an HDMI-equipped source connected to a DVI-equipped TV with an adapter, for example, the TV can receive the digital video signal, but not the audio or control. By the same token, a DVI-equipped source can send the video signal to an HDMI-equipped TV. You have to route the audio signal separately. HDMI is good choice for DVD-A/SACD players as the cable passes both the digital video and digital audio signals from all types of discs.

Need a DVI signal to your projector but the conduit's less than 1.5 inches? Pull HDMI. The cable connector is significantly smaller and easier to pull through the conduit. Use a cable adapter at both ends to connect your DVI signal to the projector.

Figure 10.22

HDMI to DVI Adapter. Cables terminated with a DVI connector on one end and an HDMI connector on the other are also available. (Image courtesy of Ultralink)

Serial digital interface

Professional broadcast studios pass digital YPrPb video signals between equipment with a serial digital interface. SDI uses a 75-ohm coaxial video cable, usually terminated with a BNC connector. The signal is unencrypted and uncompressed. It's rarely found on consumer equipment though is sometimes added as an aftermarket modification.

11

Electrical Power

Gray Davis, former governor of the state of California, will likely be the first person to tell you not to take electricity for granted. After all, he was recalled from office after the state's power grid ran short. While this chapter is not about California's electricity woes, it is about making sure you don't experience electricity-related lags in your home theater system. You can assemble the finest components there are, but if you don't feed them enough electricity they won't perform to the best of their ability. Worse, if the system's electrical wiring isn't connected properly, you can end up with audible buzzes or ground loops that mar the image and sound. It's important to consider whether or not your system is getting enough power and if the components are connected correctly to that power system.

Power Requirements

Determine Your Electrical Power Needs

The combined electrical draw from a decent home theater system can far exceed the current capabilities of your home's electrical outlet. You might not notice when you've run out of power, but your system can be affected nonetheless. If the AC line voltage sags a few volts below normal (120 V is normal), for example, your amplifier can lose as much as 30 to 50 watts at the output. If you want to use all the performance you've paid for, it's important that the wall outlet provide as much or more electrical power than the system requires.

First, though, you need to determine how much power you need. Since electrical components draw more power when they are first turned on, if you can power up all your components at the same time without tripping the circuit breaker, you'll at least know that the system won't shut down during crucial movie scenes. If you want to make sure that you have enough power to fuel the gear at its optimum level, though, check each product's manufacturer specifications for power consumption. If you don't have the manual, look at the back of your component. Every component should have a sticker or engraved label that indicates the maximum current draw for that component and should be listed in watts (W). Simply add the power draws for each component together to get an idea of your total power needs.

Figure 11.1

Electricity powers your home theater system. Treat it with the same respect you give every other component.

The electrical power "draw" for a component, like a receiver, should not be confused with its acoustical power "output," or the amount of amplifier power available to the music signal and sent to the speakers.

Figure 11.2

Check the power consumption (in Watts) of each component in your system. If it's not listed in the manual (or if you lost the manual) it should be listed on the back near the UL label.

117 VAC 60 Hz
65 WATTS MAX

As an example, my system's amplifier has a maximum current draw of 1,875W. This amplifier, by itself, is close to the maximum continuous power of a 20-amp circuit (see "How Much Power Is Available?" below). Granted, the outlet will handle brief musical peaks, but when you add the power draw for the rest of my equipment and my projection TV the power needs increase quickly.

 Even if you rent your home, or are not in a position to upgrade your electrical service, keep your system's power needs in mind when shopping for equipment. That 7-channel, 350-watt-per-channel amplifier might sound great in the store, but you might not get as much power from it when you get it home, assuming the circuit breaker can handle it in the first place.

How much power is available?

You don't need an electrician to determine how much power you have available—just a flashlight and a calculator (if that). Your home's electrical power starts at the circuit breaker box and is divided into circuits. Each circuit feeds roughly 110 to 120 volts of current to a number of electrical outlets or lighting fixtures. In some cases a single circuit feeds a single outlet intended for a high-power appliance like a pool filter or washing machine. Each circuit breaker should have an amperage label. The typical modern home uses a 20-amp circuit, which provides 2,400 watts (20 amp × 120 volt = 2,400 watts) of power. Older homes might use 15-amp circuits, which provide 1,800W. Electrical codes require that the safe capacity for a particular circuit be roughly 20 percent less than the total power capacity for that circuit.

Most power strips are rated for 15-amp circuits and have an internal 15-amp circuit breaker. Connect a 15-amp power strip to a 20-amp outlet and you've effectively reduced the outlet's power capability to 15 amps. Draw more power than 15 amps and you'll likely pop the power strip's circuit breaker.

As I mentioned, though, that one circuit might feed multiple outlets, lights, and other electrical systems in your home. Whenever possible, find a circuit that's not shared or whose other outlets are not used at the same time as the home theater. (In addition to the power benefits, using a dedicated circuit prevents electrical noise, that household appliances inject into the power line, from affecting the performance of your home theater system.)

If you can't find or install a dedicated circuit for your home theater, determine the power requirements of the other electrical devices on the circuit using the same method as I described. Appliances have power draw ratings in watts or amps. Convert amps to watts by multiplying the amperage by the voltage (110 or 120 V). Most home appliances that heat or cool things (e.g., refrigerators, toasters, hair dryers) draw a lot of power and should not share an electrical circuit with your home theater equipment. Granted, the toaster may not be running for long periods of time during a movie. Even if you have to share a circuit, avoid sharing with light fixtures; if you can't avoid this, include the power draw of the lights. Light fixtures draw power based on the bulb wattage. If you have four 80W bulbs on a circuit, they draw 240W. Hopefully there's enough left over to power your home theater system.

Power system options

If your system's power demands substantially exceed the capabilities of a single circuit you can do one of two things. One, instead of a 15-amp breaker, you can use a 20-amp or greater circuit breaker. If you want to upgrade from an existing 15-amp breaker, you will likely need to use thicker electrical wire to accommodate the greater current (see the Electrical Wire Gauge chart on page 229).

Electrical Wire Gauge

Amps	Watts	Up To 50' Gauge	Up To 100' Gauge	Up To 150' Gauge	Up To 200' Gauge	Up To 250' Gauge	Up To 300' Gauge	Up To 400' Gauge	Up To 500' Gauge
15	1800	14	12	10	6	6	6	4	4
20	2400	12	10	8	6	6	4	4	2
30	3600	10	8	6	6	4	4	2	2
40	4800	8	6	4	4	2	2	1	1/0
50	6000	6	6	4	4	2	1	1/0	2/0

(Courtesy General Cable Technologies Corporation, AKA Romex)
Gauge Guide for maximum allowable wire length, 2% nominal voltage drop (copper wire only)

Your next option is to add a second electrical circuit. I've seen many systems use a second, dedicated circuit just for a projector or video system. The apparent goal is to electrically isolate the video system, but I think it's a total waste of an electrical circuit. Unless you use a fiber optic-based video cable, the projector or TV will be electrically connected to the rest of the system through the video cable and any ground problems in the main system will make their way to the TV. Share the second electrical circuit between the projector and other components. Make sure the second circuit uses the same electrical ground as the first circuit to avoid ground loops between the two circuits.

Ground Loops

If you're satisfied that your system has enough power, make sure that the electrical service is clean and your system is connected properly. Making sure the home theater circuit isn't shared with other electrical items, particularly lights and computers, helps keep the AC signal clean. If it's not clean, you might hear hiss, static, or other noise in the background when you listen to music and you may see sparkles or other anomalies in the video image. A line conditioner can help in these situations, but it won't get rid of ground loops, which cause significant audible and visual distortions in the system.

Identifying grounding problems

Ground loops are created when two interconnected components have an unintended electrical potential through ground wires or the shields of audio or video cables, creating distortion and noise. In audio, a ground loop usually manifests itself as a buzz or hum coming from the speakers, though it can sometimes sound like excessive static. Hum is usually a 60-cycle tone corresponding to electrical power added to the audio signal. Faulty wiring or power supplies, power cables wrapped too closely to low and line-level cables, or more likely, components improperly connected to the electrical service can cause the ground loop.

Similarly, buzz is usually just distorted hum and can often be caused by the feedback from lighting dimmer systems on the same electrical circuit. If the dimmer is on a different circuit, but its power lines run parallel with wiring for the A/V system, a buzz might still occur. Buzz can also come from interconnected components that have poorly shielded transformers. Separating the two components and proper grounding should eliminate the noise.

Ground loops can take on comparable forms in video images, such as a vertically rolling ascending or descending band, or they can create a grid of diagonal noise. No matter how noise manifests itself, ground problems degrade system performance.

Eliminating ground problems

The first thing you need to do before connecting any home theater equipment to the wall outlet, and the first place to start looking if you already have one of the problems I listed above, is to make sure the outlet is wired correctly. Inexpensive testing devices called GFCI Receptacle Analyzers are available from most electrical supply and hardware stores for a few bucks. Plug the analyzer into the outlet and a series of lights tells you if the outlet is wired properly, in phase, and with proper ground. You can also use a voltmeter. Test the receptacle's two power slots relative to the ground slot. There should be 110 to 120 V between the hot wire (smaller slot) and ground (round hole), and no more than a fraction of a volt between the neutral (larger slot) and ground. If you have a second circuit, comparable measurements should give you similar readings. If you measure significant voltage between the neutral and ground, or noticeably different values from one circuit compared to another, have an electrician check and or re-wire the system.

 Cable TV companies are notorious for not properly grounding their cable signals. The RF signal needs to be grounded, preferably at the point it enters the building. If existing ground loops go away when you disconnect the TV cable, make sure the signal is properly grounded. Call a qualified cable technician or electrician to do this.

Test for proper polarity

Once you're confident the electrical system and TV cable are wired properly, check to see if your A/V equipment is connected with proper polarity. Manufacturer's may or may not wire the two-prong plug onto their equipment properly. You might need to reverse the plug at the outlet in order for the equipment's hot and neutral leads to match those of the outlet. Again, use a voltmeter to measure the difference between the equipment chassis ground, via a ground lug or chassis screw, and the outlet's ground termination. (On some units the audio and video connector ground might be floating from the chassis ground.) Reverse the plug and measure again.

Since one of the two prongs is wider than the other, you might have to use cheater plugs. These are three-prong to two-prong adapters that don't usually have the polarized prong, or at least can be filed down without permanently damaging your equipment (and voiding the warranty). The adapters cost about a buck and can be found at any electrical supply or hardware store. The connection with the lowest measurement is correct. You can also measure polarity with Audio Advisor's Elfix polarity tester, a gray handheld device that beeps and illuminates when the polarity is incorrect. Keep in mind that you can only measure for correct polarity when no other connections are made to the equipment, which means you have to disconnect everything from the component.

Figure 11.3
Cheater plugs are available for a few bucks from the hardware store. The Elfix polarity tester is available from www.audioadvisor.com.

Obviously, it's significantly easier to test for polarity before the system is connected. Disconnecting complex systems after they've been assembled is difficult enough without knowing if you'll find one or two components wired improperly. It is worth the effort, though. Only as a last resort should you revert to lifting the ground on three-pronged equipment. The ground pin is for safety, and the problem may or may not be with a grounded component. Finally, when too many grounds are lifted (or if the entire system's ground is lifted) the system will often exhibit excessive static or background noise.

Another approach that doesn't involve disconnecting the entire system is starting at one end of the audio and video signal chain and working your way to the other. It's important that you don't miss a step, though. And keep in mind that three or more components might be wired improperly. Does the volume control affect the level of the hum? If so, it's a ground loop before the amp; if not, it's a ground loop with the amp (or with a powered speaker, like a subwoofer). Lift the ground temporarily on only one component at a time, working your way through each component. Then try combinations of two components at a time, and so on. Then see if any of the ground-lifted components need to have their polarity reversed. If the only way to clear the system of buzzes and hums is to lift the ground on the entire system, you're better off starting over.

Even if you don't have to worry about being ejected from political office over state power problems, give electricity the proper respect it deserves. For starters, wear rubber boots, don't stand in puddles of water, and don't grip exposed electrical lines with both hands. Spend all the money and time you want on your home theater system, but make sure your electrical system can handle it. Take care when installing your system from the beginning and you will prevent serious headaches later on and you will optimize your system's performance.

Power Line Conditioners and Other Electrical Enhancers

The products marketed and sold as line conditioners or electrical power enhancers rarely do what their advertisements suggest, but they do often provide benefits to your system. For one thing, line conditioners act as a good-quality power strip with delayed turn-on capabilities. You can usually connect a control cable to your surround processor that will sense when the surround processor is activated. The line conditioner will then apply power to its various electrical outlets in a particular sequence, making sure that some products turn on before others.

 NOTE Power on source components first before turning on your amplifier to prevent the turn-on power spike that occurs with the source equipment from sending pops or thumps to the speakers. Similarly, turn off the amp first and let the power drain before turning off other components. The amp will absorb the turn-off spike, as well.

Most of these products provide a basic level of surge protection, which, in thunderstorm and surge-prone regions offer excellent protection against lightning strikes or wild and woolly electrical power spikes. Some products even offer a substantial amount of equipment insurance if the product fails to prevent the surge from taking out your equipment. The surge protection feature and the equipment turn-on sequences can, in and of themselves, justify the cost of the power enhancer.

One company has even introduced a power enhancement product that includes a battery backup system to make sure your system is never without power. You may not be able to watch the extended, director's cut of the *Lord of the Rings* trilogy with your full surround sound system off of a battery backup system, but it might prevent you from losing installation settings, or from missing your DVR's scheduled recording times.

Another benefit to many power enhancers, though, is actual line conditioning. Power lines are rarely the perfect 60 Hz signals we expect them to be. Minute-by-minute changes in demand and supply on the power company's grid can create unwanted spikes and dips in the electrical current. In addition, various household electrical appliances add spurious noise and electrical interference to the power line. Your electronic equipment is supposed

continues on next page

Power Line Conditioners and
Other Electrical Enhancers *(continued)*

to filter these elements out of the power signal before applying the signal to the component's electronics. How well the equipment achieves this objective depends on the quality of the product's filtering components and the amount of filtering needed for a given signal. If the signal is particularly "dirty," components with lesser filters might not sufficiently filter the power signal, which allow these spikes and dips through to the audio and video signals, thus affecting performance.

Line conditioners take the existing electrical signal and provide additional filtering to ensure that the resulting signal is clean as a whistle. In the case of AC power regenerators, the product uses the existing electrical power to run what amounts to a small generator, which creates a completely new, perfectly clean power signal. Since there's some loss in this process, AC regenerators tend to run hot and have limited output power capabilities. A myriad of products use various techniques to achieve similar results—clean power signals.

 NOTE Products called voltage regulators actually store excess current in reserve. The regulator can draw from the reserve to provide a consistent power level at the output, even when the electrical utility power signal has sagged.

I'm a strong believer that line conditioners or other power enhancers make a subtle but audible difference in a sound system, and can remove noise from a video system, but I can't verify the outrageous claims made by some power enhancement product manufacturers and dealers. Only voltage regulators can increase the power signal level, and even then it's only for short periods of time and regulators only increase the power level to where it should be in the first place. Clean, consistent power does not change the color or light output capability of your TV set. Power enhancers don't provide more power than what's available, and sometimes provide less. And they don't prevent or eliminate ground loop problems. I strongly suggest you consider a power line conditioner or similar product for your system. It can offer practical benefits and subtle performance improvements—just don't assume it will make fantastic changes.

Figure 11.4

Power line conditioner,
model M10, courtesy
of APC

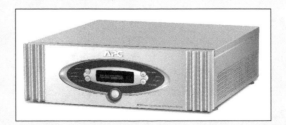

12

Sound and Room Acoustics

You can buy a sports car if you want to go fast, but if you drive in bumper-to-bumper traffic, you won't be going much faster than the guy next to you in the Geo Metro. You might be happier in a sports car than a Metro on that crowded highway, but you need a good, long empty stretch of road to really enjoy the sports car's performance benefits. Home theater isn't that much different, except that instead of a road, you need a quiet, neutral listening room to really enjoy the sonic capabilities of your equipment. In this chapter I'll talk about the science of sound and how it relates to small listening rooms. I've started with a few simple concepts and definitions of sound that will be useful later on when I talk about room acoustics.

Fundamentals of Sound

Compression and rarefaction

Sound begins when something large enough vibrates fast enough to move air molecules at a rate we can hear. Pluck an acoustic guitar string, for example, and the string will move back and forth at a rate determined by the length and size of the string. As the string moves forward, it compresses the air molecules in front of it, creating an area of high pressure. The pressure of the air molecules presses outward against the nearby molecules, which similarly compress, continuing the outward motion. Meanwhile, the guitar string is pulling away from the same spot, which causes the air molecules to spread apart or rarefy, creating an area of low pressure. Again, nearby molecules move to fill the space, creating low-pressure areas that follow behind the high-pressure areas in an ever-outward moving direction. These cycles of high and low pressure are sound waves. The point with the greatest compression is considered the peak while the point with the least compression (or greatest rarefaction) is called the dip or trough. The distance between the point of one peak and the point of the next peak is the wavelength of the frequency. Visually, sound waves are like water waves when you throw a rock in a calm pool of water, except that sound waves move spherically.

Figure 12.1

Absorption and diffusion acoustical treatments with fabric covering, model Cinepanel, courtesy of Performance Media Industries

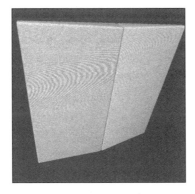

Sound, or the cycles of compression and rarefaction of air molecules move from one molecule to the next at a constant rate dependent only on atmospheric temperature and pressure. This rate is independent

Figure 12.2

Compression and rarefaction of air molecules

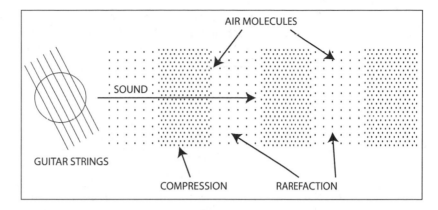

of the sound's frequency and amplitude, or volume level. At sea level, sound moves about 1,130 feet per second. How fast the string vibrates determines the number of compressions and rarefaction cycles that travel those 1,130 feet in a second. The number of waves, or cycles per second, is the frequency, and is measured in hertz (Hz). A big, slow moving string might create 100 waves per second, or 100 Hz, while smaller strings vibrate quickly and create 1,000 waves per second or 1,000 Hz (1 kHz). Divide the speed of sound, 1,130 ft/sec, by the number of waves that travel that distance in one second, say 100 Hz, and you can determine the wavelength of a frequency. Therefore, a 100 Hz tone has a wavelength of 11.3 feet.

Figure 12.3

A sound wave's frequency is defined by the number of cycles that occur within a second of travel (or 1,130 feet at sea level). The fewer cycles per second, the lower the frequency (in hertz). The wavelength of a single frequency is defined as the distance traveled during one complete cycle (dip to dip).

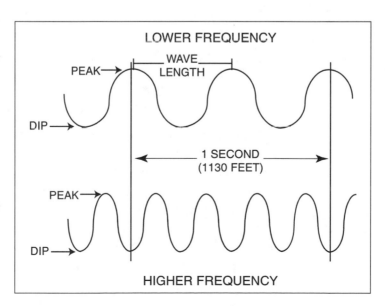

Humans hear frequencies between 20 Hz on the low end and roughly 20 kHz on the high end, though the upper end decreases with age (particularly in men). Low frequencies, below 80 Hz, tend to be visceral, and less directional (you can't tell what direction they are from) than higher frequencies.

Room Acoustics

Room acoustics have three characteristics that are important to how your audio system sounds. One is how the room's shape affects the system's response. Another is how quiet it is within the room. Third is how the room's surfaces reflect sound within the room. When all three elements of the environment are well designed and competently constructed, your audio system will achieve its peak performance. Determining and designing the room's acoustical elements, however, is a complex task that you might decide is better suited for a professional. There are a few things to consider first, though.

Standing Waves

Listening rooms and resonant frequencies

In a residential-sized space (e.g., something smaller than a cathedral), the room dimensions determine how sound waves build up, resulting in low-frequency resonances. Knowing how to calculate a room's resonant frequencies helps you design a room if you're starting from scratch, choose from existing rooms to use as your home theater, or take advantage of a room's characteristics to achieve the best sound.

A resonant frequency, or standing wave, is a frequency whose half wavelength (peak to trough) fits perfectly within a room's length, width, or height. Since the resonant frequency fits so neatly, this particular frequency builds up between the opposing surface and creates peaks and nulls of increased or decreased amplitude, or sound pressure, relative to the inherent frequency response of the speaker system. Harmonics, or multiples of the resonant frequency, will also match the same room axis and will create additional peaks at those frequencies.

Wavelengths that build up between two opposing surfaces are called axial resonances. Standing waves that occur between four or six surfaces are referred to as tangential or oblique resonances, respectively. Axial modes have the most significant impact on room acoustics.

Main Modes	Room Dim. (inches)	Room Dim. (feet)	Resonant Freq. (Hz)
Length	228.00	19.00	29.711
Width	210.00	17.50	32.257
Height	96.00	8.00	70.563
Room Volume			

Axial Resonances	1	2	3	4	5	6	7	8	9	10
Room Length	29.7	59.4	89.1	118.8	148.6	178.3	208.0	237.7	267.4	297.1
Room Width	32.3	64.5	96.8	129.0	161.3	193.5	225.8	258.1	290.3	322.6
Room Height	70.6	141.1	211.7	282.3	352.8	423.4	493.9	564.5	635.1	705.6
Sorted Res.	32.3	59.4	64.5	70.6	89.1	96.8	118.8	129.0	141.1	148.6

Figure 12.4
Resonant frequencies calculated for an 8-by-17.5-by-19-foot room. Resonant frequencies below 200 Hz are reasonably well spaced. This spacing will make it easier to find good listener and speaker positions to get good sound over a wide area.

Main Modes	Room Dim. (inches)	Room Dim. (feet)	Resonant Freq. (Hz)
Length	288.00	24.00	23.521
Width	192.00	16.00	35.281
Height	96.00	8.00	70.563
Room Volume			

Axial Resonances	1	2	3	4	5	6	7	8	9	10
Room Length	23.5	47.0	70.6	94.1	117.6	141.1	164.6	188.2	211.7	235.2
Room Width	35.3	70.6	105.8	141.1	176.4	211.7	247.0	282.3	317.5	352.8
Room Height	70.6	141.1	211.7	282.3	352.8	423.4	493.9	564.5	635.1	705.6
Sorted Res.	35.3	47.0	70.6	70.6	70.6	94.1	105.8	117.6	141.1	141.1

Figure 12.5
Resonant frequencies calculated for an 8-by-16-by-24-foot room. Since room dimensions are not well varied, resonant frequencies coincide for all three room dimensions at 70 Hz and 141 Hz. This spacing will likely cause significant level boosts at those frequencies, depending on where the listener and speakers are placed.

When you compare the resonances of one room dimension to the resonances of the other two dimensions, you'll hopefully find that few, if any, of the resonances are identical or are less than 5 percent of one another, and are evenly spaced so there are no gaps greater than 20 percent between them. Resonances of one dimension that coincide with resonances of the other dimensions might create significant peaks at those frequencies, which will make some sounds louder and more forward than others. Large gaps between resonances can create large dips in response, making certain sounds seem more quiet or distant.

If the room is 20 feet long and 20 feet wide, for example, the room will have a resonant frequency of 28 Hz in both dimensions. Particular speaker and listener positions in the room will enhance this resonant frequency (see "Speaker Placement and Resonant Frequencies" in Chapter 8), which will create even greater frequency response peaks at that frequency. A room with dimensions that are even multiples of each other (like a room that's 10-by-15-by-20 feet will also create equal resonances at multiples of the resonant frequency. While it is possible to find a good speaker and listener position for a single listener in a room with similar dimensions, it becomes increasingly more difficult to get good sound for a wider area of potential listener positions.

While there are no perfect room dimensions, the room's length, width, and height will ideally vary so that the resonant frequencies will be evenly spread throughout the lower-frequency range (below about 300 Hz in a small bedroom or 150 Hz in a larger living room). Above 300 Hz or 150 Hz other acoustic characteristics dominate or you can use other acoustic treatments.

Calculating resonant frequencies

If a room is rectangular you can predict its resonant frequencies. (Math for calculating resonances of L-shaped rooms or rooms with vaulted ceilings is considerably more complex.) These predictions are rough guidelines, at best. Compliant building materials can absorb or shift modes somewhat. The more rigid the room's walls and ceiling, the more accurate the prediction, but the more pronounced the resonances become. If you're building a room from scratch, though, you have to start somewhere. Calculate and design your room's dimensions to vary the resonant frequencies for each dimension, and the end result will be better than if you randomly picked the room dimensions.

Divide the speed of sound (1,130 ft per second at sea level) by the room's dimension, then divide the remainder by two to determine the resonate frequency between opposing room walls. For a room that's 19 feet long, the resonant frequency is roughly 30 Hz (1,130/19 = 59.5; 59.5/2 = 29.7, or 30, if we round up). Multiply this fundamental resonance by whole integers (1, 2, 3...) until the harmonic resonances are up to about 300 Hz. For a 19-foot-long room, the axial modes are at 30 Hz, 60 Hz, 90 Hz, etc. Do the same calculation for each room dimension, and then list all the frequencies in numerical order, from lowest to highest. If you want to know if two of the frequencies are more than 5 percent apart, subtract the lower frequency from the higher frequency and divide the difference between the two frequencies by the higher of the two, then multiply that total by 100. If the answer is greater than 5 percent you're OK.

You can download an Excel spreadsheet template that calculates and lists axial modes for you from www.guidetohometheater.com. Read the website's Sweet Spot feature for more information on how to use the spreadsheet.

Again, varied room dimensions give you a better chance of finding great sounding speaker and listener positions (see "Speaker Placement and Resonant Frequencies" in Chapter 8). You can get bad sound in an otherwise "good" room if you don't carefully position the speakers and listeners to avoid the room mode peaks and nulls, just as you can get good sound from a "bad" room if you place the speakers and listeners in optimum positions.

Room Construction

The main goals during the construction phase of a home theater are noise control, isolation, and sound quality. Noise control eliminates extraneous noise from within the room. Sound isolation refers to how little outside noise reaches the room, and how little of the sound in the room reaches the outside world. Sound quality refers to the types of materials used during construction and the manner in which they are used. Generally, a well-constructed room, with no rattles or buzzes or loose parts, sounds better than a room built with poorly secured materials. All materials though, have certain acoustic properties that become important when I talk about the room's acoustic treatment later in this chapter. I'll talk about common building materials and their potential effect on sound quality when I discuss the construction.

Noise criteria

Noise control is quantified with a measurement called NC, for noise criteria, which measures the amount of noise within a room. This sound can pass from another room into the listening room or from internal components. Creating a soundproof room does you no good if you install a digital projector with a whirring fan noise. A room with an NC of 20 is nearly silent and equivalent to a quiet living room late at night, while NC 30 is similar to the same room during the day. NC 30 is certainly acceptable, though not ideal. NC 40 is fairly loud. The background noise level at NC 40 will be audible and distracting.

Other occupants in your home will appreciate it if you prevent sounds from the latest action-adventure extravaganza from wafting through your home. Similarly, the less noise within your home theater room, the greater the system's dynamic range. If the ambient noise level is 40 dB and the soundtrack starts at 0 dB then no matter how loud the soundtrack gets, the bottom 40 dB is lost. Increasing the volume just compresses the dynamic range, creates distortion, or causes hearing damage. Your system will sound better if you can lower the ambient noise to hear the soundtrack's subtle details at comfortable levels.

Transmission loss

Sound travels through nearly every material. Transmission loss (TL) figures show you how much sound is lost when it travels through a given material. Transmission loss is dependent on frequency, however. Older STC (sound transmission class) ratings that provide only a single number average the amount of loss at all frequencies. Newer STC ratings list the sound transmission at different frequencies. A material that might be excellent at preventing transmission of high frequencies could have no effect at lower frequencies. Mass, an air space, and decoupling two objects or environments will create greater transmission loss. Damping materials, like soundboard, eliminate material resonances, which can also contribute to sound transmission loss. Greater mass, like heavy layers of vinyl, can also decrease the frequency at which a material absorbs sound, but it is usually expensive. (Vinyl can also act as a damping material.) Decoupling uses hanging, spring-loaded, or cushioned materials to prevent sound vibrations in one material from transferring to another. It's effective, but still somewhat expensive. Rubberized isolation bushings, like those from PAC or Kinetics Noise Control offer the equivalent transmission loss as seven layers of drywall. An air space sandwiched between materials, on the other hand, can be extremely effective at limiting sound transmission without the expense of other techniques. One of the best ways to achieve excellent noise isolation is to make the home theater a separate room, with a 1- or 2-inch air space between it and the home's adjacent walls, floors, and ceilings.

Flanking paths

It is important to consider flanking paths when handling noise isolation in room construction. These are the paths sound takes to go from one place to another. If you build a soundproof wall, the route the sound takes to get around the wall and into the room is the flanking path. Sound travels through any opening, no matter how small, and through any material, including water pipes, air conditioning ducts, air gaps around electrical outlets or light switches, and more. The more flanking paths you eliminate or alleviate, the quieter your room will be. Avoid having electrical outlets on opposing sides of the same stud bay—space between two studs and the drywall—between the home theater and an outside room, for example. Seal or isolate every link between your listening room and the outside world in equal amounts. In other words, don't build 12-foot thick concrete walls that completely block out the sound, and use a thin, hollow-core wooden door that lets the sound back in. Save money on the walls, use a thicker door, seal the outlets, insulate the air conditioning, etc.

Soundproof doors

If your home theater resides in a common area that's open to other portions of the house, consider adding a door. Popular home theater designers suggest that even double French doors enclosing an archway are a huge improvement in sound isolation. Preferably, use a prehung, exterior grade (i.e., solid core) door that includes all of the weather-stripping around the edges. You can find these doors for as little as $300 (not including installation). The door should also have a sealed threshold across the bottom, thus creating an airtight seal around the door. Dual seals are better than one. Don't simply replace a hollow core door with a solid core one, though. The weight of the solid-core door will probably rip off the weak hinges. Enclosing the room not only improves noise isolation, but also substantially improves bass output, as the subwoofer is no longer trying to pressurize air throughout your entire home.

Eliminate ringing

In constructing walls of any type, use techniques that eliminate ringing. All materials have a resonant frequency dependent on the mass of the material. Drywall mounted on 2-by-4 studs on 16-inch centers, for example, resonates somewhere between 70 Hz and 125 Hz. When sound hits the drywall, some of it (mostly mid and high frequencies) is reflected. Low frequencies pass through the drywall and are either absorbed by the insulation material behind it, continue on, or are reflected back into the room. The drywall panel will resonate, however, with sounds at or around 70 Hz to 125 Hz and will transfer sounds at those frequencies to the next room. Using soundboard material between the 2-by-4 and the drywall can eliminate the ringing. Soundboard is a pressed cardboard-like material that comes in 4-foot by 8-foot sheets. At roughly a half-inch thick, it's light enough not to affect the wall's absorption characteristics (or overall transmission loss), but reduces the panel's resonance. Increasing the space behind the wall or increasing the wall's mass also decreases the resonant frequency.

Isolating the floor

One of the best ways to achieve good isolation is to build a "floating" or suspended floor, and then construct the rest of the home theater's walls and ceiling on top of this floating structure. If you're considering this approach, you definitely need to consult a professional designer and a contractor. A floating floor is isolated from the structure below it with either a foam sheet, like Acoustical Floor Mat (part of the QuietZone line of products from Owens Corning), or neoprene pads called U-blocks (by Auralex) or Isoblocks (by Acoustic Innovations). If your floor is raised or uses floor joists under plywood, U-blocks are placed between the floor joists and the foundation below the joists. If the floor is not raised and is just a few layers of plywood on top of a flat concrete slab foundation, the Acoustical Floor Mat, a 3/8-inch-thick material that looks like pink-foam packing material, lays under the plywood and around the outside edges. You could, in theory, use both methods. With a floating floor, sounds are less likely to resonate through the floor to or from the listening area. You can even go a step further and give your home theater room its own foundation.

A raised wood subfloor provides an additional acoustical benefit in addition to the noise isolation advantage. The subfloor allows some low frequencies to be absorbed, which is good, instead of being reflected off of a denser concrete floor. A wood floor also vibrates to some extent with low frequencies, transferring the bass to the seating area through the structure, which adds a tactile experience to the sound. Using carpet or a pad doesn't affect the experience. A raised floor should have at least a 3- or 4-inch air space (use 2-by-4s or larger lumber as joists resting on neoprene pads).

Isolating the Walls

If you have a floating floor, you should build your room's walls on top of the floor, or vibrations from inside or outside the room will transmit through the wall structure. If your wall is attached to the floating floor, the walls will be acoustically suspended from the rest of the home's structure. As I mentioned, you can use both floating floor methods, in which case the walls can be built on top of the neoprene suspended floor joists, but not on top of the section with the Acoustical Floor Mat material.

Acoustics companies like Acoustic Science Corporation (ASC) and Kinetics Noise Control offer various products that decouple your home theater from the surrounding structure. These products can offer similar isolation with simpler construction techniques.

You need to isolate your wall structure whether or not you use a floating floor. Adding fiberglass or mineral wool insulation batting within the wall helps somewhat. Don't be tempted to add layers of drywall because the added mass will only marginally improve transmission loss. When the second layer of drywall is applied to the inside of your listening room's walls it also reduces the wall's ability to absorb bass resonances (explained in greater detail in "Reverberation" on page 250). It's probably better to add the dual layer of drywall to the outer sides of the listening room walls, the sides that are part of neighboring rooms that don't need any absorption benefits. You should also use a different thickness of drywall for the second layer and overlap the seams of one layer with the panels from the second layer.

Figure 12.6

Standard, single wall construction with 3.5-inches of insulation offers an STC of 36 dB (34 dB without insulation). Dual layers of drywall may increase isolation only a few dB.

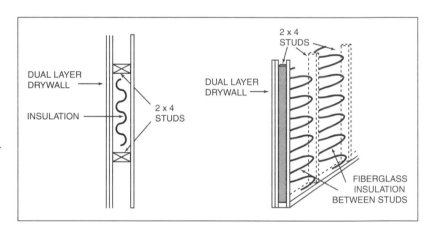

Concrete provides even greater isolation, but has almost no absorption properties. If you have, or are planning to build a room with concrete walls, build wood-framed walls on the inside of the concrete barriers. A space-saving, mass-adding alternative is to add a layer of heavy 1/8-inch vinyl ($3/sq ft from Acoustic Innovations) to the wall. I've used the material, and it's definitely my least favorite option. The material is heavy and difficult to install. Warn your contractor if you're not doing the installation. Unlike the added drywall, though, the added vinyl mass dampens the resonant frequency of the wall, reducing transmission to neighboring rooms and increasing the absorption over a broad range of frequencies.

Double wall construction, using two separate walls built on two separate base plates, is an excellent combination with the floating floor system described above. One of the walls is built on the floating floor, while the other is built on the existing, surrounding structure with a 1- or 2-inch space between the two walls. Drywall is added to both wall structures, but not to the interior portion, leaving you with the widest possible air gap. You should also add fiberglass or mineral wool insulation batting to the space between the wall studs to further reduce transmission loss. You can also utilize a double-wall construction without the floating floor (or use the Acoustical Floor Mat to isolate the floor within the room), though doing so is less effective as sounds transmit through the foundation.

Figure 12.7

Double wall construction with 9 inches of insulation can achieve an STC of 58 dB (43 db without insulation). Two separate walls are built on two separate base plates.

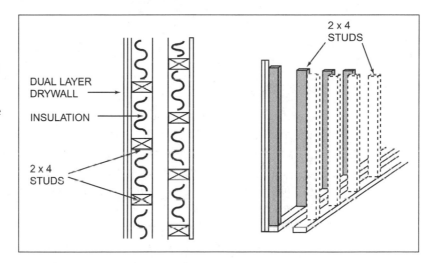

Another less expensive alternative, particularly when you don't have a floating floor is to build a wall with staggered studs. For this technique, you use only one, 2-by-6 base plate (instead of the regular 2-by-4 base plate). The 2-by-4 studs for both the inner and outer walls are set flush to the inner or outer edge of the base plate, respectively, thus preventing any physical connection between the drywall on the outer edge with the drywall on the inner edge other than through the base plate. Again, add soundboard to the inner wall and insulation material to the inside of the wall.

Figure 12.8
Staggered stud wall construction with insulation provides an STC of as much as 52 dB (42 dB without insulation). Two inter-weaved walls with staggered studs are built on top of the same 2-by-6 base plate.

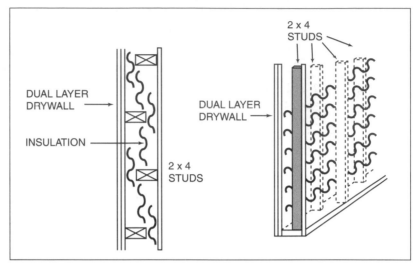

If you are retrofitting a room or are on a limited new-construction budget, consider adding resilient channel (RC) or a similar form of wall isolation device. RC is a metal track that attaches to the existing studs—you need to remove the existing drywall or at least cut out the drywall between the studs. You then hang a new layer of drywall on the track, thus decoupling the new wall from the stud framing. While this method is not as quiet as dual walls, it should be significantly better than a single wall. Unfortunately, most installers end up screwing the new drywall into both the resilient channel *and* the stud, thus coupling the whole structure and eliminating the benefit of the channel. You can make the installation easier using RSIC-1 (distributed by PAC International), a rubber puck that attaches to the 2-by-4 stud. A type of resilient channel called dual-leg furring (AKA "hat channel") attaches easily to the puck and reduces the danger of screwing the two walls together accidentally. Other products from ASC, Kinetics Noise Control, and Owens Corning offer similar techniques of wall isolation without additional wall framing.

Heating, ventilation, and air conditioning

Designing and installing a silent heating, ventilation, and air conditioning (HVAC) system requires extensive knowledge of air handling equipment and is best left to experts. HVAC is the most significant, but often-overlooked source of ambient noise in a home theater. In many cases, your HVAC system should be one of the first places to make improvements. There are a few things to consider for your HVAC system.

The goal is to move a lot of air very slowly. The faster the air moves, the more sound it makes. Decrease the velocity by increasing the size or the number of air ducts feeding the room. Use large, low-velocity (and low-turbulence) air diffuser vents, as opposed to multilouvered vents. Locate the vents away from the listening position. And try to eliminate as many objects in the air's path as possible.

The ducts should be lined with duct liner board; round metal ducts should be lined with a fiberglass blanket, such as Linacoustic. The liner absorbs noise in the duct. Use numerous right-angle bends in the duct path to help slow the air speed and deflect and absorb sound traveling through the duct. Suspend the ducts with isolation hangers where possible and include a plenum silencer near the vent.

A plenum silencer is a large fiberglass or mineral-wool lined box that acts like a car muffler. The box has a duct supplying air at one end and an output, which feeds air to the room, at the other end. The two ends should have a surface area five times the size of the supplying duct. Kinetics Noise Control makes in-line silencers, as well.

Since the room will be isolated from the rest of the house and hopefully airtight (to improve sound isolation), you need to pull air from the room with air returns in addition to providing air to the room with air supplies. Use the same philosophy and techniques with the air return as with the air supply. Noise is often heard more through the air return than through the air supply.

Another source of noise in the HVAC system can be noise passing through ducts from other rooms. Using a dedicated HVAC system for the theater room is an obvious and expensive approach. If that's not an option, consider using a separate air duct for the theater room that's not shared with other rooms in the house. If you have to use shared ducts, put the vents for the other rooms as far down the duct as possible, away from the theater's vents. Use the techniques listed here to eliminate as much noise as you can.

Fan blades can also create a significant amount of noise. Duct liner and multiple bends in the duct can help eliminate the noise, but you can also pinpoint the frequencies of the fan blade noise with sound testing equipment and can use an in-line duct silencer to eliminate those frequencies. Other general tips include locating the HVAC machinery far away from the home theater room and isolating the equipment against structure-borne vibration. This might mean having the equipment on its own foundation or using isolation hangers. (See Kinetics Noise Control products at www.kinetics-noise.com.) Talk to an acoustical designer and an HVAC expert for professional help when you need to quiet your air handling system.

Filling In the cracks

When cement sound walls are installed near freeways, nearby residents often complain that the road noise is worse after the installation than it was beforehand. The cement wall works, it's just that it works almost too well. It reduces the road noise significantly, but the cab portion of tractor-trailers now extends above the wall height. The engine sound of the tractor-trailer, which had previously been masked by the ambient traffic noise, now stands out on its own. The sporadic nature of the big rig noise ends up being more annoying than the constant rush of traffic. The same is true in a well-insulated home theater. As you reduce the major sources of noise and sound transmission in and around your room, previously insignificant sources of noise become substantially more audible. It's important to consider all noise sources, no matter how small, and deal with them accordingly.

Acoustic Treatments

Reverberation

If you've ever sung your favorite tunes in the shower (and come on, who hasn't?) or listened to a chorus in a cathedral, you know how reverberation can improve the sound of music. The hard surfaces in the shower or the church create a series of sound reflections that trail off almost endlessly. The trailing off of reflections into a fully scattered, randomized, nondirectional fog or mist of sound energy is reverberation.

(Echoes, by comparison, are distinct packets of repeated sound.) Reverberation time, or decay rate, is important and is a measure of the amount of time it takes the reflections (or reverberation) of the initial sound to diminish or decay by 60 dB. This decay is designated as RT60. The materials and room surfaces determine the amount of reverb time in a room.

RT60 is typically applied to large rooms (concert halls and cathedrals), which can take a long time for sounds to die out. Strictly speaking, reverb is never achieved in small rooms. Sounds die out in small rooms quickly, through multiple absorptions and reflections, and can drop 60 dB before a fully random sound field is achieved. The rate of sound decay in residential rooms that are less than a few thousand cubic feet is important, though, and this decay rate can vary based on frequency. In other words, some frequencies decay faster than others. Your goal is to make sure that all frequencies decay at roughly the same rate.

While long reverb times make some sounds better (like your voice in the shower), it wreaks havoc on more complex music or home theater soundtracks, creating an incoherent, blurred mess. You won't hear distinction or detail between sounds. Similarly, if a room is too absorptive or has an excessively short reverb time, it can suck the life out of the music and make it sound dry, lifeless, and dead. And because materials affect reverberation differently at different frequencies, you can have too much reverberation in one range of frequencies and not enough at others.

Figure 12.9 on page 252 is a graph of ideal reverb times, per ITU standards, for rooms of various sizes (by volume). If you're good at math, you can divide the volume of your room by 3,532 (a constant that relates to human preferences). Then multiply the cube root of that number by 0.3. Slightly longer reverb times are acceptable at lower frequencies (increasing below 250 Hz).

Once you know the ideal RT60, or decay rate of your room, you can calculate the actual RT60 of various frequencies in the existing room. If you're building the room from scratch, you can calculate the RT60 of the room, as it will be, unfurnished (see Calculating RT60, on page 253).

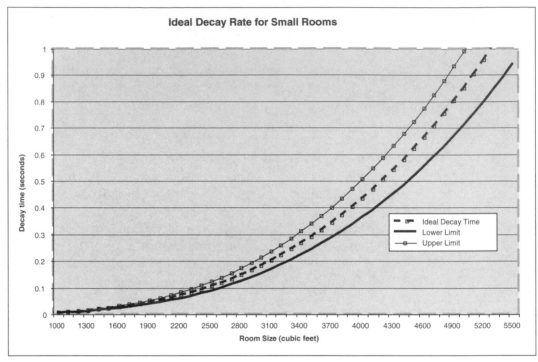

Figure 12.9
Reverb goals for small rooms

Acoustical Characteristics of Materials

Every room surface has an acoustical effect on sound that determines the room's decay rate. What the effect is depends on whether the material is absorptive, reflective, or diffusive.

Soft, fuzzy, and/or porous materials absorb sound, thus reducing the reverberant signal's energy and amplitude (volume level) by transforming it into heat through friction of the fibers. The range of frequencies that a material absorbs depends on the thickness of the material. For example, 1-inch-thick, high-density fiberglass placed flat against a wall absorbs sound evenly down to 1 kHz. The amount of absorption lessens at lower frequencies. Below about 500 Hz, the 1-inch-thick material has little or no effect. You can improve the low-frequency absorption of a material by positioning it away from the wall. Thicker absorption materials (2 to 4 inches or more), or specially designed low-frequency absorbers are needed to help absorb sound over a broad frequency range.

Hard, flat reflective surfaces (like drywall or cement) don't reduce the sound level as much as point it in a new direction. The reflected angle is equal to the angle at which the sound hits the surface. Reflecting sounds is useful if you're trying to direct early reflections away from the listening area, but it might not be as ideal as using diffusing material. Diffusing materials are reflective, but have a varied or convex curved surface instead of a flat surface. They are usually collections of small blocks placed at mathematically determined but varied heights, but sometimes can be as simple as bookshelves. Diffuse surfaces reflect sound in multiple directions, which in turn reduces the signal level in any one direction, while preserving most of the sound's energy in the room.

Many materials, however, are reflective and absorptive at the same time. A single layer of regular drywall, mounted on normal wood framing (2-by-4-inch studs placed 16 inches on-center), for example, will absorb some sound below 250 Hz, but reflect frequencies above that point. You also need to consider the combined effect of materials. The 1-inch-thick fiberglass mentioned previously, if mounted on drywall, absorbs frequencies above 500 Hz, but passes frequencies below that frequency to the drywall. The drywall then absorbs some of the energy below 250 Hz. Sounds between 250 Hz and 500 Hz are then reflected back into the room.

Calculating RT60

To achieve the reverberation decay rate (RT60) goal mentioned previously, you will probably need to add acoustic materials to your listening room. What kind of materials depends on the difference between the room's existing or initial reverberation decay rate and the goal rate. Calculating RT60 requires that you know the absorption characteristics of various materials at various frequencies, the surface area of that material, and the total room volume.

The best way to determine how much and what type of material to use on the walls is to measure the room's reverberant character with test equipment and compare that figure with the goals for a room of that size (see **Figure 12.6**, reverb goals for small rooms). Since neither you nor many dealers actually have this test equipment, and measuring small rooms is problematic anyway, I suggest you estimate the theoretical decay rate and then use trial and error. First, calculate the room's RT60 time based on equations created by Wallace Clement Sabine. (Newer techniques by Eyring or Arau-Puchades are considered more accurate, but are more complicated.) Try combinations of various materials until things sound the way you want. The formula is simple; multiply the material's absorption characteristic at each frequency (found in acoustic texts or product specifications) by the surface area of the material, in square feet, to get the subtotal of absorption for that material, in a unit of measurement called Sabines. Then add all the subtotals for the room's different materials at each given frequency. Multiply the room's total volume by a constant (0.049) and divide that number by the total absorption figure.

Figure 12.10

RT60 calculations for a typical room. The top trace is the expected decay rate in an unfinished room. The bottom trace is the calculated RT60 for the same room with wall-to-wall thick carpet and 164 square feet of 4-inch pressed fiberglass. (Owens Corning 703)

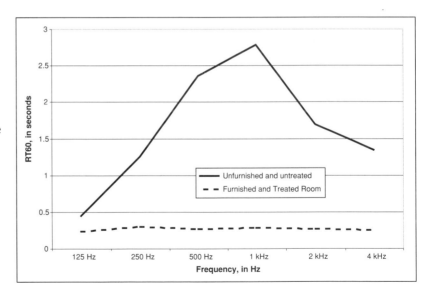

The problem with these calculations is that they are only as accurate as the number of surfaces accounted for. For example, it's not likely the entire carpet will be exposed, so you have to subtract a certain amount for the areas of carpet that are covered with other items. Then you have to calculate the absorption of those items, assuming you can find all the absorption specifications. As I mentioned, some materials may only partly obscure others at certain frequencies and will be nearly invisible at other frequencies, like the 1-inch-thick fiberglass mounted on drywall. Therefore, you might need to determine the surface area of a given material differently at one frequency than another, depending on what frequencies get absorbed.

For example, if you cover the drywall with a 2-by-4-foot sheet of 1-inch-thick fiberglass, fiberglass absorbs sound at frequencies above 500 Hz. You'll have to subtract the absorption coefficients at frequencies above 500 Hz from the corresponding area of covered drywall. But fiberglass passes frequencies below 500 Hz, so the covered area of drywall will absorb those frequencies.

Compare the results of the Sabine equation in each frequency range with your goal reverb time that you calculated in the Reverberation section. If the goal is lower than your existing number, add some material that will absorb sound in that frequency range. If the goal is higher, you might need to replace some existing absorbent material with a similar amount of diffusive material. A number of companies offer a wide array of acoustical materials that fit your needs. Again, you might want to fine-tune the results by ear with some trial and error.

 Your room doesn't have to look like a test lab with random materials on the walls. Many acoustical treatments can be wrapped in acoustically transparent cloth colored to match your room's décor. Or you can use a fabric track to stretch acoustically transparent fabric across an entire wall, hiding any and all materials behind it.

Placing acoustical treatments

Positioning acoustical treatments is as important to your system's sound quality as having the treatments in the first place. To properly reduce the overall reverb time, the acoustic materials should be placed somewhat randomly throughout the room. In other words, there should be an equal amount of absorption, reflection, and diffusion on each wall. Generally you don't want to put all of the absorptive material on one wall, with all of the diffusive material on another wall. Instead, a consistent interleaving of absorption and diffusion will smooth out the room's acoustical thumbprint.

Offsetting various materials, so that absorptive materials are across from diffusive or reflective materials, also helps eliminate slap echo. Slap echo is a "zinging" effect that occurs when sound bounces between two flat, parallel surfaces.

Another goal when acoustically treating the room is to eliminate first-order reflections. These are the first reflected sounds that reach the listener just after the direct sound from the speaker. (See the Secrets section in Chapter 8 on page 181.) These reflections bounce off one nearby surface and are detrimental to the sound quality of the speakers (floors and ceilings in particular). Adding absorption or diffusion to these reflection points greatly improves the sound quality of the system.

Room acoustics isn't voodoo, but it can make substantial improvements to the sound of your home theater. If you're planning to spend a decent amount of money on home theater equipment, you should also consider spending something on room acoustics. Even a few well-placed book-shelves and drapes can help make any system sound better. Consider hiring an acoustical designer, though, if you want a top-notch system to sound its best.

System Setup

Installing a home theater system is a bit like solving a Rubik's cube.
There can be any number of ways to get to the ultimate solution, but
in the end you need to listen to music and watch movies. Describing
how to connect all your equipment in every possible system configuration is impossible given the wide variety of individual components.
You will have to consult your owners' manuals for some specifics. If I
break down your system to its core components, though, I can describe,
generally, how things should go together. The capabilities of your
system will then determine your installation method, of which there
are two general approaches. One, you can route everything through
an audio/video switcher. Two, you can send video signals directly to
the TV and audio signals to the surround processor and speakers.

Conceptually, think of your system as having four major parts. Most of the electronics are considered source components. These include the DVD player, cable box, AM/FM radio, satellite receiver, and other components that create, play back, tune, or otherwise output audio and video signals generated from within or from removable media. These are the starting points for the audio and video signals that drive your system.

The next part of the system is the A/V preamp/processor or receiver, also known as the controller. As outlined in Chapter 6, the controller can take on any number of functions, but almost every controller includes an audio-video switcher in addition to its surround processing functions. The switcher is the important part for our discussion, as it routes the signals to its ultimate destination and, as I'll describe later, the capabilities of the switcher help determine the installation approach of your system.

The last two parts of the system are the video and audio playback equipment. These are the components that reproduce the respective signals. The video playback device is your TV, which can be a plasma monitor, front projector, direct view CRT, or any other type of video display. The video processor is considered a part of the TV or video playback system. The audio playback system refers to the speakers, but can also include the power amplifier, crossovers, and equalizers. Essentially, everything within the audio signal path that comes after the audio-video switcher and surround processor is part of the audio playback system.

The Simple Solution

Your two main goals when configuring your system are to obtain the highest possible signal quality, yet still make the system easy to use. If you have a high-end system you should be able to take the approach outlined in **Figure A**. This method routes all the audio and video signals coming from the source components through the audio-video controller. You select the desired source on the controller, which then sends the processed signals to the video display and speakers. With the right components, and when set up correctly, this type of system is simple. You only need to worry about switching sources on the controller.

Select DVD, for example, and the DVD signal should appear on the TV while the 5.1 audio soundtrack should play back over the audio system.

Figure A:
A simple system configuration routes all audio and video signals from the source components, through the A/V preamp processor or receiver to the TV and speaker system. Ideally, you will only need to select the source on the A/V pre-pro or receiver to get the image to appear on the TV and to hear the sound through the speakers.

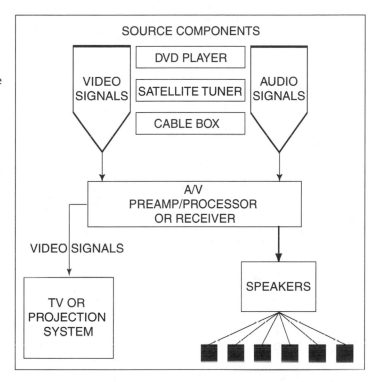

This seemingly simplistic method can have some significant drawbacks, though, and can become as complicated as the alternative approach depending on your system limitations. For one, only higher-end controllers can actually pass high-quality video signals like DVD, and particularly HDTV, without degrading the picture quality. Most controllers just don't have the bandwidth to pass the signal. Some of the signal quality will be lost and the controller will output an ever so slightly softer image than if you just connected the video source directly to the display. Components that cost more than a few thousand dollars, and that include a broadcast quality video switcher, are more adept at the task.

Even if the controller can pass the signals, you might still need several video connections from the controller to the TV. If you connect composite,

S-Video, and component video sources to the controller, and the controller doesn't include any transcoding or upconversion features (as described in Chapter 6), so as to make all of these signals available from a single video output, you will need to route one each of the same signal types to the display. Most TVs won't allow you to connect composite, S-Video, and component signals to the same input and only use the active signal, for example. You have to use separate inputs on the TV, which means that when you select a source that's connected to the controller with an S-Video cable, you still have to switch to the S-Video input on the TV. Switch to a component video source and again you'll have to switch the TV to the component video input. If you don't have a macro-based or automation-type universal remote control (see Chapter 9) that can switch all of this, it will be difficult to make the system work for you or for the rest of your family.

If you don't mind sacrificing picture quality for convenience—and when it comes to domestic harmony, such a sacrifice might not be a bad idea—you can route all the video signals to the controller using the same video signal type. For example, in many systems you could connect S-Video signals for most components. S-Video still provides a substantially better signal than composite connections for NTSC sources, and doesn't give up too much of the quality compared to component signals (except with progressive or high-definition sources). Cable manufacturers even make composite-to-S-Video signal converters that allow you to connect a legacy component like a VCR to the controller with an S-Video cable. With all the equipment connected through the one signal type, you don't have to switch to different inputs on the TV for each source.

The Performance Solution

In an entry-level system, the controller probably won't have the input connections to handle the high-quality signals from your better video devices. Many receivers don't have component video inputs, for example, let alone DVI or HDMI. If that's the case, and you still want the highest-quality picture, you have no choice but go with the second option as outlined in **Figure B**. In this scenario, all the audio signals from the source components are routed directly to the controller, and all the video signals are sent straight to the video display (the TV). Since there are fewer components in the video signal path between the source components and the TV, more signal quality is preserved but system simplicity is not. You must select the desired audio source on the controller and the corresponding video source on the TV. Again, this configuration can be just fine if you have a good automation remote control. Without that remote, you may end up significantly frustrated.

Figure B:

If you want the best performance from any system, you may have to route all your video signals directly to the video display or TV. Audio signals will still connect to the A/V preamp processor. The drawback is that you will have to select the source on the A/V pre-pro or receiver to hear the sound and will need to switch to the appropriate input on the TV to see the picture.

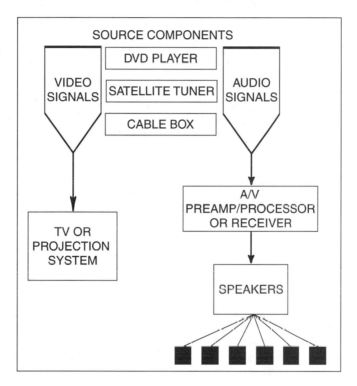

 Another option is to use either composite or S-Video signals through the controller for every piece of equipment, but also run higher-quality signals—like S-Video, component, or DVI— separately to the TV or video display. The advantage to this approach is that family members can utilize the simpler setup that routes all signals through the TV's composite or S-Video input. Then you'll only need to switch the source on the controller. If you're more technical or advanced, you can still switch both the controller and video display inputs to access the higher-quality video signals, when desired.

With the proliferation of progressive scan DVD signals and high-definition television signals, it's becoming more and more difficult to route all the signals to the controller and then to the TV without switching inputs on more than one component. When you add in the need to adjust aspect ratios, audio surround modes, and any number of other parameters, you can see the importance of a good automation remote control. As I said, there's no right or wrong way to connect your system. Look at your system's capabilities and choose the installation path that seems to make the most sense. You might choose to sacrifice some picture performance for the sake of simplicity. If that means you'll use the system more often, it's worth it. If you set up the system for the best performance, and can keep track of all the switching that needs to happen to make the system work, more power to you. So long as you end up watching and listening to music and movies in the end, that's all that matters.

Glossary

.1: The point-one channel of a five-point-one (5.1) system. .1 is a low-frequency effects channel (LFE) that augments the bass response with additional bass sounds. Since the channel doesn't support a full-range signal, it doesn't earn a whole integer. .1 is not necessarily a subwoofer channel, though most home surround processors mix the low-frequency signals from the other five channels with the LFE to create a subwoofer output. See Dolby Digital or DTS.

4:3: The nearly square aspect ratio of a 35mm film frame and NTSC television. Read "four by three." Also referred to as 1.33:1 (one point three-three to one).

480i: Signal format designation for basic, analog NTSC signals (or standard definition digital television signals) that indicates the signal is made up of 480 active, interlaced lines.

480p: Signal format designation for progressive scan DVD (or extended definition digital television signals) that indicates the signal is made up of 480 active, progressively scanned lines.

5C: Copy protection system used with a DTV FireWire signal.

5.1: Designation for a discrete, 6-channel digital surround soundtrack. Uses three main front channels (left, center, and right), two surround channels (left surround and right surround), and an LFE or low-frequency effects channel. Read as "five-point-one." See also Dolby Digital and DTS.

5.1 EX or **5.1 ES**: See Dolby Digital EX or DTS ES.

6.1: Generic term used to describe Dolby Digital EX, DTS ES, and other similar types of processing. Offers three front speakers, three surround speakers, and a subwoofer or LFE. Only one center surround or surround back speaker channel is used.

7.1: Generic term used to describe Dolby Digital EX, DTS ES, and other similar types of processing. Offers three front speakers, four surround speakers, and a subwoofer or LFE. The two surround back speakers are used even though the signal is mono. Various signal processing techniques can be used to create a quasi-stereo signal to the surround back channels.

720p: Signal format designation for high-definition digital television signals that indicates the signals are made up of 720 active, progressively scanned lines.

1080i: Signal format designation for high-definition digital television signals that indicates the signal is made up of 1080 active, interlaced lines.

16:9: The wide-screen aspect ratio of HDTV. Read as "sixteen by nine." Also labeled as 1.78:1 (one point seven-eight to one).

A

AAC: Advanced Audio Codec. Used separately by Apple's iTunes and Dolby Labs for shrinking down the file size of music or other audio to easily transferable sizes with minimal loss in performance.

Absorption: Reduction of acoustical energy usually by converting it into heat via friction using soft, fibrous materials.

AC-3: Audio Codec 3. Original and more technical name for Dolby Digital compression. Used in commercial movies, DVD, DTV broadcasts, video games, satellite and cable channels, DVD-Audio discs, and some laser discs. Name changed when marketing mavens at Dolby realized the company name wasn't a part of the title.

Academy Curve: An intentional reduction of amplitude at progressively higher frequencies above ~2 kHz (to –18 dB at 8 kHz) in a theatrical system's playback response to minimize noise in the mono optical track. A few home processors have an Academy filter option, making them a must for old-movie buffs. The filter has been used theatrically since 1938.

Acoustic Suspension: A sealed speaker enclosure that uses the air trapped in the cabinet as a reinforcing spring to help control the motion of the woofer(s).

Active: Powered. Audio signals are divided through a crossover prior to amplification.

Advanced Audio Codec: See AAC.

Affiliate: In TV broadcasting, affiliate refers to independent TV stations that are contracted or "affiliated" with a national broadcast network that doesn't have an owned and operated station. The local NBC affiliate for a particular area is the channel you turn to when you want to watch NBC TV programs.

Ambience/Ambient Sounds: Sounds that relate to the atmosphere or immediate surrounding area.

Amplifier: Device that uses electrical power to increase the gain or power level of line-level audio signals.

Analog: A signal or mechanism represented by continuously variable physical quantities.

Analog Terrestrial TV: See NTSC

Anamorphic: In film, it's a process of optically squeezing a wide-screen image onto the square-ish (1.33:1) 35mm film frame. An anamorphic lens placed on the theater's projector un-squeezes the image as it's projected on screen. In a DVD, it's an electronic process that squeezes a wide-screen, 1.78:1 (16:9) aspect ratio into the 1.33:1 (4:3) shape of the disc's video frames. This preserves 25 percent more vertical resolution than letterboxing the same image down to a 1.33:1 shape. Requires a wide-screen TV to see any benefit. Note: Wide-screen movies with aspect ratios greater than 1.78:1 are letterboxed to fit the 1.78:1 frame before being anamorphically squeezed down to 1.33:1.

Aspect Ratio: Ratio of screen width to height. Television shapes are usually described in terms of the least number of whole units that can be divided into the horizontal width. Theatrical aspect ratios are expressed as the width divided by the height. For example, NTSC television uses an aspect ratio of 4 by 3. Theatrically, this is expressed as 1.33:1.

ATSC: Advanced Television Systems Committee. Consortium of manufacturers that originally proposed competing HDTV formats to the FCC before agreeing to collaborate on a single system that used the best components of each separate system.

Attenuate: To turn down, reduce, decrease the level of; the opposite of boost.

Audio/Video Switcher: Device that accepts audio and video signals from numerous source components and switches between them. Usually incorporated into a pre-pro or receiver.

Automation Remote Control: Remote control that allows automated functions of an audio/video system. Macro controls activate several functions at once, such as turning on the power for any appropriate components, switching those components to their appropriate inputs.

A/V: audio/video

A-Weighting: Measurement based roughly on the uneven frequency sensitivity of the human ear. The influences of low and high frequencies are reduced in comparison to midrange frequencies because people are most sensitive to midrange sounds.

B

Balanced Input: A cable connection with three separate wires and three separate connector pins: Two identical wires and pins are 180 degrees out of phase with each other, the third is a ground. This type of connection is very resistant to line noise.

Bandpass Filter: Crossover filter that utilizes low and high pass filters to allow only middle frequencies to continue through.

Bandwidth: In audio, the range of frequencies a device operates within. In video, the range of frequencies passed from the input to the output.

Bass: Low frequencies; those below approximately 200 Hz.

Bass Reflex: Type of speaker cabinet that uses a vent, or port to direct additional low-frequency sound captured from the rear wave of the driver to the outside of the cabinet. Bass reflex or ported speakers typically have more bass at the low frequencies above the cutoff frequency, but tend to roll off quickly below that frequency. See Port. Opposite of acoustic suspension.

Beta: Now-defunct videotape format originally championed by Sony Electronics. Center of the landmark lawsuit against Sony by Universal Studios that tried to deem time-shifting illegal. Universal lost.

Black Level: Light output level in the darker portions of a video image. A black level control sets the light level of the darkest portion of the video signal to match that of the display's black level capability.

Boost: To increase, make louder or brighter; opposite of attenuate.

Bridge: Combining two channels of an amplifier to make one channel that's more powerful. One channel amplifies the positive portion of an audio signal and the other channel amplifies the negative portion, which are then combined at the output.

Brightness: For video, the overall light level of the entire image. A brightness control makes an image brighter; however, when it is combined with a contrast, or white level control, the brightness control is best used to define the black level of the image (see Black Level). For audio, something referred to as bright has too much treble or high-frequency sound.

Burn in: Condition in a CRT or plasma display where a static image (like a television channel identification logo) or a quasi-static image (like the news or stock ticker at the bottom of the screen) excessively wears the phosphors in that area of the screen. This uneven wear causes the image to have noticeable bright and dark spots that are viewable all the time.

C

Cascading Crossovers: Two crossovers used in series on the same signal in the same frequency range causing greater attenuation of the out-of-band signal. For example, using the crossover in a receiver's bass management setting and the one in a subwoofer simultaneously creates an exaggerated loss of signal.

Cathode Ray Tube (CRT): Analog display device that uses an electron gun to drive a layer of phosphors to create an image.

CD: Compact disc. Ubiquitous digital audio format. Uses 16-bit/44.1 kHz sampling rate PCM digital signal to encode roughly 74 or 80 minutes of 2-channel, full-range audio onto a 5-inch disc.

CD-R: Recordable compact disc that offers record-once capability. Once information is recorded, it cannot be erased.

CD-RW: Recordable compact disc that offers rewritable capability. Information can be erased and re-recorded multiple times.

CDS: See Cinema Digital Sound

CEA: Consumer Electronics Association. A consortium of manufacturers organized to create standards and promote the industry.

Celluloid: The photographic film used for making and projecting motion pictures. A type of transparent plastic made from nitrocellulose and a plasticizer.

Center Channel: The center speaker in a home theater setup. Ideally placed within one or two feet above or below the horizontal plane of the left and right speakers and above or below the display device, unless placed behind a perforated projection screen material. Placement is important, as voices and many effects in a multi-channel mix come from this speaker.

Channel: A single path for an audio signal typically designated for one speaker, though a single surround channel can be played back through multiple surround speakers. Two discrete channels may contain matrixed signals for one or more derived channels. Also, the portion of a frequency spectrum set aside for a specific purpose, such as a television or radio broadcast frequency.

Chrominance: The color portion of a video signal. Often designated with a C.

Cinema Digital Sound (CDS): The first digital audio soundtrack system used with motion pictures. The system used a 6-channel configuration—that later became known as a 5.1 soundtrack—with the 1990 release of the movie *Dick Tracy*. Developed by Eastman Kodak and the Optical Radiation Corporation.

Coaxial Cable: An audio or video cable with a single center pin and a shield or ground.

Coaxial Digital Audio: Type of digital audio connection that uses an RCA or phono-type connector (single center pin with a grounding shield) on a coax cable (single conductor with shield). Carries a line level, electrical SPDIF digital audio connection.

Codec: Compression-Decompression. Mathematical algorithms used to compress large data (audio and video) signals into small, easily transferable file sizes with minimal perceived loss of information or quality.

Color Decoder: An internal TV component that converts composite, S-Video, and component video signals into the separate red, green, and blue signals that the TV uses to create the image.

Component Video: Video signals divided into three wires. One carries luminance (Y), the other two carry the difference between the original red and the luminance signal (Pr) and the original blue signal and the luminance (Pb). Pr and Pb are usually called red difference and blue difference (or color difference) and carry substantially greater color bandwidth than S-Video or composite. They are sometimes inappropriately labeled as R-Y, B-Y or Cr, Cb on consumer equipment. Cables are color coded green or black for Y, red for Pr, and blue for Pb.

Composite video: Basic video connection that uses a single wire with a yellow color-coded connector. S-Video's chrominance signal has been modulated onto the luminance signal, which creates numerous artifacts in the image.

Compression: Process of shrinking the amount of information used to represent images or sounds by eliminating redundant or supposedly unnecessary information.

Conductor: Solid wires or collection of stranded wires that are bound together to pass electrical signals.

Contrast: Relative difference between the brightest and darkest parts of an image. A contrast control typically adjusts the peak white level of a display device.

Controller: Device that includes audio-video switching, surround sound processing, and volume control. A receiver, integrated amplifier, or preamplifier.

Crossover: Speaker component that divides the audio signal into frequency ranges that are then sent to specific drivers. An active crossover is powered and divides the line-level audio signal prior to amplification. A passive crossover uses the signal's existing power, either at line level or, more commonly, at speaker level to divide the signal after amplification.

Crossover Frequency: The frequency at which an audio signal is divided. 80 Hz is a typical subwoofer crossover point and is the recommended crossover point in theatrical and home THX systems. Frequencies below 80 Hz are sent to the subwoofer; signals above 80 Hz are sent to the main speakers.

CRT: See Cathode Ray Tube.

D

Damping: Controlling the excessive electrical or mechanical vibration of a material.

DBS: Direct Broadcast Satellite. Small dish satellite systems that deliver hundreds of digitally encoded channels directly to your home.

De-interlace: Process of eliminating a signal's interlace pattern and outputting a progressive signal. Subsequent fields are stored in a memory buffer, re-assembled, and then output as one, progressive frame (then repeated to maintain the signal timing). Often incorrectly referred to as "line-doubling" because the output has twice as many lines as the original signal, though none of them have been "doubled" or duplicated. If proper care is taken to assemble the correct fields, the signal will look excellent and will only contain original information. See Line Doubling and Interpolating.

Decibels (dB): A unit of relative sound loudness, electric voltage, or current equal to ten times the common logarithm of the ratio of two readings.

Diffusion: Scattering of sound or light waves, thus reducing the sense of localization.

Diffusor: Acoustical device that reflects the incident sound in multiple directions equally, thus reducing the energy level of the sound at its reflected angle.

Digital Cinema: The next technological advance in motion pictures; uses digital images (typically sourced in high-definition formats) transmitted to and projected through a massive digital video projector onto theater screens. Since no degradable filmstrip is used, each presentation is as good as the last one. Debuted with *Star Wars: Episode 1-The Phantom Menace*.

Digital Theater Systems: See DTS.

Digital TV: A new television format adopted by the FCC in 1997 for the United States. Uses the ATSC system for transmitting anywhere from five standard definition channels to one or two high-definition channels.

D-ILA: JVC's proprietary version of LCoS technology.

Dipole: Speakers with drivers on opposite sides that are wired electrically out of phase, creating a null, or area of cancellation to the sides. THX recommends using dipole surround speakers, with null directed at the listener, to create a more ambient and nonlocalizable surround effect.

Direct Broadcast Satellite: See DBS.

Direct Radiator: See Monopole.

Direct-Stream Digital: Compression scheme sometimes used in digital audio mastering and used on SACD to squeeze up to six channels of high-resolution audio onto a DVD-type disc. It uses a 1-bit encoder with a sampling rate of 2,822,400 samples per second (verses 44,100 for CD).

Direct-View Television: Display whose image is created on the same surface from which it is viewed.

Discrete: Completely separate and unconnected.

Dispersion: The scattering or distribution of sound (or light) within an area or space.

DLP: Digital Light Processing. A Texas Instruments process of projecting video images using a light source reflecting off of a DMD, or an array of tens of thousands of microscopic mirrors. Three-chip versions use separate DMDs for the red, green, and blue colors. Single-chip DLPs use a color-filter wheel that alternates each filter color in front of the DMD array at appropriate intervals.

DMD: Digital Micromirror Device. Texas Instruments engine that powers DLP projectors. Uses an array with tens of thousands of microscopic mirrors that reflect a light source toward or away from the lens, creating an image. Each mirror represents a pixel and reflects light toward the lens for white and away from it for black, modulating in between for various shades of gray. See DLP.

Dolby Digital: Digital audio compression system that encodes up to 5.1 channels of audio into a bitstream of data that fits onto film soundtracks, DVD recordings, HDTV broadcasts, video games, and some satellite and cable network channels. Provides up to five discrete, full-range main channels (front left, center, and right), two surround channels (left and right), and an LFE or low-frequency effects channel for added bass effects below 120 Hz. Can be used to deliver 2-channel and monophonic signals instead.

Dolby Digital Surround EX: Extension of Dolby Digital. A center surround channel is matrix encoded, in phase, within the surround left and right channels and provides an effective

6.1 channel output that is backwards-compatible with 5.1 Dolby Digital equipment.

Dolby Pro Logic: Full consumer implementation of Dolby Stereo and an upgrade from Dolby Surround. Offers left, center, right, and monophonic surround channels. Most processors add a crossover to create a subwoofer output. Pro Logic adds steering logic that subtly boosts the speaker level for dominant sounds and diminishes the levels of other speakers to improve perceived separation. Surround channels are bandpass filtered to frequencies between 100 Hz and 7 kHz.

Dolby Pro Logic II: An enhanced version of Pro Logic. Derives a 5.1 signal with stereo surround channels from any 2-channel source.

Dolby Pro Logic IIx: An enhanced version of Pro Logic and Dolby Digital. Derives a 7.1 (Surround EX) signal with stereo surround and back channels from any two or non-EX 5.1 channel signal.

Dolby Stereo: Created in 1974, Dolby Stereo is the commercial or theatrical version of Dolby Pro Logic or Dolby Surround. The system encodes four separate audio channels (left, center, right, and mono surround) onto a 2-channel soundtrack, then decodes those tracks at the theater.

Dolby Surround: Initial consumer version of Dolby Stereo. Used a monophonic surround signal, derived from left and right main channels, and fed to left and right surround speakers.

Dot Crawl: An artifact of composite video signals that appear as a moving, zipperlike vertical border between colors.

DSD: See Direct-Stream Digital.

DSP: Digital Signal Processing. Manipulating an audio signal digitally to create various effects at the output. Often refers to artificially generated surround effects derived from and applied to 2-channel sources.

DSS: Digital Satellite System. Original name DirecTV used to describe its direct broadcast satellite system. See DBS.

D-Theater: Copyright protection system used in JVC's D-VHS players. Studios can release pre-recorded D-VHS tapes with high-definition content in the D-Theater format that can only be played back on D-Theater-equipped VCRs.

DTS: Multichannel digital audio system first used with the theatrical release of *Jurassic Park*. Uses a timecode signal recorded on the filmstrip to sync the image with the soundtrack, which is recorded onto accompanying CD-ROMs. Jointly owned by DTS, Steven Spielberg, and Universal Studios. Home version records 5.1 discrete channels of audio onto a handful of laser discs, CDs, and DVDs. Requires a player with a DTS output connected to a DTS processor.

DTS ES: 7-channel digital audio system used for both theatrical and consumer movie soundtracks. A seventh main channel is added to the 5.1 mix as a center surround channel. The seventh channel can either be matrixed from the left and right surround channels or it can be a completely discrete signal altogether.

DTV: See Digital TV

DVD: A 5-inch optical disc format that uses smaller pit sizes than CD, combined with MPEG2 compression to store between 4.7 (single-layered, single-sided) to 17 GB (dual-layered, dual-sided) high-quality video, enough for a full-length feature film and supplemental material. Also uses Dolby Digital, PCM and/or DTS compression algorithms to provide up to 5.1 channels of discrete digital audio in various languages. Originally called Digital Video Disc, the name was later "changed" by marketing departments to Digital Versatile Disc to accommodate both its video and audio capabilities (see DVD-Audio).

DVD-Audio: A DVD disc devoted almost entirely to audio. The disc uses Meridian Lossless Packing (MLP) to encode up to six channels of high-resolution audio with up to 24-bit word depths and 192 kHz sampling rates. The disc producer can determine the number of channels or the bit and sampling rates used. A portion of the disc can contain some video, usually reserved for on-screen album graphics, band photos, or liner notes.

DVD Forum: Consortium of DVD player manufacturers and Hollywood studios that handles licensing for the DVD format. The Forum adopts and certifies changes to the existing format or accepts new formats that incorporate DVD technology.

DVD-R/RW: One of several recordable DVD formats. DVD-R is a write-once format that allows you to record onto a DVD one time. DVD-R requires that discs be finalized but are compatible on many but not all DVD players (more than other recordable formats). DVD-RW is a rewritable format that requires DVD-RW discs and allows you to record onto the same DVD over and over, up to 100,000 times. DVD-RW is not as compatible with players as DVD-R or +R.

DVD+R/RW: One of several recordable DVD formats. DVD+R is a write-once format that allows you to record onto a DVD one time. It requires DVD+R discs, which are compatible on many but not all DVD players and are compatible with fewer players than DVD-R. Finalization times are much shorter than with DVD-R discs. DVD+RW is a rewritable format that requires DVD+RW discs and lets you record onto the same DVD over and over, up to 100,000 times. DVD+RW is not as compatible with other players as is DVD+R.

DVD-RAM: One of several recordable DVD formats. DVD-RAM is a rewritable format that is mostly used in camcorders and computer drives. Data can be recorded and/or accessed to or from anywhere on the disc at any time. You can play back a recorded program while recording new material. DVD-RAM is only compatible with drives specifically made to accommodate the discs and is therefore the least compatible of all recordable DVD formats.

D-VHS: Digital VHS. Advanced videotape system that stores digital information on tape, which provides for substantially more storage capacity—enough to store two to four hours of high-definition video. Uses 5C copy protection.

DVI: Digital Visual Interface. A digital video connection originally created to connect computers to flat panel (LCD) monitors. Now used between digital video components, including DVD players, satellite receivers, digital cable boxes, and digital

TVs. Carries decompressed video data from the DVD or digital tuner to the TV. Often uses HDCP. Replaced by and is compatible with HDMI. An adapter will connect HDMI and DVI components, but will only transfer the video signal.

DVR: Digital Video Recorder. Computer hard drive with a program schedule grid used to record video programs.

E

EDTV: Enhanced definition digital television. Designation created by the CEA to differentiate between standard definition digital television (SDTV, or 480i DTV signals) and high-definition digital television (HDTV, or 720p and 1080i DTV signals). EDTV refers to products with a native resolution greater than 480i but less than 720p, which generally means 480p products but can also include SVGA.

Electrostat: Speakers with an electrostatic drive element, a charged Mylar material sandwiched between electrically charged grids. The signal is applied to the grids, which react electrostatically (instead of electromagnetically) with the Mylar material.

Emulsion: A thin coating of light-sensitive material, typically silver bromide or silver halide on photographic film.

Equalizer: A component designed to boost or cut individual bands of frequencies in order to improve the frequency balance of an audio signal.

F

Fantasound: The groundbreaking multichannel soundtrack to Disney's 1940 release of *Fantasia*. Leopold Stokowski recorded an orchestra with nine separate optical tracks that were then mixed down to four master surround sound tracks and played back on special equipment synchronized to the film.

FCC: Federal Communications Commission. Government body responsible for overseeing and standardizing satellite, radio, cable, television, and telephone services within the United States.

Fiber Optic Cable: Glass, plastic, or hybrid fiber cable that transmits digital signals as light pulses.

Field: Half of a video frame. Interlaced video frames are divided into two fields.

Finalize: Process of formatting a recordable DVD so that it can be played back on DVD players.

FireWire: 4- or 6-pin square connector used to network digital video components, including DVD players, D-VHS recorders, DVRs, camcorders, satellite receivers, cable boxes, integrated HDTVs, and more. Transfers compressed video signals. Fifth and sixth pins carry power. Term originally trademarked by Apple Computer.

Flicker: An unsteady or wavering light. Our eye is more sensitive to flashing light than flashing images. As the light gets brighter, the flicker is more noticeable. If a light flickers fast enough the human eye perceives the light source as consistent. Movie images are shuttered at 48 frames per second to prevent noticeable flicker; video is displayed at 60 frames (or fields) per second.

FM: Frequency modulated.

fps: Frames per second. See Frames.

Frames: Individual movie or video images shown successively to create moving images. Usually expressed as frames per second or fps. Film uses 24 fps but is shuttered at 48 frames (see Flicker). Video uses 30 fps but is often interlaced to 60 fields.

Frequency: The number of cycles (vibrations) per second. In audio, audible frequencies commonly range from 20 to 20,000 cycles per second (Hz). In video, frequency is used to define the image resolution. Low-frequency video images depict large objects or images. Higher frequencies depict smaller objects (finer details).

Frequency Response: A measure of the frequencies a speaker can reproduce and how accurately they are reproduced. Presented graphically, frequency is represented on the horizontal or X-axis with the sound pressure level output noted on the Y-axis. If the speaker's output level is equal at every frequency, the graph will have a flat line across the middle. This consistent output versus frequency is referred to as a "flat" response and will drop or roll off at an upper and lower limit. A measurement of 20 to 20,000 Hz ± (plus or minus) 3 dB means those frequencies between 20 and 20,000 Hz can be reproduced no more than 3 dB above or below a reference frequency level.

Full-Range: A speaker designed to reproduce the full range (20 Hz to 20 kHz) of audible frequencies.

G

Gain: Increase in signal level or amplitude.

Gray Scale: A video display's ability to reproduce a neutral image color with a given input at various levels of intensity. Various shades of gray are measured with a color analyzer.

H

Hanging Dots: An artifact of composite video signals that appear as a stationary, zipperlike horizontal border between colors.

HDCP: High-bandwidth digital content protection. Copyright protection on digital signals that pass through an HDMI.

HDMI: High-definition multimedia interface. A digital audio and video connection between digital video components, including DVD players, satellite receivers, digital cable boxes, and digital TVs. Carries decompressed audio, video, and control data from the DVD or digital tuner to the TV. Uses HDCP. Replaces and is backwards-compatible with DVI. An adapter connects HDMI and DVI components, but cannot carry the audio or control signals.

HDTV: See high-definition television

HDTV-compatible: Television that can display an HDTV signal with 720 vertical lines or higher, but lacks a digital TV tuner.

Heliograph: Sun drawing. Nickname for the first photograph.

Hi-Fi: High fidelity. Dated term used to describe electronic equipment used to reproduce high-quality music.

Hi-Fi Stereo: Feature found on VCRs that records or plays back stereo soundtracks with improved fidelity compared to using the linear stereo tracks.

High-Definition Television: Part of a new television format adopted by the FCC in 1997. Several signal resolutions can be transmitted in the ATSC system; high-definition signals include a vertical resolution of 1080 interlaced or 720 progressive active lines, a 16:9 shaped picture, and 5.1 Dolby Digital audio.

High Gain: Output is greater than the input. In screen material, the screen reflects (or transmits) more light than a reference material.

HTIB: Home Theater in a Box. An all-in-one system that includes five main speakers a subwoofer and an audio/video receiver. Newer systems can include a DVD player with SACD, DVD-Audio, or DVD recording functions.

Home Theater in a Box: See HTIB.

Home Video: Though semantically this could refer to any movie available electronically in a consumer medium, it usually refers to videotape.

Horizontal Resolution: Number of on/off (white/black) transitions measured from left to right across a portion of the screen proportional to the height.

Hz: Hertz or cycles per second.

Hybrid: In SACD (and now DVD-Audio), hybrid discs can include both a regular CD player-compatible signal and a high-resolution, multi-channel audio signal.

I

IEEE-1394: See FireWire.

iLink: See FireWire.

Integrated Amplifier: Combination of an audio-video switcher and two or more amplifier channels. Usually includes a surround sound processor. A preamp-processor lacks the amplifier. A receiver adds an AM/FM radio.

Interlace: To decrease the size of the signal, each frame is split into two fields, making 60 fields per second. Each field contains every other line of the original frame. If you numbered the lines of each frame from top to bottom, the first field of each frame would contain the odd lines (1, 3, 5 ... 479) while the second field would display the even lines (2, 4, 6 ...480). Each field is shown quickly and offset by one line space so that if there's no motion between them, persistence of vision will blur the two fields together and you will see them as one frame.

Interpolate: A processor that creates additional information in an image by determining what types of new pixels should be created between existing pixels. Better interpolaters look at adjacent pixels in an existing frame as well as at pixels in previous and later frames.

Imaging: The ability to localize the individual sound sources in three-dimensional space.

Impedance: A measure of the impediment to the flow of alternating current, measured in ohms at a given frequency. Larger numbers mean higher resistance to current flow.

J

Jack: Slang term for an audio/video connector.

Jack Pack: The back panel of an audio/video component that contains numerous audio and video connections.

K

kHz: Kilohertz. 1000 Hz.

L

Laser Disc: Now-defunct home theater video format that provided superior picture and sound quality to a VHS videocassette. Information was stored with analog frequency modulated signals onto a 12-inch optical disc.

LCD: Liquid Crystal Display. A transmissive display technology that consists of two polarizing transparent panels and a grid of liquid crystals sandwiched in between. Each liquid crystal represents a picture element, or pixel.

Voltage is applied or disabled to certain areas of the panels, depending on whether a portion of an image should be light or dark, causing the crystal to become opaque or remain translucent. A light source behind the panel transmits through transparent crystals and is mostly blocked by opaque crystals, projecting an image.

LCoS: Liquid Crystal on Silicon. Display technology that uses translucent liquid crystals placed above a reflective surface. (See LCD). Light is directed at the liquid crystals, which when voltage is applied become opaque. Translucent crystals pass the light through to the reflective layer, which redirects the image to the projection lens.

Letterboxed: Process that adds black bars above and below an image to fit a wide-screen movie into a film frame, video frame, or TV screen that is not as wide as the original movie. The film's original aspect ratio is maintained, but some active lines are sacrificed to record and transmit the black bars.

LFE: Low-frequency effects channel. The ".1" channel in a 5.1, 6.1, or 7.1 system. Often misconstrued as a subwoofer channel, the LFE is more of a boom track, added for additional emphasis at low frequencies and augments the low frequencies that come from the full-range main channels. In nearly every home surround processor, the LFE channel is mixed with the low-frequency signals of the main channels, thus creating a subwoofer output.

Line Doubling: Increasing the scan rate of lower-resolution signals by duplicating every line of information. Better line doublers are in fact de-interlacers.

Line-Level (Low-Level): Electrical signals that are too low in level to make the average speaker vibrate sufficiently. Amplifiers receive line-level signals and amplify them to speaker level.

LNB: Low Noise Blocker. The reception arm of a digital satellite dish.

Luminance: The black-and-white, (or Y) portion of a composite, Y/C, or Y/Pb/Pr video signal. The luminance channel carries the detail of a video signal. The color channel is laid on top of the luminance signal when creating a picture. Having a separate luminance channel ensures compatibility with black-and-white televisions.

M

Macro: Remote control function that transmits a string of commands that activate several audio/video components to achieve a specific function with the touch of a button. A macro can turn on the receiver, TV, and DVD player; switch the receiver to the DVD input; switch the TV to the component video input, and play the disc in the DVD player without any additional input from the user.

Magnetic Soundtrack: Audio signals recorded as magnetic polarizations on metal oxide coated sections of a plastic tape or a filmstrip.

Matrixed: Mixed together. A matrixed audio system, like Dolby Stereo, mixes an equal portion of the center channel, in phase, into the left and right channels, while equal parts of the surround channel are mixed, out of phase, into the left and right channels.

Microdisplay: Technical term used to generically refer to newer, solid-state rear-projection television technologies. DLP, LCD, and LCoS all use imaging devices the size of a thumbnail to create the image, thus the term microdisplay, even though the projected image can be up to 82 inches diagonally.

MLP: Meridian Lossless Packing. Lossless compression scheme used on DVD-Audio discs to encode up to six channels of high-resolution audio with as much as 24-bit word depths and 192 kHz sampling frequencies.

Mono or Monophonic: One. As in a single channel of audio: monophonic sound.

Monopole: Speaker that projects sound in one direction.

MP3: MPEG-1, audio layer 3. A compression/decompression format that reduces CD music files by as much as 12 times allowing songs to be transferred over the Internet and stored in portable players and digital audio servers.

MPEG: Motion Pictures Experts Group. Committee that adopted and standardized audio and video compression algorithms (MPEG1, MPEG2) that are used in DVD, satellite broadcasting, DTV, and other digital video formats.

Multicasting: Process of using available 6 Mhz broadcast spectrum to transmit up to five or six standard definition TV channels instead of one or two high-definition channels.

Multichannel: More than one. Typically refers to a 5.1 or greater sound system.

Multiroom: System that provides audio or video signals from one source at a time to multiple areas in a home.

Multizone: System that provides different audio and video signals from multiple sources into multiple areas simultaneously.

N

Negative Gain. Output is less than the input. In projection screen material, the screen reflects (or transmits) less light than a reference material and can improve a projector's black level performance.

NTSC: National Television Standards Committee. Government organized body that created the original color television standard in 1953, which is scheduled to be replaced by the ATSC system in 2006.

Null: Dead spot. Point in space where positive and negative sound waves meet and cancel each other out.

O

Octave: The difference between two frequencies where one is twice or half the other. For example, 100 Hz is an octave higher than 50 Hz. 1,000 Hz is one octave higher than 500 Hz.

Off-Air: See Terrestrial.

Ohm: A unit of electrical resistance between two points on a conductor (like a cable). Higher numbers mean greater resistance.

Optical: Of or relating to light. Optical film soundtracks use images analogous to the soundtrack to record audio signals.

Optical Digital Outputs: see Toslink.

OTA: Over the air. See Terrestrial.

Over the Air (OTA): See Terrestrial.

Owned and Operated: TV stations that are owned and operated by a broadcast network and broadcast that network's programming. If a network doesn't own a station in a particular market, they contract with an independent station to be an affiliate.

P

Pan and Scan: Wide-screen movies don't fit regular 4:3-shaped TVs. Movie studios often crop the image to fit the TV and then electronically pan the image to center on the action (if it's not in the middle of the scene). This not only sacrifices information at the edges of the frame, but also creates undesirable motion as the video now has additional pans that were not a part of the original movie. See Letterboxed.

Parametric: Equalizer with adjustable parameters, such as center frequency and bandwidth (or Q), as well as amplitude.

Passive: Opposite of active. A passive crossover comes after the system amplifier and uses the amplified signal's power to drive the crossover components. A passive speaker does not have built-in amplification.

PCM: Pulse Code Modulation. Method of converting analog audio sound waves into the ones and zeros of digital audio signals with 16 bits and 44.1 kHz sampling rates. Used on CDs and a few DVDs.

Peak: Loudest. Highest. Greatest. Area of excessive sound pressure level (see SPL).

Persistence of Vision: The lingering effect of images on the human retina. The eye retains images for 1/14th of a second before it obtains a second image. This effect prevents you from seeing black when you blink. The brain blurs the successive images together to create the perception of a constant image, regardless of whether the scene being viewed is actually constant or is a collection of still drawings or photographs flashed repeatedly.

Phase: Time relationship between signals.

Pixel: Individual picture element. The smallest element of data in a video system.

Plasma: Type of video display that uses pockets of gas plasma that, when charged, ignite and emit light thus creating a picture. Displays as large as 60, 70, or 80 inches diagonally are only 4 inches thick.

Port: The vent tube of a bass reflex, or ported, loudspeaker.

Power Amplifier: See Amplifier.

Preamplifier: Device that includes an audio-video switcher and a surround sound processor. An integrated amp includes two or more amplifier channels. A receiver adds amplifiers and a radio.

Preamp-Processor or Pre-Pro: A combination preamplifier and surround processor

Pre Outs: Connectors that provide a line-level output of the internal preamp or surround processor.

Processor: Component that takes an incoming signal and decodes or enhances the signal. Surround sound processors decode Dolby Digital bitstreams into as many as seven channels of audio.

Progressive: Opposite of interlaced. Designated with a p. Each frame of a video image is scanned completely, from top to bottom.

Pro Logic: See Dolby Pro Logic

Pulse Code Modulation: See PCM.

Q

Q: The magnification or resonance factor of any resonant device or circuit. Also the width of affected frequencies in an equalizer. Shaped somewhat like an adjustable-width bell curve.

R

RCA Jacks: Connections for coaxial cables carrying line-level audio signals. Also called phono-type connectors.

Re-EQ: Short for Re-equalization. A feature found on THX-certified receivers and pre-pros. Movie soundtracks are mixed for theaters or far-field monitors with an expected high-frequency roll-off otherwise known as an X-curve. If these soundtracks are not remixed for home use, they sound too bright when played back through home speakers or near-field monitors. Re-EQ inserts an X-curve response into the signal to compensate, which takes out some of the soundtrack's excess edginess or brightness.

Rear-Projection Television (RPTV): Display that projects an image on the backside of a screen material, usually after having been reflected off of a mirror.

Receiver: Device that integrates an audio-video switcher with an AM/FM radio and two or more amplifier channels. Usually includes a surround sound processor. An integrated amplifier lacks the radio. A preamplifier lacks the radio and amplifiers.

Resonant Frequency: Certain frequencies whose wavelengths fit into twice the room dimensions, creating peaks and nulls throughout the room.

Reverberation: The sound within a closed space that's been reflected off of boundaries enough times to achieve a fully randomized, nonlocalizable, fog-like ambiance.

Reverberation Time. The amount of time it takes the reverberation of sound in a room to decay 60 dB from the level of the original impulse sound.

RF: Radio Frequency. Carrier signals for remote controls (as opposed to IR or infrared) or terrestrial television.

RF Amplifier: Indoor signal booster for antenna and analog cable signals. Often includes a splitter with multiple outputs. Best if used at a point closest to where the signal enters the home before the signal is split off to multiple TVs.

RF Preamp: Indoor/outdoor signal booster for antenna and analog cable signals. Usually consists of a power supply and amplifier. The power supply connects to an indoor electrical outlet located near where the antenna feed enters the house. Power is sent up the antenna signal wire to the mast-mounted amplifier. The amplifier boosts the signal before it has a chance to degrade, but without lengthy extension cords.

RF Taps: A TV signal splitter that allows you to daisy-chain or link the signal from one TV location to another.

RGB, RGBHV: Red, green, and blue. Typically refers to the video signal that carries information for each primary color separately. HV stands for horizontal and vertical synchronization signals, which can be carried on separate cables as in 5-wire RGBHV; combined into one separate signal as RGB+ composite sync; or combined with the green signals as RGB with sync on green.

RMS: Root mean square, method of measuring and describing a power amplifier's continuous power output.

RPTV: See Rear-Projection Television.

RT-60: See Reverberation Time.

S

SACD: Super Audio Compact Disc. A DVD-type disc that devotes the majority of storage capacity to audio. Uses DSD compression to record up to six channels of high-resolution audio onto a DVD-type disc. A portion of the disc can contain video, usually reserved for on-screen album graphics, band photos, or liner notes.

Sampling Frequency: Number of times a digital sample is taken of an analog wave. The more samples taken, the more accurate the recording will be. You need to sample at a minimum of twice the highest frequency you want to capture. For example, the 44.1-kilohertz sampling rate of a CD cannot record sounds higher than 22.05 kilohertz.

Scaler: Video processor that takes incoming video signals and converts them to a higher scan frequency.

Scan Lines: The lines a CRT's electron gun draws to make up the picture. Drawn horizontally, from left to right, starting at the top left and working to the bottom right.

Scan Rate: The number of horizontal lines drawn, from top to bottom in an image. NTSC's scan rate is 480i. HDTV can be either 720p or 1080i.

SDDS: Sony Dynamic Digital Sound. 7.1 digital surround sound system used on theatrical film releases. First used with *Last Action Hero*.

SDTV: Standard definition television. Lower-resolution subset of the ATSC's DTV system. 480i is typically accepted as an SD signal. Digital broadcasters can offer multiple subprograms at SDTV quality, as opposed to one or two HD programs. Digital satellite and digital cable often refer to the majority of their programs as SDTV, somewhat erroneously, as neither system has anything to do with DTV, though both, technically, consist of a digital 480i signal.

Sealed: See Acoustic Suspension.

Sensitivity: In speakers, a measure of the acoustical power output with 1 watt input measured from 1 meter away.

Sensurround: Inaudible tones recorded onto an optical control track, in conjunction with the 4-channel magnetic soundtrack, that signals subwoofers in specially equipped theaters to play low-frequency vibrations (5-40 Hz) during the movie. Used on films like *Earthquake* (1974) and *Battlestar Galactic* (1978).

Soundfield: The total acoustical characteristics of a space, such as ambience; number, timing, and relative level of reflections; ratio of direct to reflected sound; RT-60 time, etc.

Sound Pressure Level: See SPL.

Soundstage: The sonic impression that two speakers are creating phantom sound sources between the speakers that correlate with the music. Like a real stage, a soundstage should have width, depth, and height.

Source Components: Components that generate audio or video signals. DVD players, VCRs, DVRs, digital TV tuners, cable boxes, music servers, and multichannel audio disc (SACD and DVD-Audio) players are all source components in a home theater.

SPDIF: Sony Philips Digital Interface. Interconnect protocol for PCM digital audio.

Speaker: A component that converts electrical energy into acoustical energy.

SPL: Sound Pressure Level. Acoustical output of sound, measured in decibels (dB).

Splitter: Device that takes one input and creates two duplicate outputs.

SR-D: Original name for the theatrical version of Dolby Stereo Digital. Included an analog, matrixed, 2-channel optical soundtrack with SR noise reduction and a 5.1 digital optical soundtrack that used AC-3 compression.

Standard Definition Television: See SDTV.

Standing Waves: See Resonant Frequency.

Stereo or stereophonic: Audio system that uses two or more audio signals to reproduce recorded music.

Subwoofer: A speaker designed to reproduce very low bass frequencies, usually those below about 80 Hz.

Surround Back Channel: Audio signal in a 6.1-type format that is reproduced from speakers placed directly behind the listener.

Surround EX: See Dolby Digital Surround EX.

Surround Processor: Component that decodes 2-channel analog audio or digital audio bitstreams into multichannel soundtracks. See Processor.

SVGA: Computer format with a resolution of 800 by 600 pixels.

S-VHS: Super VHS. Enhancement to regular VHS that offers improved luminance resolution (400 lines or so).

S-Video: Video signal with two coaxial cables. One cable carries the luminance signal (Y). The other cable carries a chrominance (C) signal, a compressed and combined version of a component video signal's red and blue color difference signal. S-Video uses a single wire and connector with four pins and a round casing.

SXGA: Computer format with a resolution of 1280 by 1024 pixels.

T

Taps: See RF Taps.

Terrestrial: Uses airborne signals. TV reception that uses rabbit ears or a rooftop antenna.

THX: Quality certification program originally created by Lucasfilm to ensure moviegoers experience the same technical presentation performance of a film that the director intended. Similar standards applied to home theater equipment and software. Acronym for Tomlinson Holman's eXperiment, after the name of the program's original creator, and George Lucas' first feature film, *THX-1138*.

THX Select: Certification program for speakers and receivers that assures a base level of quality and performance when played in a room size between 2,000 and 3,000 cubic feet.

THX Surround EX: Original consumer term applied to the Dolby Digital Surround EX format. Adds a sixth matrixed center surround channel to the existing 5.1 format. Is completely compatible with existing 5.1 systems and software.

THX Ultra: Certification program for speakers, receivers, and amplifiers that assures a base level of quality and performance when played in a room larger than 3,000 cubic feet.

THX Ultra2: The newest certification from THX, THX Ultra2 requires amplification for seven channels, boundary compensation for subwoofers, and stricter requirements for amplifiers and speakers than THX Ultra. Dipole speakers are used for the side surround channels. Monopole speakers are used for the surround back channel and are placed next to each other. The Ultra2 processor accommodates both 5.1 EX/ES soundtracks, as well as multichannel audio recordings by directing ambient sounds to the dipole speakers and discrete effects/sounds to the surround back channels.

TiVo: One of the more popular stand-alone and satellite digital video recorder services. TiVo is included with many DirecTV satellite receivers. Often used as a verb, as in "I TiVo'd that show last night."

Toslink: Term trademarked by Toshiba Corporation for a SPDIF-format, fiber optic digital audio interface. Uses a squarish plastic plug and transfers digital audio with pulsed light.

Tracks: Separate sections of a magnetic tape where a single channel is recorded, usually designated for a specific speaker. See channel. Also, single songs from a music album.

Transcoding: Converting one type of video signal into another (i.e., to transcode composite signals into S-Video or component).

U

Unity Gain: Output that equals the input. In screen material that reflects (or transmits) as much light as a reference material.

Universal Remote: A single remote that can control several different electronic devices from the same or different manufacturers.

Upconversion: Process of converting low-resolution signals to match the scan rate or pixel density of higher-resolution displays so that the signal is compatible.

V

VCR: Video Cassette Recorder. Typically uses VHS technology (now that Sony has ceased Beta production) to record low-resolution audio and video signals onto magnetic tape.

VCR Plus: VCR feature that, once programmed, allows the user to input the TV guide code for a program into the VCR, which is then automatically set to record that program.

Vented: See Ported.

VGA: Computer format with a resolution of 640 by 480 pixels.

VHS: Vertical Helical Scan. Nearly obsolete method of recording audio and video signals onto magnetic tape. Allowed for longer playing and recording time than now-defunct competitor Beta. Sometimes defined as "Video Home System."

Video Cassette Recorder: See VCR.

W

Watt: International unit of power equal to 1 amp times 1 volt: Abbreviated as W.

WMA: Windows Media Audio. An advanced audio compression format used to shrink the file size of music (or other audio) into easily transferable sizes with minimal loss in audio quality.

Woofer: A large speaker driver designed to reproduce low frequencies.

WXGA: Wide-screen computer format with a resolution of 1366 by 768 pixels.

X

X-Curve: An intentional roll-off in a theatrical system's playback response above ~2 kHz at 3 dB per octave. The system's frequency response should measure flat up to 2 kHz and then gradually decrease at higher frequencies above 2 kHz. Home THX processors add this roll-off (called Re-EQ), when THX processing is enabled so that a home video soundtrack has the same response as it would in a theatrical setting.

XGA: Computer format with a resolution of 1024 by 768 pixels.

X-Over: See Crossover.

Y

Y/C: Abbreviation for luminance/chrominance. See S-Video.

YPrPb: 3-wire component signal. Y stands for luminance, a black-and-white signal. Pr carries a red signal while Pb transfers blue signals. Pr and Pb are referred to as a color difference signals, as they only contain the difference between the Y signal and an original RGB signal, from which the YPrPb signal was derived.

Z

Zone: Speakers and TVs in an area of a home (one or more rooms, hallways or open spaces) that can access and play back the audio and video signals from a particular source (i.e., a DVD or CD player). No matter how many TVs or sets of speakers are used in that zone, they cannot play back different sources simultaneously.

Index